ATLANTIC

D1554606

B

A

SANTIAGO

DAIQUIRI

The
ARIZONA
ROUGH RIDERS

Rough Riders On Parade At San Antonio: Col. Leonard Wood (left) and Lt. Col. Theodore Roosevelt (in light uniforms in foreground) are shown in this photograph of the 1st Volunteer Cavalry (The Rough Riders) on horseback. The white horses of Troop D are seen in center behind headquarters unit. (*Courtesy Sharlot Hall Museum.*)

The
ARIZONA
ROUGH RIDERS

Charles Herner

THE UNIVERSITY OF ARIZONA PRESS
Tucson, Arizona

About the Author ...

The famous Rough Rider monument in Prescott, Arizona, and the oft-told tale of the classic version of the death of Captain Buckey O'Neill caused CHARLES HERNER to wish to know more about the Arizona Rough Riders. Following his military service in an armored unit Herner began to explore the story of the Rough Riders in depth, to use it as the basis for a master's thesis in history at the University of Arizona. Finding numerous errors, misconceptions, and omissions in previously published versions of the Rough Riders' story, Herner delved deeper and uncovered new and heretofore unpublished facts which he now presents in this book. A native Arizonan, Herner is a teacher and head of the history department in a public high school in Tucson.

UNIVERSITY OF ARIZONA PRESS

I.S.B.N.-0-8165-0206-4
L.C. No. 73-121894

For
Harlan R., Thelma,
  Beryl,
Harlan L., and Katie

Acknowledgments

THE ENCOURAGEMENT OF FRIENDS and acquaintances to set down this chronicle of the Arizona Rough Riders in book form was largely responsible for my decision, and I am most grateful to those individuals for spurring me to this end product. It has been a fascinating experience. Additionally, the book has provided the opportunity to correct numerous errors about the Rough Riders which were being circulated widely.

In particular, I wish to thank Harwood P. Hinton, my thesis advisor at the University of Arizona, for suggesting this topic originally. Special thanks are extended to John A. Carroll for his help and cooperation. Other historians and authorities intimately in touch with Arizona events who gave me valuable assistance were Odie B. Faulk, Andrew Wallace, Sidney Brinckerhoff and Bert Fireman. Information from the National Archives was obtained through Benjamin Sacks of Baltimore as well as Senator Carl Hayden and Representative Morris Udall. My aunt, Myra Ellen Jenkins, state archivist of New Mexico, provided information on the troopers from New Mexico.

Acknowledgment should be made to Mrs. Georgia Muir, Mrs. Mary Delanie, Robert L. Patterson, the late General Geoffrey Keyes, Mrs. Gwendolyn Penniman and Hermann Hagedorn for contributing information and family records.

During my research, I was fortunate in being able to contact six surviving Rough Riders: George Hamner of Hollywood, Florida; Jesse Langdon of New York; Arthur Stockbridge of Phoenix; Charles Hopping of Long Beach, California; Frank Brito of Las Cruces, New Mexico; and Arthur Tuttle of Salinas, California. All cheerfully provided information and reminiscences, and I have quoted them extensively, just as I have made full use of the manuscript accounts left by their comrades. To preserve the color and authenticity of these first-hand accounts, I have quoted them without alteration or correction. Errors have been identified by the customary *sic* only to call attention to a specific mistake.

Of the surviving Rough Riders at the time of my research, Arthur L. Tuttle was particularly helpful. I am deeply indebted to him. As a native of Arizona, the last survivor of the Arizona squadron of the Rough Riders and an eyewitness to the death of Buckey O'Neill, his recollections were extremely significant. He had a remarkable memory and the details provided by him have been found to be very accurate. Moreover, I thoroughly enjoyed the two long visits I had with him and his charming wife.

Without someone's belief that the knowledge I had acquired was worth sharing, however, my reaching the sources would have been without much significance. I am particularly appreciative of the teamwork and the professional skill devoted to this book by the University of Arizona Press, through which publication has been effected. My special words to Jack Weadock, the editor who helped bring the final version into a comprehensive flow.

Finally, I wish to thank my wife, Beryl, for her patience in quietly tolerating the trips out of town, the many evenings alone while I worked in the library, and the inconvenience of having the house cluttered with documents and half-completed sections of manuscript. She became an expert at cleaning around piles of books and papers. Without her indulgence this study could not have been completed.

My thanks to all.

CHARLES HERNER

Contents

ILLUSTRATIONS

Prologue

A DEEP-ROOTED CONTROVERSY between Spain and the United States came to its ultimate conclusion on April 25, 1898. On that day, partially in response to popular demand, the United States declared war.

The problem between the two nations was Cuba. For seventy-five years the American people had watched the Cubans struggle to free themselves from Spanish rule. The last outbreak in a long series had burst into open warfare in 1895. In attempting to suppress this rebellion, the Spanish government, utilizing methods which worked more hardships on innocent civilians than on the belligerents, alienated the American people beyond hope of reconciliation. The final blow came when the USS *Maine* mysteriously blew up in Havana harbor. Inflamed by a bellicose press, public opinion in the United States favored an immediate declaration of war. Young men from all over the country began clamoring to enlist. None had more enthusiasm than an exuberant group of cowboys and miners from the Territory of Arizona. Joined by men from New Mexico, Oklahoma and Indian Territory, they were molded into a regiment of fighting men destined to become famous as the Rough Riders. Cowboys, miners, executives and laborers, clerks and preachers, hunters and former soldiers they enlisted for their short, but dramatic appearance on history's stage.

February 15, 1898, began like any other day in port for the officers and crew of the USS *Maine,* which had swung at anchor in Havana harbor since January 25. The crew was following routine procedure which included normal security precautions commensurate with the political situation and mission of the vessel. That evening Captain Charles B. Sigsbee was in his cabin writing a letter to his wife. At 9:40 P.M. a tremendous explosion shook the battleship, which first rose with the violence of the blast and then immediately began to settle. Stumbling out of his cabin, through dark, debris-strewn passageways, the stunned commander made his way to the main deck to supervise rescue operations. Long boats arrived quickly from other vessels in the harbor as well as from shore. Within fifteen minutes ninety survivors, out of the three hundred and fifty officers and men on board, had been moved to safety.

Aboard the *City of Washington,* a transport which had received a number of survivors, Captain Sigsbee wired his preliminary report to John D. Long, Secretary of the Navy. He concluded it with what proved to be an unrealistic plea: "Public opinion should be suspended until further report."

The *Maine* was in Havana harbor because the Cubans again were trying to secure their independence. Early in the Nineteenth Century there had been several desultory revolts, but the mass of Negro slaves along the coast and poor whites in the mountains had not supported them and they had failed.

The United States offered a nearby sanctuary, however, and the Cuban patriot leaders had sought refuge there between revolutions. The Cubans found most Americans favorable to their cause. They were able to arouse American filibustering expeditions to land supplies and arms for the rebels. Sometimes these United States citizens went ashore to join in the fighting.

The most serious Cuban outbreak, usually called the ten year revolt, began in 1868 and ended a decade later. During that struggle Spanish officials committed a serious political blunder. They executed some American gunrunners. During the ensuing furor Secretary of State Hamilton Fish avoided a crisis by convincing a wavering President Grant that intervention at that time would be a mistake. As a substitute, Fish dispatched a grim warning to Madrid that Spain must either effect a reconciliation on the island or prepare for intervention by other governments. Three years later, in 1878, a change of government in Madrid finally brought peace to the island. Fearing reprisal, the die-hard revolutionary leaders took refuge in the United States and continued to plot.

At his headquarters in New York, the leader of the Cuban Revolutionary Party, Jose Julian Marti, waited for an opportunity to launch another revolt. It came in 1893 when the panic of that year ruined the sugar business in Cuba. The following year the sugar industry suffered another setback when the Wilson tariff restored duty on that Cuban staple. With the economy of the island disrupted and bandits loose in the hills, Marti saw his opportunity to take personal command of the revolutionary forces in the field. He sailed for Cuba. Scarcely had he landed when he blundered into a Spanish patrol and was killed. Leadership then devolved on Maximo Gomez, a ruthless native of Santo Domingo. He was determined to win at any cost by fighting a war of attrition. Starting in eastern Cuba in the summer of 1895, Gomez carried westward a campaign of unrestricted destruction of both Cuban and Spanish property. In the following spring, with the smoke of burning plantations visible in Havana and the collapse of Spanish control clearly imminent, Spain sent General Valeriano Weyler to restore order.

By the fall of 1896 Weyler had made considerable progress in breaking up Gomez's *Insurrectos*. To combat the guerrillas' habit of posing as innocent peasants working in the fields by day and then seizing arms to harry the Spaniards by night, Weyler implemented his famous *reconcentrado* orders. The Cubans were restricted to living in towns or villages, and no food could be sent out of settled communities into the countryside. Weyler knew that in order to defeat a guerrilla force it was necessary to sever its supply lines by isolating it from a sympathetic civilian population. He was successful and effectively prevented the insurgents from receiving many supplies or recruits. Meanwhile, his troops kept constant pressure on the guerrilla bands. By the summer of 1897 Weyler was on the verge of complete success. He had cleared the western end of Cuba and was moving rapidly eastward.

General Weyler's *reconcentrado* policy, although successful, worked hardships on the civilians. The burning of plantations by both Weyler and Gomez created a food shortage, causing a famine to sweep the island. The American press, universally in favor of the Cubans, overlooked the destruction of food by Gomez's forces and heaped abuse on Weyler, calling him the "butcher." This was in part the result of extremely effective Cuban propaganda. Utilizing a complex network of spies and rumormongers, the Cubans fed vivid descriptions of Spanish atrocities to gullible American correspondents. This propaganda was so effective that American diplomats in Madrid began to demand the recall of Weyler. In August, 1897, the liberal party, which was opposed to Spain's harsh colonial policy, took control of the Spanish government and shortly thereafter recalled Weyler. It was too late. The American people were demanding action.

The famous circulation battle between the publishers of the New York *Morning Journal* and the New York *World* contributed to the emotional involvement of the American people. In the fall of 1895 William Randolph Hearst bought the *Journal* and immediately engaged Joseph Pulitzer, owner of the *World,* in a bitter struggle for journalistic supremacy. Cuba provided the sensational field upon which the two publishers struggled. Both sent some of their best correspondents to Cuba and each tried to outdo the other with garish and often fanciful tales of starvation in concentration camps, pitched battles and Spanish atrocities. Such constant, biased presentation of the Cuban affair had an incendiary effect on the American people. They were convinced that it was the destiny of the United States to extend military help to the Cuban people in their struggle for freedom from Spanish tyranny. Demands for intervention came from both political parties.

In spite of this pressure, President Grover Cleveland consistently refused to deviate from his policy of asking Spain to solve the Cuban problem. He had no intention of committing his Democratic administration to armed intervention. In the summer of 1895, shortly after the revolt started, Cleveland proclaimed American neutrality and actively enforced our neutrality laws until he left office in the spring of 1897. In his negotiations with Spain, Cleveland kept asking that the revolt be brought to an end. He also made it clear that the United States had no designs on the island. By December, 1896, with no end to the revolt in sight, Cleveland warned Spain that she could not expect the United States to remain patient forever. He did not wish to further commit the incoming administration and did not press the point.

This was the situation when President William McKinley took the oath of office on March 4 1897. Having no desire for war, McKinley initially followed the basic policy laid down by his predecessor. In June he suggested that Spain work out with the insurgents a peaceful solution to the Cuban question. Specifically, he suggested the reconcentration end; the fighting stop; relief be extended to the Cuban people and Spain reform her colonial policy toward Cuba. As an alternative, McKinley warned, the United States might have to intervene. Of course, any settlement between Spain and the Cubans would have to receive the approval of the insurgents, who were not prone to acquiesce as long as the citizens of the United States supported their demands for complete independence. Consequently, no satisfactory progress was made. McKinley felt it necessary to turn the diplomatic screws again early in the fall by demanding that Cuba be given some form of autonomy. In November the Queen Regent responded by announcing a plan of autonomy for Cuba. It pleased no one. To the Cubans and to McKinley it was not autonomy at all. To the man on the street in Madrid it was virtual independence. The fighting in Cuba continued. In January, 1898, the battleship *Maine* was ordered to Havana. Ostensibly the ship was on a courtesy visit, but many believed it was there to protect American citizens from civil disorders.

The destruction of the *Maine* on February 15 set in motion the final moves which preceded the declaration of war. Within two days the New York *Journal* had published diagrams showing exactly how the bomb — the "infernal machine" — had been placed which blew the *Maine* into scrap iron. Other papers followed suit, and the press reported that the whole thing was a Spanish plot. The country was incensed. Meanwhile, a court of inquiry went to Havana and inspected the hulk of the shattered vessel. The report, released to Congress on March 28, concluded that the ship had been destroyed by a submarine mine which ignited at least two of the forward magazines. No conclusions were drawn as to who was responsible, but popular opinion blamed Spain. Delegations from both parties approached McKinley with the suggestion that his next message to Congress be decidedly belligerent.

During April President McKinley made his last attempts to resist the nation's demands that he ask Congress to declare war. Still attempting to settle the problem through diplomatic channels, he asked the Spanish government to call an armistice, to revoke the reconcentration orders, and to grant Cuba "full self-government." The Spanish reply was deemed inadequate. The Spaniards were perfectly willing to grant an armistice, and the reconcentration orders already had been revoked. They were willing to grant the island autonomy, but they were determined not to extend independence. This point had now become the major obstacle to peace. Neither nation would accept compromise. On April 11 McKinley sent a message to Congress asking that he be authorized to end the fighting in Cuba. Congress responded on April 20, giving the President power to use military force to secure independence for the island. Five days later the United States declared war.

Within ten days the Arizona Rough Riders were enroute to San Antonio to secure their place in history.

This is their story.

```
                    OFFICIAL BUSINESS

                 WAR DEPARTMENT TELEGRAM


                                        April, 25 1898.


To
     Honorable Myron T. McCord,

            Governor of Arizona,

               Phoenix, Arizona.

     The President directs that Captain Leonard Wood of the

United States Army be authorized to raise a regiment of cowboys

as mounted riflemen, and to be its Colonel, and has named Hon.

Theodore Roosevelt as Lieutenant Colonel.  All other officers

will come from the vicinity where the troops are raised.

What can you do for them?  Answer immediately.


                         R.A.ALGER,

                            Secretary of War.
```

The Call To Arms: War Department telegram sent to
Gov. Myron T. McCord authorizing the organization
of the unit which was to become the Rough Riders.
(*Copy Courtesy National Archives.*)

CHAPTER 1

To Tender Our Services

SPRING CAME EARLY to Arizona in 1898. By April the residents of Phoenix, the territorial capital, had started to complain about the unusually warm weather. But on Monday, April 25, it was neither the unseasonal heat nor the cloudless sky which bothered Governor Myron Hawley McCord as he drove to his office in the capitol building. He was more concerned with the political temperature of Congress. On this day it was expected to declare war with Spain and to authorize President William McKinley to intervene with military force to assist Cuba in its battle for independence. Two days before the Phoenix *Daily Republican* had predicted that war would come and that President McKinley would issue a call for volunteers. McCord's personal contacts in Washington, acquired during a long association with the Republican party, had intimated the same thing.[1]

Shortly after arriving at the capitol building, McCord received the expected news that Congress had declared war. Later that same day another telegram arrived from Secretary of War Russell A. Alger. This message informed McCord that Alger was forming a special regiment of volunteer cavalry as authorized by the Volunteer Bill of April 22. It was to be an exclusive unit, composed of men from the territories of Arizona, New Mexico, Oklahoma and from the unorganized area known as the Indian Territory. Arizona was called upon to furnish one hundred and seventy men for this regiment, which was designated the First United States Volunteer Cavalry.

Alger's request for volunteers came as no surprise to McCord or the citizens of Arizona. The governor had been requesting permission to form such a unit for two months. But the small quota for Arizona proved disappointing. As official spokesman for several ambitious Arizonans, McCord since late February had been petitioning the President for authority to muster a complete regiment of 1,000 men from Arizona. McKinley consistently refused the request, but McCord was confident that a declaration of war would induce the President to accept the offer. Consequently, when McCord received instructions to furnish a token force of two troops of but one hundred and seventy men, the governor was both disappointed and angry. In an attempt to increase the allotment, McCord immediately wired the War Department and made a final plea that the entire regiment be recruited in Arizona. Secretary Alger refused, but granted McCord the right to name the senior regimental major. That same evening McCord instructed his nominee, Alexander Oswald Brodie, a mining engineer and former Regular Army officer, to select the men and gather them at Whipple Barracks, a Regular Army post located near Prescott, the county seat of Yavapai County.

Whipple Barracks was an obvious and excellent choice as the rendezvous for the Arizona men. Located three miles northeast of Prescott, it had adequate transportation facilities provided by the Santa Fe, Prescott and Phoenix railroad. It could be reached from the south via Phoenix and from the east through Flagstaff. The fort had adequate quarters in the old masonry barracks, and sufficient rations were available. Historically, the post had been closely identified with Arizona's progress since the establishment of the territorial capital in nearby Prescott thirty-four years before. It had been headquarters of the Military Department of Arizona during the command of the redoubtable General George Crook, among other leading military figures of the grim Apache wars which had terminated in the territory a dozen years before.[2]

Moreover, the residents of Prescott long had been aroused over developing conditions in Cuba and had called for American intervention many weeks earlier. This feeling had intensified with the destruction of the *Maine* on February 15. A week later two Cuban officers, touring the West to plead Cuba's cause, lectured in the mountain city. On February 22 a Captain Mahoney and a Lieutenant Cordier, identified only as "two Cuban patriots," addressed a large crowd in the Yavapai Court House. In vivid terms they described the tyrannical Spanish colonial policy, the infamous *reconcentrado* orders and compared the motivation of the Cuban struggle for freedom with the spirit of the American Declaration of Independence. Mayor William "Buckey" O'Neill was presiding, and when they finished, the crowd passed a resolution calling on Congress to recognize the belligerents and to furnish them with assistance. A substantial sum was pledged to the war coffers of the insurgents.

Under such conditions it is not surprising that a plan to form a regiment of volunteer cavalry for service against Spain mushroomed at Prescott. On February 22, the same day that the two Cubans lectured in the court house, the Associated Press flashed the news across the nation that recruits were being accepted for a regiment of cavalry to be raised in Arizona and commanded by Alexander O. Brodie, a former Regular Army officer. Within a week Brodie was receiving applications from as far away as California.

Although the first news releases did not explain fully the plan of organization, details already had been carefully worked out. In its final conception, as approved by the governor some two months before the declaration of war, the plan called for a regiment to consist of twelve troops divided among three squadrons. Each squadron would contain four troops, and each troop would consist of one captain, two lieutenants and eighty-five enlisted men. Mayor "Buckey" O'Neill, of Prescott, would recruit men for six troops from the counties in the north. A Phoenix free-lance journalist, James Harvey McClintock, agreed to form six troops in the south. The enlisted men would elect their own troop officers, who in turn would select squadron commanders. It was expected, of course, that O'Neill and McClintock each would be elected to command a squadron with the rank of major. The colonel commanding the regiment would be Brodie, who would select the assistant regimental commander and the staff.

A simple and workable plan it appears to have been, but its origin still is not clear. McClintock, who was to be the de facto historian of the Arizona recruits for thirty years, always maintained that O'Neill conceived the idea and that together they approached Brodie with the proposal that because of his experience and leadership Brodie should command the unit. This version has been accepted without reservation by friends and biographers of O'Neill. Some have even asserted that O'Neill actually formed the regiment while waiting for authority to do so from the War Department. Undoubtedly this is an exaggeration for there is no record of O'Neill ever having made application to either Governor McCord or Washington. Moreover, contemporary newspaper accounts usually credited Brodie with initiating the plan.

Although the original and exact relationship between Brodie and O'Neill is not clear, there never was any doubt that the command would be offered to Brodie. In addition to his obvious qualifications, he was well liked in Arizona.

Fortunately, Alexander O. Brodie was available to head

the proposed Arizona regiment. Born in Edwards, Saint Lawrence County, New York, in 1849, he had entered West Point at the age of seventeen. After graduation in 1870, ranked twenty-seventh in a class of fifty-eight, the new second lieutenant reported to Fort Apache, in the White mountains of eastern Arizona, for duty with the First Cavalry. There he trained Indian scouts and actively campaigned in the field. On June 24, 1871, Brodie was wounded when his small detachment was ambushed by a large band of hostile Apaches near the fort. A few weeks later the Secretary of War, in a speech to the graduating class on the plains at West Point, described this action and praised the young officer's conduct. The wound healed without complications and Brodie was able to participate in General Crook's famous campaign of 1872-73 in the pine-shrouded Tonto Basin and other Apache strongholds north of the Salt River in eastern and northern Arizona. The following year the First Cavalry moved to Washington Territory, and there Brodie took the field against the Nez Perce of Idaho under the noted Chief Joseph. In 1877 he was saddened by the passing of his wife of only one year, the former Kate Reynolds of Walla Walla, Washington, who died in childbirth. The infant daughter died a few weeks later. Notwithstanding his promotion to first lieutenant, Brodie terminated his promising Regular Army career by resigning.

For the next few years Brodie was ranching in Kansas. The lure of military life, however, proved to be irresistible. In August, 1883, Brodie turned up at Jefferson Barracks, Missouri, and enlisted in the cavalry. Within a few days he was enroute to Arizona for field service with M Troop, Sixth Cavalry.

There is no satisfactory explanation as to why Brodie chose to enlist, but it may have been because of a desire to participate in the Apache wars which again had broken out in Arizona. In September, 1882, Brodie's old commander from his days at Fort Apache, General George Crook, had returned to take command of the Department of Arizona. Early the following May Crook had swept into Mexico at the head of a column composed of a troop of the Sixth Cavalry under Captain Adna R. Chaffee and a group of Apache scouts.[3] The scouts were commanded by the ill-fated Captain Emmett Crawford.[4] Within a few months some four hundred Apaches under Geronimo and several lesser chiefs had been enticed out of Mexico to settle on the San Carlos Reservation in central Arizona.

If Brodie enlisted with the anticipation that he would see field service against these hostiles with the Sixth Cavalry his timing was unfortunate, for with Geronimo and his warriors on the reservation the frontier was relatively peaceful until another outbreak occurred in 1885. Garrison duty as an enlisted man did not appeal to Brodie and he was discharged in February, 1884.

Brodie stayed in Arizona after his discharge and three years later became superintendent of the Walnut Grove Water Storage Company near Prescott. In that capacity he supervised the installation of a dam on Walnut Creek. In 1890, when he was no longer associated with the firm, the dam burst following a period of prolonged rainfall. The resulting flood caused some loss of life. Brodie could not be blamed for this disaster because he had advocated publicly an increase in the size of the spillways. Following this tragedy the operating company became bankrupt. Brodie, almost alone among the early promoters, was so respected that he was named receiver of the Walnut Grove Water Storage Company. Because of law suits filed against the property, Brodie retained the connection for a dozen years.

Brodie also had an interest in politics. He served a short time as colonel of the Arizona National Guard and, in 1892, was elected recorder of Yavapai County on the Republican ticket. He served one term. A mining enterprise then took Brodie into the Bradshaw mountains southeast of Prescott. He and his associates opened a group of potential mines including the Yankee Boy, Yankee Girl, Silver King and Crown Point. Brodie felt that the gold deposit at the latter claim was the most promising, and he personally took up residence at the mine site, while maintaining another home in Prescott for his second wife, the former Mary Hanlon of that community. She was the daughter of the original owner of the Walnut Grove Water Storage Company.

Tragedy again struck Brodie's personal life in 1896, when the first son of his second marriage, Alexander O. Brodie, Jr., died. On April 20, 1898, however, Mary presented him with a second son who was given the same name, thus keeping alive an ancient Scottish tradition. Brodie's full name was Alexander Oswald Brodie the XVI.

Brodie had all the characteristics desired in a military officer. He was a large man, standing just under six feet, with the physique and rugged, sun-bronzed features of an out-doorsman. Dark brown eyes and a drooping, brown mustache complemented his tanned face. By 1898 he had lived in Arizona for most of sixteen years and had made many friends because of his intelligence, his gentlemanly deportment and his ability to mingle socially with people from all walks of life. He could converse with people of high society one moment and equally be at ease with a group of cowboys the next. Firm and just in administering discipline, he held the respect of all. "He never looked down on anyone," recalled Arthur L. Tuttle, one of the recruits from Safford.[5]

In organizing the proposed Arizona regiment, Brodie received the most help from the young mayor of Prescott, William Owen "Buckey" O'Neill. Born in Ireland in 1860, O'Neill had come to Phoenix in 1879, giving for reasons, probably political, either Washington, D.C., or St. Louis as his birthplace. He revealed his Irish origin for the first and only time when he enrolled in the army in 1898. A printer and typesetter by trade, O'Neill moved to Prescott two years after arriving in Arizona. There he started and operated a livestock newspaper, the *Hoof and Horn*. It was also at

Prescott that his friends began calling him "Buckey" because he liked to play faro or "buck the tiger" as it was called.

Politically oriented, O'Neill became a probate judge in Yavapai County in 1886. Two years later he was elected sheriff and received wide publicity for his tenacious pursuit and capture of three men who robbed a train at Canyon del Diablo, northeast of Prescott. Impressed by the reform movement, which was sweeping the West in that decade, O'Neill ran for delegate to Congress on the Populist ticket in 1894 and again in 1896. Both times he was defeated. He continued to criticize the Republican party and finally incurred the political enmity of Governor McCord for his outspoken opposition to the practice of contracting prison labor to private corporations. McCord's retaliatory opposition, however, did not prevent O'Neill from being elected mayor of Prescott in 1897.

A man who enjoyed life, O'Neill had a vibrant, magnetic personality which made him popular with both men and women. Standing almost six feet, he cut a dashing figure with his dark brown hair, neatly trimmed mustache and infectious grin. Women considered him to be quite handsome. His military experience was limited to some service with a militia company, the Prescott Grays, where an interesting aspect of O'Neill's character was revealed. On one occasion his troop turned out to act as guard at a legal hanging. Just as the trap was sprung under the condemned man — O'Neill fainted dead away. After the Prescott sports had reminded him of this incident for a dozen years, the danger of the battlefield held no fresh horrors for Buckey. He gave Brodie his whole-hearted support.

As a third member of the triumvirate, Brodie and O'Neill selected James H. McClintock, a broad-shouldered Phoenix journalist who had known O'Neill for nineteen years. Born in Sacramento, California, in 1864, McClintock had come to Arizona to visit his brother in 1879. He liked the territory and decided to stay. During the next few years he held several jobs, including employment on the Phoenix *Salt River Herald* and the Prescott *Journal*. Later he was employed by the adjutant general's office at Fort Whipple during the last campaign against Geronimo. This was his first close association with the military and he never forgot it. McClintock returned to Phoenix and enrolled in the new Tempe Normal School, later Arizona State University. After one year he was qualified to teach school and he went into the Tonto Basin north of Globe as a teacher. Journalism remained his real interest, however, and soon he returned to the Salt River Valley to pursue that line of work.

Politically, McClintock affiliated himself with the Republican party, but this did not preclude his association with members of the opposition. He retained his close friendship with O'Neill, who was moving to Populism, and with Carl Hayden, who later became the traditional vote-getter of the Arizona Democrats.[6] McClintock also served as secretary of the Republican party in Arizona while working for the *Arizona Republican* of Phoenix and as a special correspondent for the Los Angeles *Times*. When the war clouds began to gather in the spring of 1898, McClintock was running a news service in Phoenix and doing free-lance writing. Like O'Neill, he was anxious to lay down the pen and pick up the sword.

In March Brodie took preliminary steps to make his proposed regiment a reality. Early that month, after publicly announcing his intentions, he tried to secure official authorization from Washington. On March 3 he sent telegrams to both President McKinley and Governor McCord offering his services in the event of war and requesting permission to raise a regiment of cavalry. In his telegram to the President, Brodie made the alternative proposal that he be reinstated in grade to rank with his class at West Point if the decision was made to increase the size of the Regular Army rather than call for volunteers. A week later Brodie renewed his application. In a handwritten letter, he invited attention to his personal qualifications and ventured an opinion as to the military potential of the Arizonans. On March 10 Brodie wrote:

> Prescott, Arizona
> March 10, 1898
>
> To the President
>   Washington
>   D.C.
> Sir —
>
> On March 3rd I telegraphed tendering my services to the Government in the event of war with Spain and requesting authority to raise a regiment of volunteers in this Territory for active service in the field, and failing a call for volunteers but increase of regular army, made application for appointment in the line in rank with my class, 1870 U.S.M.A.
>
> I have the honor Mr. President to renew in writing my tender of service and to request, in case of war and call for volunteers, authority to organize a regiment, Cavalry preferred, for duty in the field, and I feel qualified to assure you that no better material can be found than in the men of this Territory.
>
> My record as an officer of the 1st Cavalry U.S.A. for over some 7 years, will be found on file in the War Department and in event of hostilities I shall be pleased to furnish testimonies as to my standing as a citizen.
>
> In addition to my services [words illegible] Army I was appointed Colonel of and organized 1st Regiment National Guard of Arizona.
>
>   I am Sir
>   Very respectfully
>   Your Obdt Servant
>   Alex O. Brodie[7]

Similar testimonials came from the chief executive of the territory. Governor McCord was in Washington when Brodie made his original application, but acting governor Charles A. Akers endorsed Brodie's request with the recommendation that he be allowed to "organize, and lead on the field of battle, a regiment of cavalry."[8] Brodie sent this endorsement forward on March 15.

When Governor McCord returned to Arizona later that same month, Brodie prevailed upon him to provide another endorsement. On April 2 the governor wrote a long letter to the President requesting that Brodie be authorized to raise a regiment in Arizona. McCord assured McKinley that "no better material for cavalry purposes can be found anywhere in the world, than among the cowboys of Arizona." He pointed out that the members of such a unit would require little training as they already possessed skill with horses, fire-arms and camp equipment. Many of them had campaigned against Indians and therefore had experienced hostile gun-fire. They would be particularly well-suited for outpost and scouting duty because of their self-reliance and knowledge of Spanish. Moreover, they could take the field immediately, because the men would be able to furnish their own horses — horses that they could ride day after day without additional training as opposed to recruits from "older settled sections," who would have to learn all this at government expense. Coming from the southwest, McCord continued, the men from Arizona "would be better prepared for campaigning in semi-tropical countries than men secured from the colder climates."[9]

Although his requests failed to produce immediate authorization, Brodie gathered the names of those in Arizona who desired to join such a unit. By the end of the first week in April, O'Neill, working closely with Brodie, had a recruiter in each of the six counties north of Maricopa. In Mohave County W. W. Dunbar and Kean St. Charles of Kingman had agreed to recruit; while Ralph Cameron, A. C. Stark and J. W. Francis of Flagstaff were active in Coconino County. A. F. McAllister of Winslow was working in Navajo County, and Walter G. Scott of St. Johns was gathering the men in Apache. Henry W. Nash, a school teacher in the little town of Strawberry in the shadow of the Mogollon Rim, had taken up recruiting duty in Gila County. O'Neill, of course, per-sonally handled the applications in Yavapai.

Brodie instructed his assistants to continue to accept volunteers until the War Department granted the expected authorization. At that time Brodie planned to travel to each county, oversee the formation of the troops and preside over the election of officers. It is not known how many men expressed an interest during March and early April, but, on April 4, recruiters in Jerome, a picturesque little mining town clinging to the east slope of Mingus Mountain in Yavapai County, promised to furnish O'Neill one hundred good men.

McClintock, meanwhile, had less success in the southern part of the territory than had O'Neill in the north. Tradition holds that this occurred because McClintock actively recruited only in Maricopa County and merely wrote letters of invitation to a few friends in other areas. This tradition is supported by the correspondence concerning the regiment which was printed in the newspapers. Invariably these letters were between the local recruiter and either O'Neill or Brodie. Nevertheless, by April 6 recruiters were working in four of the six southern counties. They were: Wiley S. Jones in Graham County, Captain William P. Long in Cochise and Bernabe Brichta with the help of Mose Drachman in Pima. McClintock, of course, was in Maricopa. Yuma and Pinal counties were not represented. McClintock's limited success is reflected in a comparison with the situation in the north. On the same day that recruiters in Jerome had promised to furnish O'Neill with one hundred men, McClintock estimated that he had a total of sixty. Yet, in spite of his limited success, the journalist expressed satisfaction with his progress, especially in the quality of his recruits. Early in April he reported to Brodie that "an excellent class of men" had expressed a desire to join.

Within this same letter, which McClintock wrote to Brodie in Prescott on April 5, there is some explanation for the newspaperman's failure to recruit as energetically as O'Neill was doing in the northern tier of counties. McClintock already was thinking of himself in a command position and was imparting to Brodie his intimate feelings about recruiting problems:

My Dear Colonel:

Glad to hear from you. Believe the best rendezvous would be Whipple, though it is possible that troops along the line of the S.P. might better be gathered at Tucson till removed from the Territory. Political significance counts nothing in this case. Do not believe there is any likelihood of going other than as cavalry — I have an excellent class of men on the roll. Yesterday two model cavalrymen came in. One had just arrived from Mexico, coming from the Yaqui river to fight for the Union. Few or none are of the blustering mouthing kind. Several are substantial merchants and farmers. Somehow the "tin soldier" element is very shy of the proposition. Guess its members all want to be colonels or majors. About a third of my enlistment have an eye on a lieutenancy, but they seem to have agreed without discussion on a captain. I have told them that you will be here and preside at the organization meeting and that such meeting will be a quiet affair. There's very little brass band about the outfit. Yours sincerely,

(s) Jas. H. McClintock.[10]

McClintock's confidence about the selection of the captain was well placed. Brodie, McCord and the men were all satisfied with him.

During March and April, while Brodie gathered prospective recruits in Arizona, at least two other men in western areas came up with similar proposals. On March 8, just five days after Brodie's initial request, a member of the Wyoming legislature, Jay L. Torrey, wrote the governor of Wyoming to inquire if the governor would support a plan to form a regiment of cavalry in that state. Two days later Torrey met President McKinley and asked for authorization to proceed with his plan. Still another request was made on March 23 when Melvin Grigsby, a Civil War veteran and adjutant general of South Dakota, asked permission to form a volunteer regiment of cowboys from the West. Although both Torrey and Grigsby actively continued to press for authorization to proceed with their plans, apparently neither of them actually initiated steps to form their regiment as did Brodie.

Grigsby's enterprise and interest, however, was to save the day for the Arizonans within a few weeks.

As recruiting continued, Brodie found that his plans had the enthusiastic support of newspapers throughout the territory. Most editorial comments on the idea agreed that Brodie was an excellent choice to lead the regiment and predicted great success. The Prescott *Journal Miner,* reflecting the unparalleled enthusiasm of Yavapai County, kept its readers well informed of progress as reported by Brodie and O'Neill. Although supporting President McKinley's reluctance to send a premature war message to Congress over the *Maine,* the editors predicted that Arizona would demand acceptance of Brodie's regiment should war be declared.

In southern Arizona the Tucson *Arizona Weekly Star* gave its complete support. Suggesting that the command be christened "the Arizona Flying Cavalry Squadron," the *Star* treated its readers to an eloquent display of braggadocio in praising the military potential of the Arizona cowboys. All the troopers would be inured to the climate of Cuba and able to "shoot to kill on a fly as well as at a dead rest." If given the opportunity this regiment of Arizona boys would "sweep over the island of Cuba like a tornado, and would do more execution than ten ordinary regiments of cavalry."[11]

As the diplomatic relations between the United States and Spain continued to deteriorate late in April, Brodie became concerned over the War Department's failure to act on his request. He realized that war might come at any time. To ensure that everything was ready, Brodie had O'Neill write to each assistant and request a report on the status of recruiting. In these letters O'Neill emphasized the need for haste. He pointed out that Brodie had promised the President he would form his command within ten days after authorization. In his letter to McClintock, written April 23, O'Neill revealed that recruiting was not progressing satisfactorily — especially in the south. After stating he had nearly three hundred men pledged to join his northern battalion, O'Neill made a rather pointed offer to furnish men to McClintock if the southerners failed to respond. "I want to see your troop thrown into this battalion," O'Neill wrote, "unless you can raise two troops in the Salt River Valley, in which case we can throw another troop to you from the north making a full battalion."[12]

Within this same letter, which revealed that Brodie only had approximately half the number he had promised to enlist, O'Neill went on to suggest that McClintock approach McCord with the proposition that the governor travel to Washington and personally press for official sanction of the regiment. O'Neill indicated that five hundred dollars could be raised to defray expenses. This plan, however, was never pushed. On April 22 Congress passed the Volunteer Bill and three days later declared war.

As originally written, the Volunteer Bill of April 22 did not provide for the acceptance of units such as the one proposed by Brodie. Fortunately, the bill was amended at the last possible moment. In early April, as the nation drifted closer toward open conflict with Spain, it was obviously necessary that the size of the army had to be increased in order to place the nation on any kind of a war footing. Several plans to accomplish this had been discussed. By the middle of the month, the decision had been made to form a Volunteer Army by accepting National Guard units on a voluntary basis. This plan was incorporated into appropriate legislative form and submitted to Congress by the administration. At the last moment, however, this concept was altered by the efforts of Adjutant General Melvin Grigsby of South Dakota. When Grigsby realized that National Guard units might be the only ones accepted, he made a fast trip to Washington, and presented an amendment to Senator Francis X. Warren of Wyoming, who was then debating the proposed Volunteer Bill in joint committee.

Grigsby's amendment was accepted and incorporated

into the bill exactly as he had written it. As amended, Section 6 provided that "the President may authorize the Secretary of War to organize companies, troops, battalions, or regiments, possessing special qualifications, from the nation at large not to exceed 3,000 men, under such rules and regulations . . . as may be prescribed by the Secretary of War."[13] With this authority Secretary Alger decided to form three regiments of Volunteer Cavalry to come from the states and territories of the far West.

In keeping with the provisions of the legislation, Secretary Alger specified that these three regiments of cavalry were to be composed "exclusively of frontiersmen possessing special qualifications as horsemen and marksmen."[14] The first regiment was to be raised in the four territories, the second in Wyoming and the Third in the Dakotas. To command the First regiment, Alger named Leonard Wood as its colonel. Wood, a captain in the medical corps, was well known in Arizona. While still an assistant civilian contract surgeon waiting for his pending commission in the medical corps, he had won the Medal of Honor in 1886 while commanding troops from Fort Huachuca in the closing campaign against Geronimo. His commission had come through in the midst of that campaign. The lieutenant colonel of the regiment was to be Theodore Roosevelt, then Assistant Secretary of the Navy and known in Arizona only by his reputation as a fervent jingo. The Second U.S. Volunteer Cavalry regiment was to be commanded by Jay L. Torrey of Wyoming, and the Third regiment by Melvin Grigsby.

Colonel Wood's command would have a strength of seven hundred and eighty men. One hundred and seventy would be drawn from Arizona, an equal number from the Indian Territory, three hundred and forty from New Mexico and eighty from Oklahoma Territory. The War Department gave Colonel Wood a free hand in organizing his command. With characteristic energy and speed Wood drew up his plan of organization, designated San Antonio, Texas, as the training camp — and wired Brodie to call up his Arizona squadron.

It was a great disappointment to Brodie, but the Volunteer Bill of April 22 washed out his ambition to lead an entire regiment from Arizona. He and Governor McCord had done their best, but the law specified that only three regiments of volunteer cavalry could be organized. Arizona did not have enough political significance to be allowed to furnish one complete regiment. As a result, a limited number of Arizonans were being placed in a regiment shared by three other geographical areas. Some of the men realized that this might be a blessing in disguise. Any force which included Theodore Roosevelt would probably get into action, for "Teddy" was the kind of man who would pull any string — political or personal — to get his men on the field of battle.

On the afternoon of April 25, after receiving confirmation of his majority and official authorization to form the squadron from McCord, Brodie modified his plan to organize two troops instead of a regiment. Brodie divided the Arizona quota among the counties to provide one troop from the north and one from the south. Using voting registration as the guideline, the northern troop was to be composed of six men each from Apache, Navaho and Mohave counties. Coconino was to furnish fourteen volunteers, Graham sixteen men and five recruits were to come from Pinal. Yavapai was allotted the lion's share of thirty volunteers. The southern troop was to be made up of thirty-eight men from Maricopa, fourteen from Cochise, fifteen from Pima, twelve from Gila and six from Yuma. Brodie advised his recruiters to gather their men and report to Whipple Barracks on April 29-30. In those areas where he had no active recruiters he asked the county recorder to enlist the men. Brodie cautioned them to accept only those applicants who were between the ages of eighteen and forty-five, physically sound, good riders and proficient with firearms.

During the next three days, while the recruits gathered in their respective counties, Brodie completed the final details. As captains he nominated O'Neill for the northern troop and

McClintock for the southern troop. Apparently the decision had been made not to trust the men with the important task of selecting troop commanders. Brodie forwarded the nominations to McCord, for Secretary Alger had directed the governors of the territories to appoint all company grade officers. Appointments to the staff and field grade positions would come from the War Department. McCord agreed to appoint McClintock without argument, but hesitated at commissioning his old political enemy O'Neill. McCord finally agreed, however, after McClintock and several others visited the governor and strongly insisted that O'Neill be given the position. One of O'Neill's friends is reported to have advanced the logical argument that O'Neill would not be able to embarrass the governor with editorials while campaigning in the wilds of Cuba.

On the evening of April 27, the chief officers of the Arizona group, Brodie, McClintock and O'Neill, were honored at a banquet in Phoenix. The adjutant general, R. Allyn Lewis, proposed a toast: "Now we drink the soldier's toast — death or a star!" O'Neill jumped to his feet.

"Who would not gamble for a new star?" he challenged.[15]

In later years O'Neill's enemies cited this quotation as evidence that O'Neill was driven by excessive ambition and thirst for personal glory. His critics maintained that the star he envisioned was that of a brigadier general on his own shoulder. Others more charitably contend that O'Neill's statement reflected his optimism that Arizona's reward for full cooperation in the war with Spain would be a new star in the blue field of the nation's flag. There is no doubt that O'Neill long had been interested in statehood for Arizona. He had promised to work for that goal when he ran for Congress.

Additional evidence has come to light that supports the contention that O'Neill was thinking initially of his adopted Arizona. In the Sunday supplement of the New York *Journal* of July 15, 1898, a letter from Buckey to his friend, the New York author Thurlow Weed Barnes, was published. Written between May 7 and May 20, while O'Neill was still in training at San Antonio, the letter clarified beyond all reasonable doubt O'Neill's meaning. After speculating on the forthcoming campaign in Cuba, O'Neill closed with the significant observation: "Who would not gamble for a new star in the flag?" It is unfortunate that O'Neill failed to make his meaning clear when he accepted his commission in Phoenix.

With his key officers appointed, Brodie made arrangements to provide for the men. He secured the services of private physicians in Phoenix and Tucson to conduct preliminary examinations as the men passed through on their way to Prescott. He also arranged for railroad transportation. Then, just before ordering the men to rendezvous, he received notice that Arizona's quota had been increased to an even two hundred because the regimental strength had been raised from the original seven hundred and eighty to 1,000 men. Brodie thus informed O'Neill and McClintock that they each would need one hundred men rather than eighty-five as originally planned.

The first recruits for O'Neill's troops began arriving in Prescott on their own initiative immediately after the declaration of war. Most came from the nearby ranches and mining towns, but some came from other areas. Two residents of California — William Greenwood, who had served under Brodie in the First Cavalry, and Charles Hodgdon, a prize fighter — heard of the Arizona contingent and came to Prescott to join. As no orders for formal enlistment had been received at Whipple Barracks, the men stayed in town at their own expense. This had a beneficial effect on the local economy. The hotels filled and restaurants did a thriving business. During the afternoons and evenings the men crowded into the saloons along Prescott's famous "Whiskey Row." One in particular, the Palace, run by Robert Brow, proved especially attractive. On the morning of April 27 O'Neill set up recruiting offices in Aitken and Robinson's cigar store in downtown Prescott. By noon he had over fifty signatures, and more recruits were on their way from Flagstaff, Jerome, Kingman and Camp Verde.

In contrast to the speed shown by O'Neill in selecting his men, McClintock took five days to gather a group for his command. On the evening of April 29, McClintock departed Phoenix with forty-five men from Maricopa County, the first detachment of his southern Arizona troop. The recruits had been examined by Dr. Henry V. Clymer and Dr. Win Wylie in Phoenix that morning. At 2:00 P.M. that afternoon the group had been formed in front of McCord's residence to listen to an emotional address by the governor. Among other things McCord pleaded with the men to "conduct themselves as to reflect credit on the territory."[16] The governor then shook hands with each man. When it came time to leave that evening, the National Guard company of Phoenix, a local band and a group of Civil War veterans had accompanied the volunteers to the depot of the Santa Fe, Prescott and Phoenix railway. There a large crowd gathered to say goodbye and see the boys off. Amid the bursting of firecrackers, the strains of the "Girl I Left Behind Me" and watched by a few tearful women, the train had pulled out of the station at 9:00 P.M.

As his coach rolled past Glendale and climbed toward Wickenburg and Congress Junction, McClintock settled back with obvious satisfaction. He was positive that his recruits constituted the first organized group of volunteers in the entire nation to physically respond to the President's call for men. His troopers were thinking of something else. There was a decided chill in the air. The balmy spring weather of the past few weeks had been dispersed by a cold front moving in from the coast. Already there was some snow and rain falling in the higher mountains. Many of the men had not anticipated this change in the weather and had failed to bring suitable clothing. They were to regret this before the night was over.

With the exception of the group from Maricopa County, the largest number of recruits for the southern troop came from Pima County. Although Bernabe Brichta and Mose Drachman had originally agreed to act as recruiters in Pima, the actual task of gathering the men fell to Eugene W. Waterbury, a twenty-four-year-old clerk of the Orndorff Hotel in Tucson. Waterbury began contacting prospective recruits on April 6 and estimated he had over thirty men lined up when the call came to rendezvous. Unfortunately, the Pima quota had been set at only fourteen men. Brodie, however, advised Waterbury to report with "two or three extra."[17] Consequently, twenty-one applicants presented themselves to Dr. Walter E. Gould of Tucson for examination. The eighteen who passed left Tucson on April 29. According to the Tucson *Arizona Weekly Star* they were: Waterbury, Agricol Roca, Tom Rynning, Frank T. Fitzgerald, Sam W. Noyes, Joseph McGinty, Albert Townsend, Frank Harmson, Fenn S. Hildreth, B. C. Powers and Sol Drachman from Tucson; while Marshall M. Bird, Louis H. Van Treese and Gilliat S. Hitchcock came from Nogales, then a part of Pima County. There were also four others identified only as Matney, Gustaf, Allen and King. These last four, in addition to Roca, Powers and Hitchcock, failed to pass a second medical examination in Prescott. Another Tucsonian, David L. Hughes, the son of a long time Tucson resident, Samuel Hughes, was working in Bisbee and therefore enlisted with the group from Cochise County.[18]

The recruits from Cochise County passed through Phoenix on April 30. They had been gathered by Joel Rex Hall, editor of the Bisbee *Orb,* who apparently had replaced Captain Long as the recruiter sometime in April.[19] A man who traveled extensively in the West while working at odd jobs,

Rex Hall, as he liked to be called, had no known family or relatives. He had begun recruiting in April. Hall's contingent was made up largely of Bisbee miners — some of whom had been taken off their work shifts early in order for them to depart on schedule. The group included: George J. McCabe, John Foster, Alex S. Keir, Jackson H. Misner, William S. Snodderly, Jesse T. Toland, Thomas W. Wiggins, David Hughes and Hall himself.

A great deal of confusion surrounded the departure of the eight recruits from Yuma. On Tuesday, April 26, County Recorder Cornelius P. Cronin received a telegram from Brodie asking that he recruit six good men for the volunteer regiment. Upon publicizing this request, Cronin was immediately besieged by more than fifty applicants. At a mass meeting of all interested persons held in the court house the next day, a three man committee consisting of Cronin, Mulford Winsor and U. G. Wilder was appointed by C. L. Brown, who had been elected chairman, to screen the applicants and select the six men to represent Yuma County. After some deliberation, during which the Yuma allotment was increased by two and the departure of the group was postponed from April 29 to April 30 in order that the committee could select the final candidates, the three men finally agreed on James Maxey, Willis O. Huson, William E. Marvin, George Neville, Harry Moss, Albert Wright, James Denmark and Al Houser. At Prescott Denmark, Moss and Houser were rejected, but they were replaced by William Sexsmith and Edward Moffet who had traveled to Prescott on their own initiative and without official sanction of the Yuma selection committee. The eighth member of the Yuma contingent was Cornelius P. Cronin. When Cronin, who had accompanied the group to Prescott out of curiosity and interest, learned that Brodie would accept applicants who were not cowboys, he immediately enlisted.

The sixteen-man detachment from Graham arrived in Prescott on May 2. Gathered by Robert S. Patterson, a young Safford rancher, the boys from Graham traveled by train, arrangements having been made by George Bugbee, one of the recruits who had resigned as division superintendent for the Southern Pacific. In addition to Patterson and Bugbee, the contingent included: Wilber D. French, George A. McCarter, Fred W. Bugbee, who was a brother to George, Bruce Weathers, Frank Paxton, Wallace J. Stark, Arthur Tuttle, John W. Parker, William Asay, Walter W. Griffin, James A. May, Charles Skogsberg, Adelbert D. Webb and Frank Van Siclin. Ed Wild also accompanied the group as a substitute, but he was not enlisted at Whipple Barracks. The riding ability of this group was open to question. Tuttle and Patterson had some experience with horses, but only May and Van Siclin had earned the title of cowboy.

The last contingent to arrive at the rendezvous was the group from Gila County. Recruited by Lieutenant H. H. McNelly of the Globe unit of the Arizona National Guard, the fifteen men from Gila left Globe on May 2 in two coaches drawn by four horses each that had been furnished by E. C. Hockett of Globe. At Riverside, a popular crossing of the Gila River north of Florence, the recruits found that the river was in flood and they had to wait eight hours for the water to recede. They reached Phoenix on May 3 and arrived in Prescott the next day. Representing Gila County were: Harry Pollack, Clifton Middleton, David Logue, Jerry Lee, Ed Collier, Sebird Henderson, William Owen, John Swetman, Frank Ward, William Davidson, Alva Eakin; James Goodwin, J. F. Gray, H. Graham, David Warford and E. R. Cline. All were accepted except Gray, Cline and Graham.

Brodie had hoped to begin formal enlistment at Whipple Barracks on April 29, but he had not yet received the necessary authorization. With some men already in Prescott and more scheduled to arrive the next day, he wired Colonel Wood to get the necessary instructions from the War Department. Brodie pointed out that he had already ordered the men to rendezvous, and they would need barracks and rations. He also indicated that a mustering officer and examining physician would have to be detailed. Brodie concluded his request by urging that Wood take immediate action. In

the meantime, Brodie planned to quarter the men in the
Yavapai Court House and livery barn offered by Sheriff
George C. Ruffner. Fortunately, this did not become neces-
sary as the orders to commence enlistment arrived at Whipple
Barracks that same afternoon.

On the afternoon of April 29 a towheaded young officer,
Second Lieutenant Herschel Tupes of the Fifteenth Infantry
who was stationed at Whipple Barracks, received orders to
formally enroll the two hundred members of Brodie's squadron.[20] As fast as the recruits arrived in Prescott they were
interviewed by Brodie, O'Neill and later McClintock in the
court house. Those who passed the interview were marched
to the fort in small groups. Some of the men interviewed by
O'Neill later recalled that he appeared very business-like as
he sat behind a large desk, smoking a brown paper cigarette,
and questioning the applicants in tones clipped with authority. Upon arrival at Whipple, the men were greeted by Lieutenant Tupes, examined by a physician and assigned a bunk
in one of the barracks. Each recruit received one blanket and
his mess equipment. In spite of the fact that the post was
virtually abandoned by the Regular Army and there were
several barracks available, the men expressed dissatisfaction
with the accommodations. They found the barracks cold and
full of bedbugs. Some of the volunteers were satisfied with
the army rations of coffee, bacon, beans, hash, beef and soup,
but others preferred to walk into town to supplement their
diet in the restaurants.

With one exception, Lieutenant Tupes delayed formal
enrollment until the next morning, April 30. On that day he
enlisted forty-nine men. The first volunteer to be enrolled,
however, was Captain O'Neill, who always took pride in
pointing out that he was the first volunteer to be accepted
into federal service for the war with Spain. It is suspected that
O'Neill and Tupes deliberately created this situation, for
O'Neill was the only man to be enrolled on April 29. All

others were accepted no sooner than April 30. Another member of the squadron, Tom Rynning, later expressed the opinion that he might have been the first to enlist. The official records show that Rynning joined on May 1.

Most of the men behaved themselves during their stay at Whipple Barracks, but one elderly recruit had to be dropped from the rolls. He had an uncontrollable affection for liquor. It seems that a man by the name of Adams reported to Whipple Barracks one night in a state of complete intoxication. Arthur L. Tuttle of Safford and several others were ordered to keep him under guard. That night it snowed and Tuttle laughingly recalled that the inebriate, who was well fortified with alcohol, was much warmer than his guards. The next morning Adams was taken quietly away and nobody saw him at the post or in Prescott again. Brodie had no difficulty in securing a replacement from the 1,000 or more applicants.

While waiting for the muster to be completed, Captains O'Neill and McClintock took steps to organize their troops. From the strange assortment of cowboys, miners, gamblers, journalists and one college instructor — Thomas C. Grindell who resigned his position in the English department at the Normal School in Tempe to enlist in McClintock's troop — they selected those with Regular Army experience to conduct dismounted close-order drill and other activities calculated to introduce the Volunteers to army routine. The men presented a ludicrous sight. No uniforms or equipment were available for issue, and the distinct unmilitary appearance of Stetsons and high-heeled boots hampered their efforts. Nevertheless, the Volunteers enjoyed the novelty of their clumsy attempts to learn drill in the unseasonably chilling wind that had deposited a light snow on the parade ground.

The selection of the junior officers was the last detail of organization to be concluded at Whipple Barracks. Each troop would have a captain, a first lieutenant and a second lieutenant. On April 27, the day that McCord had issued commissions to O'Neill and McClintock, he had also made a Phoenix attorney, Joseph L. B. Alexander, a first lieutenant under McClintock. Alexander turned out to be a fine choice. Born in Los Angeles in 1858, he had become a Democratic politician and, like O'Neill, had opposed McCord's administration while practicing law in Phoenix. The troop second lieutenant was not appointed until after the troop was formed at Prescott. Tradition holds that the person had already been selected, but when the men arrived they protested the decision to the extent that it was decided to fill the vacancy by election. This may or may not have been true — but an election was held.

There were several candidates after the appointment for, as McClintock had confided to Brodie a few weeks earlier: "About a third of my enlistment have an eye on a lieutenancy."[21] The choice was soon narrowed to George B. Wilcox, of Bisbee and Cornelius Cronin of Yuma. Wilcox, who was born in New York in 1864 and who had served as an enlisted man in the Fourth Cavalry, won the election in spite of McCord's preference for Cronin as stated to McClintock. On May 3 McCord wired: "If lieutenancy between Willcox [sic] and Cronin, I think Cronin the more entitled as he has spent time and money recruiting."[22]

It is not clear how the officers were selected for O'Neill's troop. None of them was chosen until after the troop had started to form at Whipple Barracks. There is no evidence that they were elected. According to the Prescott *Journal Miner,* the three men who applied for commissions were Eugene Brady O'Neill, Buckey's brother, Kean St. Charles, the recruiter in Kingman, and Frank Frantz, a native of Illinois who was a clerk for a mining company at Richenbar, a few miles southeast of Prescott. It was Frantz who eventually won the coveted shoulder straps of the first lieutenant.[23] As his second lieutenant O'Neill accepted Robert S. Patterson, a twenty-nine year old rancher who had brought the group from Graham County. Patterson's appointment may have resulted from the visit he had with McCord on May 2, when he passed through Phoenix on his way to Prescott.

On May 4, with the examination and enlistment of the group from Gila completed, the Arizona squadron was ready to leave. Brodie had received a telegram from Colonel Wood requesting that the Arizona men leave for San Antonio as soon as possible, and he was anxious to comply. G. M. Sargent, the General Passenger Agent for the Santa Fe, Prescott and Phoenix railroad, had arranged for a special train of four passenger cars and one combination car. Clearance had been secured for a departure at 6:00 P.M. from Prescott. The initial plan called for the Volunteers to ride the Santa Fe line all the way to San Antonio via Oklahoma, but at the last possible moment the route had to be changed because of washouts. As an alternative the squadron was to change to the Southern Pacific at Albuquerque and proceed to San Antonio by way of El Paso.

Sargent later may have regretted his willingness to cooperate with McCord and Brodie. Based on several communications with the War Department, McCord assured Sargent and several others that the federal authorities would defray all expenses incurred in gathering the Volunteers. When Sargent submitted his vouchers to McCord for payment, he found that matters were not quite that simple. McCord had not been able to get the federal government to make payment. There was some question as to the proper forms to use and which of the many departments was responsible. Indebted to the amount of $2467.62, Governor McCord first made application to the Treasury Department, but was told to resubmit his claims to the different "supply departments."[24] It was not until late in 1899 that the matter was finally straightened out. By that time it was settled by Governor Nathan O. Murphy who had replaced McCord.[25]

Governor McCord resigned in August, 1898, to assume command of the First Territorial Volunteer Infantry regiment, which had been authorized by the second call for

Recruits at Prescott: Lined up in civilian clothes at Prescott, the Arizona volunteers prepare to leave for San Antonio. (*Courtesy Sharlot Hall Museum.*)

Volunteers on May 25. Because his command never got into action or even left the United States, McCord may well have felt that he had made a mistake by resigning his position as Governor of Arizona.

In April, however, everyone was more concerned with the necessity of getting the Volunteers to San Antonio than they were with securing payment for transportation costs. On the afternoon of May 4, amidst the greatest demonstration in Prescott history, the Volunteers prepared to leave for war. At four o'clock, preceded by the Prescott Brass Band, the group marched onto the grounds of the court house. Formed in ranks on the north side of the plaza near the bandstand, the men stood under a leaden sky and listened to an inspirational address by McCord, who had arrived that morning from Phoenix with the contingent from Gila County. He brought with him a silk flag hand-sewn by the Women's Relief Corps of Phoenix, an affiliate of the local chapter of the Grand Army of the Republic. Lacking a suitable cord, the ladies had

decorated the top of the staff with tricolored satin ribbons. In presenting the flag to the Arizonans, McCord charged them with the responsibility of keeping his promise to the ladies of Phoenix that it "would be carried by this battalion to the front and would be found, like the plume of Henry of Navarro, waving in the forefront of battle."[26] Major Brodie accepted the handsome standard on behalf of the Volunteers, and the plaza rang with lusty cheers from the large crowd which, in spite of the threatening storm, had gathered to witness the ceremony.

Other presentations followed. The territorial adjutant general, R. Allyn Lewis, presented the officers' commissions to McClintock, who responded with a short speech. Reese M. Ling, the Prescott city attorney, called O'Neill to the stand and, on behalf of the city council, gave him a beautifully engraved sixshooter with holster. Each trooper received a colored hat band identifying him as a member of the "First Volunteer Cavalry — Arizona Column." Those in O'Neill's troop received red bands; McClintock's men got blue ones. Robert Morrison, a member of the city council, made the final presentation of the regimental mascot — a young mountain lion called "Josephine." Donated by Robert Brow, the saloon keeper whose establishment had done such a thriving business during the past week, the puma stood as a symbol of the fighting spirit of the Arizona boys.

Upon completion of the ceremonies at the plaza, the citizens accompanied the troopers to the depot at the northern edge of town. The Prescott band, a group of Civil War veterans, the fire department, the school children and the governor with his staff marched with the Volunteers down Montezuma Street, still muddy from the recent storm. Upon arrival the recruits found the cars decorated with red, white and blue streamers. They were identified by such slogans as "Remember the *Maine*," the "First Arizona Volunteer Cavalry" and "The Arizona Cowboy Regiment." The cars also were filled with provisions. Over five hundred dollars had been raised that morning to stock the combination car with boiled ham, fresh mutton, pigs' feet, canned fruit, bread and pickles. The Volunteers expressed particular satisfaction with the three barrels filled with bottles of beer. They also found three hundred corn-cob pipes. At 7:15 the train slowly pulled out of the station through a "perfect sea of handkerchiefs and parasols" that waved goodbye.[27]

The departure of the Arizona column on May 4, 1898 satisfied Brodie's persistent efforts to gain active duty in the war with Spain. His endeavor had been supported by the governor, the newspapers and the citizens in general. A unique organization in the history of Arizona, Brodie's command was the first group to go forth as an organized unit for military service outside the territory. As the first of four contingents slated to compose the First United States Volunteer Cavalry, its departure was widely heralded in newspapers across the nation. But few in Arizona were yet calling them the Rough Riders.

CHAPTER 2

Training At San Antonio

CONFUSION AND HARD WORK GREETED MAJOR BRODIE and his Arizonans on arrival at San Antonio for rendezvous with the remainder of the First Volunteer Cavalry. Well aware that their chances of getting into action depended largely on the speed with which they could get the command ready for field duty, the officers tackled the job of building a regiment from the ground up. Many factors worked in their favor. Colonel Wood's experience and organizing ability, Lieutenant Colonel Roosevelt's political contacts and enthusiasm in procuring equipment and Major Brodie's Regular Army background proved to be invaluable. Although untrained, the Arizonans were outdoor men, with some experience with firearms and horses. Moreover, they were willing to learn and morale remained high. In a short period of time, the men were uniformed, mounted and drilled. In short, they were becoming soldiers.

The journey to San Antonio was a memorable and satisfying experience. With the exception of the populace of

Albuquerque, townspeople all along the route had turned out in large numbers to welcome the Volunteers. Of these demonstrations, the one at Flagstaff, held at 2:30 A.M. in a heavy snow storm, had been the most impressive. At El Paso some of the troopers appropriated a stray Skye terrier, while others made strenuous efforts to entice an attractive young Negro girl aboard the train. She was willing, but the troop officers forced the entire project to be abandoned. These incidents evidently escaped the eyes of the reporters who lauded the Arizona boys for their "intelligence and gentlemanly deportment [which] excited the admiration of all."[1]

The Arizona men also paused to gloat over their being the first to leave for San Antonio. At Isleta, a small railroad stop just south of Albuquerque, the Arizonans sent a triumphant telegram to the New Mexico contingent which was then gathering at Las Vegas, New Mexico. It read:

Roosevelt's Troopers, Santa Fe.
Isleta, N.M., May 6, — Wat 'ell matter with New Mexico. Come running or will never get to Cuba.
Brodies Arizonians, 200 Strong.[2]

Rolling into San Antonio during the chilly, gray hours just before dawn on May 7, the troopers found that Colonel Wood had made provisions to receive them. The travel-weary men boarded street cars provided by the Edison Car Line, and rode three miles south from the city to the grounds of the International Fair Association at Riverside Park on the banks of the San Antonio River. After depositing their belongings on the floor of the barn-like exposition building, they ate a hot breakfast which had been prepared for them and inspected their bivouac. A high board fence enclosed the six-hundred acre park. It received particular attention from all who anticipated routine military restriction on personal movement. They noted all holes and loose boards as well as the ample cover afforded by the profuse growth of pecan, sycamore and cottonwood trees along the banks of the river.

As the first recruits to rendezvous, the Arizona Volunteers appropriated the most satisfactory facilities before others arrived. They had to work fast for the other groups were right behind them. On the afternoon of May 7, the same day that Brodie's men came in, the contingent from Oklahoma also marched into the fairgrounds. The troop had been raised by Captain Robert D. Huston, a lawyer from Guthrie, Oklahoma. He had formed his command by the unique procedure of selecting the six best men from each militia company in the territory. The eighty-three Oklahomans came through the sally port in a double column at 4:30 P.M. News of their arrival brought the Arizonans to the entrance to greet their comrades, according to the San Antonio *Express*, with "three roaring cheers and a thundering tiger."[3]

Three days later, May 10, three hundred and forty Volunteers from New Mexico unloaded from a special train of twelve cars. These New Mexicans, commanded by Major Henry B. Hersey, made up the largest single contingent. Hersey had resigned his position of territorial adjutant general to become the second ranking major in the regiment. His command was the only one to bring military equipment. Each man was outfitted in the regulation blue uniform, drawn from the militia stockpiles at Santa Fe. Repairs to many of the uniforms had to be made immediately, for winsome Texas girls at the small railroad stops in west Texas had begged the soldiers to cut off their brass buttons to provide the girls with souvenirs. Bent nails served as temporary replacements.

A week later First Lieutenant Allyn Capron, on detached service from the Seventh Cavalry, brought in one hundred and seventy troopers from Indian Territory. These men arrived late because the officers' commissions had to come from Washington, for the territory was not officially organized and there was no chief executive. Capron had been detached from the Seventh to recruit the men and get them to camp.[4] Except for the few troopers to be gathered from the nation at large, the arrival of this group completed the number to be collected at the rendezvous.

In contrast to the Volunteers from the territories, the recruits from the East came on their own initiative. Shortly after Colonel Wood left for San Antonio on May 2, Lieutenant Colonel Roosevelt, who had been directed by Wood to stay in Washington and expedite delivery of the regimental supplies, learned that the War Department had increased the authorized strength of the regiment from seven hundred and eighty to 1,000 men. There is some evidence that Colonel Wood was not even aware of this change when Roosevelt began taking advantage of it and accepting recruits from Harvard, Yale and Princeton. Many of these men had already been contacted by Guy Murchie of Harvard, and were waiting to be called.

The first of these "dudes," as the Arizonans called them, arrived at San Antonio on Monday, May 9, and quickly were assigned to one of the troops. Guy Murchie of Calais, Maine, Charles Bull of San Francisco, and Stanley Hollister of Santa Barbara, California, joined Captain O'Neill's troop. Dudley Dean of Boston, David Goodrich of Akron, Ohio, and Wellman Saunders of Salem, Massachusetts, were assigned to Captain McClintock.

The arrival of these easterners cast a new perspective on the character of the regiment. Because many of them came from families prominently associated with Eastern society, the reporters took particular care to cover their arrival and subsequent participation in the organization and training of the regiment. Sometimes the accounts were derisive. The troopers from the East were often referred to by the press as the "Fifth Avenue Boys," the "la da dah boys," the "millionaire recruits" or simply the "swells." Actually, the easterners got along very well with the men from the West. Sergeant David L. Hughes, a member of B Troop from Tucson, had this to say about them:

We had always considered the Eastern man as a 'tender foot' but now we met a different Easterner than we had been used to meeting. He was an athlete, husky, strong, but refined. They were not used to the carefree ways of the Western men. They were more careful and reserved. They were not used to handling stock or the harder outside work but it only took a short time after we began working together to understand one another and we became welded into one large family; the millionaire, the cowpuncher, the prospector, were working side by side and many are the life-long friendships that sprung up between these men after they become acquainted.[5]

Of course, not all of the new recruits came from colleges in the East. It seems that every day a few individuals came out to the camp to enlist. Some of them came from Arizona. One of the first to arrive was a man who had been in trouble with the law in Arizona and had gone to Mexico to avoid arrest. The identity of this individual is not known, but the story goes that when he turned up at San Antonio, Buckey O'Neill personally made a successful appeal to Colonel Wood that the man be accepted. Tradition also holds that neither Wood or O'Neill ever had reason to regret the decision. Another Arizonan was George Truman, the only recruit to come from Pinal County. Truman traveled to San Antonio from his home in Florence and was enlisted on May 28. Still another was Charles E. Mills, superintendent of the Detroit Copper Company at Morenci, Arizona. Mills first arrived in San Antonio on May 27, then returned to Morenci to put his affairs in order and rejoined the regiment to be enlisted on June 5. Like Truman he served the entire time as a private. Truman, however, did make an unsuccessful attempt to secure a commission.

The regimental chaplain, the Reverend Henry A. Brown of Prescott, also joined at San Antonio. Born in Paulding, Ohio, in 1864, Brown graduated from Oberlin College in 1888. He had come to Prescott from San Bernardino, California, in 1896 to become minister of St. Luke's Episcopal Church. Brown had a keen interest in world affairs and at Prescott he had taken an active role in supporting the *Insurrecto* cause before the United States entered the conflict. When the two Cuban officers had visited Prescott in February to drum up support, it was he who had collected donations for the Cubans. When Colonel Wood began forming his command, Brown, realizing that the regiment was authorized a chaplain, contacted Governor McCord and requested that McCord try to get the appointment for him.

It is not clear exactly what happened, but evidently McCord issued the Reverend Brown a commission on May 7 before the question of who would get the appointment was definitely settled. Lieutenant Tupes had no instructions to cover this situation. When Brown presented his commission with the request that Tupes enroll him and authorize his departure for San Antonio, the young lieutenant wired Washington for guidance. On May 9 the assistant adjutant general frostily replied: "It is understood Governor recommends Reverend H. A. Brown as Chaplain for Colonel Wood's regiment. All officers of that regiment are appointed by Secretary of War."[6] In spite of this mild rebuke for what the War Department considered McCord's infringement on the prerogatives of the Secretary of War, the governor's "recommendation" was accepted and Brown got the appointment.

Colonel Wood won the approval of the Arizonans for the skill he demonstrated in organizing the regiment. Born in New Hampshire in 1860, the muscular colonel had accumulated a wealth of experience during the fourteen years he had served as an army physician. His most exciting period of duty occurred during his tenure at Fort Huachuca from 1885 to 1886, where he may have become acquainted with George Wilcox, who was a hospital steward there.

Everyone in the Arizona column knew the story of how Wood had left Fort Huachuca with Captain Henry W. Lawton's detachment of the Fourth Cavalry for the wilds of northern Mexico in pursuit of Geronimo in the summer of 1886.[7] During this historic campaign, made through some of the most difficult terrain conceivable and filled with almost unbelievable hardships, Wood had proved that he was the physical equal of an Apache. He also had learned a great deal about military psychology and equipment which he wisely incorporated into the plans and handling of his own regiment thirteen years later. Wood's reputation among the Arizona men was based largely on the feats of strength and endurance he demonstrated during the march through Mexico.[8]

Although Colonel Wood and the Arizona men had something in common in that they both knew the mountains and deserts of Arizona, there was no particular bond between them. The colonel was considerate, but he made friends with no one. "He was reserved, cool, cautious, deliberate, and had what we term a 'poker face' hard to read," wrote Sergeant David L. Hughes of B Troop. "He would go to the end for one of his men, but he was not showy about it."[9] In Wood's calm and efficient manner the Arizonans saw a reflection of Brodie. The characteristics of both, they noted, contrasted vividly with the bellicosity of the lieutenant colonel of the regiment.

Colonel Wood did not wait for all arrivals in order to form his regiment. He and Major Brodie organized the Arizona squadron immediately after the Oklahoma group arrived on the afternoon of May 7. Apparently Wood originally had planned on having two squadrons, but when the Secretary of War increased the authorized strength to 1,000 on April 28, he had specified that each Volunteer regiment would consist of three squadrons of four troops each. There would be approximately three hundred and twenty enlisted men in each squadron. To provide Brodie four troops without breaking territorial integrity, Wood decided to give Brodie the Oklahoma troop and divide the two hundred Arizonans into three troops of approximately sixty-five men each. These three units could then be assigned enough new men to bring them up to the authorized strength of seventy-seven to eighty-one men each.

To command this new Arizona troop, Captain McClintock's popular first lieutenant, Joseph L. B. Alexander, was made captain. His junior officers were First Lieutenant Robert Patterson, promoted and transferred from O'Neill's troop,

and Second Lieutenant Hal Sayre of Denver, who had arrived
with Colonel Wood on May 5. In Captain O'Neill's troop,
Quartermaster Sergeant Joshua D. Carter of Prescott was
promoted to replace Patterson. McClintock advanced George
Wilcox to first lieutenant and held the remaining vacancy
open until May 21, when his first sergeant, Harbo T.
Rynning — or "Tom" Rynning as he liked to be called —
was commissioned second lieutenant.

By virtue of their early arrival, the Arizonans assumed
all seniority rights and corresponding troop designations.
O'Neill became the senior captain of the regiment and his
command was designated A Troop. McClintock's and Alexander's units became B and C respectively. These three commands, together with Huston's Oklahoma D Troop, composed
the Arizona or first squadron under Brodie, the ranking
major.

The reassignment of personnel to the newly created C
Troop took place the next day. On Sunday, May 8, notices
of the new organizations appeared on the bulletin boards
with the request that those who wished to transfer sign the
attached roster. Thirty-seven members of McClintock's B
Troop signed — but only one man from O'Neill's A Troop.
McClintock selected thirty-two names from the list and sent
the men to Brodie to be transferred; while O'Neill had the
names of his troopers placed in a hat and the first sergeant
drew out thirty-one to join the solitary malcontent.

Captain O'Neill's magnetic personality had so affected
his command that those selected to transfer tried their best
to avoid it. Wilbur D. French of Safford, upon having his
name drawn, offered a more fortunate comrade, Jimmy
Boyle, an itinerant miner from Prescott, $67.00 to transfer
in his place. But, French later related: "The dirty, ragged
Irish bum scornfully repulsed me."[10] Prior to this reorganiza-
tion the county groups had been kept intact. Now they were
separated. The men expressed dissatisfaction with having
their county unity destroyed.

With the reassignment completed, the commanders selected their key noncommissioned officers. Experience and
recruiting efforts were considered. For the first sergeant of
A Troop O'Neill had already named William Greenwood,
affectionately called "grandma" by his men. He had retired
after twenty-three years in the Regular Army. Probably older
than his admitted age of forty-four, Greenwood had been a
sergeant under Brodie in the First Cavalry. He was one of the
first to come to Prescott when he learned that his old lieutenant planned to form a regiment. McClintock appointed
Tom Rynning first sergeant of B Troop until May 21, when
he replaced Rynning with William A. Davidson, a thorough
and deliberate ex-first sergeant of Regular Cavalry. For his
first sergeant, Alexander named Willis O. Huson, a lawyer
from Yuma.

In addition to Davidson and Greenwood, there were
other men with prior military service. In A Troop Sergeants
Charles McGarr from Phoenix and Robert Brown from Prescott were veterans, as was Wagoner John H. Waller and
Private Arthur M. LeRoy from Prescott. Waller had served
two years in the Confederate Army where, as a guerrilla
fighter, he had lost his right index finger in a shotgun blast.
He never did explain exactly how it happened. In B Troop
McClintock had Sergeants Stephan A. Pate from Tucson,
John E. Campbell, Elmer Hawley and Private Richard Stanton from Phoenix. Stanton, who had served two enlistments
in the Fifth Cavalry, always resented McClintock's refusal to
make the soldier a noncommissioned officer. McClintock later
admitted that Stanton lost no opportunity to "rag" the captain, although he did it carefully so as to avoid breaking
regulations.

Other experienced men in B Troop were Sergeant David
L. Hughes from Tucson and Private George Truman, who
came to San Antonio from Florence, Arizona, on May 28.
They had been commissioned officers in the Arizona National
Guard. Alexander's command, having been created from the

two original troops, could not muster as many experienced men and acquired the unfortunate reputation of having inferior personnel.

The Arizona squadron was officially formed on May 17, the same day that Capron's group reported to Camp Wood. On that day Lieutenant Tupes and Captain Henry Cooper, who had enlisted the New Mexicans, arrived to muster the regiment into the Volunteer Army. Most of the Arizona boys believed that this muster was necessary because errors had been made in the enlistment at Prescott. Lieutenant Rynning later said that Tupes had enlisted them into the Regular Army at Prescott and had to come to San Antonio to get them into the Volunteer Army where they belonged. The situation is not entirely clear, but apparently the men had enlisted as individuals in their respective territories. At San Antonio they had to be mustered in by troops.

When Lieutenant Tupes arrived to muster the Arizonans, he found that several changes had occurred since the men had left Prescott. In addition to the new recruits enlisted by Roosevelt, several men were absent. Sergeant Cornelius Cronin had fallen sick with rheumatism and had been sent to the hospital at Fort Sam Houston. Marshall Bird was at the same hospital with a severe head injury. Private Bird, a young recruit from Nogales, was one of those few individuals who had the opportunity to read his own obituary. Two days after his arrival at Camp Wood, Bird was thrown from a horse while returning from water call. His head struck a fence post and he was sent quickly to Fort Sam Houston with a fractured skull. Someone sent a telegram back to Arizona reporting that the young trooper had died. His obituary appeared in the territorial papers on May 19. Bird did not die, however, and he was discharged on August 8 for disability incurred in line of duty.

There were other problems connected with the muster. One Robert M. Hicks, who had enlisted at Whipple Barracks, had somehow become involved with civilian authorities and had deserted to avoid being apprehended. He never was located. Another trooper, Frank W. Schneck from Phoenix, also had disappeared. Lieutenant Tupes reported him as A.W.O.L., but he was enrolled upon returning to duty a few days later. Contrary to popular belief, Schneck originally enlisted in Prescott and did not work as a short-order cook in San Antonio as Edward Marshall stated in his book, *The Story of the Rough Riders*. Marshall claimed incorrectly that Captain O'Neill needed a cook and recruited Schneck out of a nearby restaurant.

Lieutenant Tupes also refused to enroll Arthur L. Tuttle of Safford, because the eighteen-year-old Volunteer had fraudulently given his age as twenty-one when he had enlisted at Whipple Barracks. Somehow Tupes had found this out. Tuttle appealed the decision to Major Brodie, who prevailed upon Colonel Wood to have the mustering officer of the New Mexico squadron accept Tuttle. Family influence may have been a factor here. Tuttle's father, who had come to Arizona in 1862 as an officer in the California Column, and Brodie were old friends. Lieutenant Tupes indicated his displeasure with the situation in his official report. After explaining why he had refused to accept Tuttle, Tupes angrily concluded: "The Colonel of the Regiment accepted and mustered him in with a troop that was not assigned to me for muster-in."[11]

With the completion of the muster on the afternoon of May 17, the Arizona contingent had been made an official part of the United States Volunteer Army. It consisted of O'Neill's A Troop with three officers and sixty-eight men, McClintock's B Troop of two officers and sixty-five men and Alexander's C Troop of three officers and sixty-seven men.

Recruiting for the Arizona squadron continued, for the troops were not up to authorized strength. On April 28 the War Department had spelled out a specific table of organization. Each troop was to have one captain, one first lieutenant, one second lieutenant, one first sergeant, one quartermaster sergeant, six sergeants, eight corporals, two farriers and black-smiths, two trumpeters, one saddler, one wagoner and not less than fifty-five or more than fifty-nine privates. This meant that a maximum of forty-three privates could still be enlisted for the three Arizona troops. All positions of rank, of course, had been filled.

It is significant that this table of organization contained certain weaknesses. There was no troop clerk or mess section. The troop commander, obviously, found it necessary to detail line troopers to perform these important functions. The position of wagoner appeared to be superfluous. There were no wagons assigned to the regiment.

Upon completion of the muster on May 17, the First Volunteer Cavalry regiment consisted of three squadrons of four troops each. In the Arizona squadron were A, B and C Troops from Arizona and D Troop from Oklahoma. The second, or New Mexico squadron under Major Hersey, had the four troops from New Mexico lettered E, F, G and H. Frederick Muller from Santa Fe, Maximilian Luna from the same place, William Llewellen from Las Cruces and George Curry from Tularosa were the respective commanders. Each of the New Mexico troops had been reduced from eighty-five to sixty-five men upon arrival at San Antonio, and the superfluous troopers placed in I Troop under Captain Schuyler A. McGinnis of Oklahoma. This unit, along with K, L and M Troops composed the third squadron under Major George M. Dunn, a native of Denver and a close personal friend of Roosevelt. Captain Micah John Jenkins of South Carolina, a West Point graduate, commanded K Troop, which had been created for the Eastern recruits. One group from the Indian Territory elected Capron the captain and became L Troop. The remaining Volunteers from Muskogee, lettered M Troop, were placed under Captain Robert H. Bruce from Mineola, Texas.

Again, certain organizational weaknesses existed at the regimental level. The table of organization specified that the

Officers of the 1st Volunteer Cavalry at San Antonio with "Josephine" the mountain lion, their mascot. (*Courtesy Sharlot Hall Museum.*)

1. Col. Wood	11. Lt. Patterson	21. Lt. Goodrich	31. Capt. McGinnis
2. Lt. Col. Roosevelt	12. Capt. Alexander	22. Lt. Winchey	32. Lt. Devereaux
3. Maj. Brodie	13. Lt. Nichols	23. Lt. Wilcox	33. Capt. Llewellyn
4. Maj. Hersey	14. Capt. Huston	24. Lt. Greenway	34. Lt. Kane
5. Maj. Dunn	15. Capt. Luna	25. Capt. O'Neill	35. Lt. Green
6. Lt. Hall	16. Capt. Bruce	26. Lt. Frantz	36. Surgeon Church
7. Lt. Schweitzer	17. Lt. Weakley	27. Lt. Ballard	37. Lt. Day
8. Lt. Carr	18. Capt. Muller	28. Lt. Kelly	38. Lt. Haskell
9. Lt. Sayre	19. Lt. Griffin	29. Capt. Capron	39. Lt. Leahey
10. Capt. McClintock	20. Capt. Curry	30. Lt. Keyes	40. Lt. Rynning

command element of regimental headquarters would consist of one colonel, one lieutenant colonel and three majors. The commissioned staff included one first lieutenant as adjutant; one lieutenant as quartermaster; one surgeon, whose rank was not designated, but the position was filled by a major; two lieutenants as assistant surgeons and one chaplain. Enlisted personnel included one sergeant major, three hospital stewards, one quartermaster sergeant, one chief musician, one saddler sergeant and one chief trumpeter. The obvious weaknesses included a lack of mess personnel and clerks. Other sections, notably the hospital and quartermaster, were badly understaffed. There were not enough enlisted personnel in headquarters to provide runners, orderlies or even a color sergeant. Colonel Wood alleviated some of these shortages by detaching personnel from the line troops. This did not make the troop commanders happy, but under the circumstances they had no alternative.

For transportation the regiment had a pack train of one hundred and eighty-nine stout Missouri mules. On May 6 the animals had arrived from St. Louis on the International and Great Northern Railroad. They were under the experienced eye of Chief Packer Mickey O'Hara. For years civilians had been hired by the War Department to serve as packers, and O'Hara had seen considerable service. He and Colonel Wood were old friends, for O'Hara had been one of the packers with Wood on the Geronimo campaign. O'Hara also knew Tom Rynning of B Troop.

Lieutenant Colonel Roosevelt arrived at Camp Wood on May 15. Resplendent in a new uniform made of material which resembled brown duck and accompanied by a personal valet, he was escorted to camp by Colonel Wood in early afternoon. Roosevelt desperately had wanted to come sooner, but he had been ordered by Wood to stay in Washington and expedite delivery of the regimental supplies. This was an excellent decision. Roosevelt's appointment as Assistant Secretary of the Navy in 1895 had given him the opportunity to form influential friendships in the right places. By his own admission he had loudly and forcibly advocated that it was "our duty to intervene in Cuba and to take this opportunity of driving the Spaniard from the Western World."[12] With this attitude he had become well known to all those members of Congress and others who were interested in a war with Spain. Consequently, his subsequent appeals as a lieutenant colonel to the quartermaster and ordnance departments for equipment were received on a personal as well as a political basis. Roosevelt had much more success along these lines than did other Volunteer officers.

It was this same aggressive spirit that had brought Roosevelt his appointment to the regiment in the first place. Back in April, when President McKinley and Secretary of War Alger first began discussing the various appointments to be made in the Volunteer Army, it logically followed that the outspoken Assistant Secretary of the Navy was one of the first to be considered for a line command. Initially offered the colonelcy of the First United States Volunteer Cavalry, Roosevelt, out of consideration for his lack of experience, proposed that Wood be given the command instead. Roosevelt went on to add, however, that if this were done he would consent to go as the lieutenant colonel. This proposal was entirely agreeable to McKinley, who made the necessary arrangements. Wood had then entrained for San Antonio after instructing Roosevelt to hound the various departments until the necessary equipment was secured and sent to the rendezvous site.

The very characteristics that later impressed the Arizona men also popularized Roosevelt with the general public via the prolific and friendly efforts of the press. Disregarding his lack of military knowledge, Roosevelt expounded on tactics, strategy, discipline and logistics to any reporter who took time to visit him. This made great copy and the Eastern papers devoted considerable space to his candid observations. On the same day that he received his commission, Roosevelt confided in considerable detail the plans for the regiment. In a description of the rank and file, he created an unusual image of his troopers while cleverly taking particular care to indicate that he expected no weakness to appear in the recruits who came from the East. The interview was reported as follows:

"They [the bad men] will be turned out as quickly as they make a break," said Mr. Roosevelt, who knows the type thoroughly. "Some weaklings there will be, too, from the towns, especially perhaps, the southwestern towns, who know nothing of the wild life, but who like to put on a broad hat and be called cowboys. These, too, will break down and be dropped in a hurry. . . . The fighters will remain, rough riders all, but no 'terrors.' "[13]

Turning to the battle tactics of the regiment, Roosevelt related that the men would fight dismounted with every fourth man detailed to secure the horses in the rear. Then, with a wonderful disregard for consistency, he went on to explain that the men were already skilled marksmen — they only had to be taught not to fire until their horses touched those of the enemy! Just how his men could be dismounted and yet hold their fire until their horses touched those of their opponents, Roosevelt did not explain.

Although Roosevelt enjoyed wide popularity in the East, he did not favorably impress the westerners at first. To the cynical boys from Arizona this thirty-nine-year-old politician looked too much like a dude with his bull neck, his flashing teeth and his small eyes protected by unusually thick lenses. But the strong personality of this remarkable man could not long be denied, and the troopers changed their opinion of him. His ability to make quick decisions, his unwavering energy and enthusiasm, and his friendly manner soon overshadowed his physical appearance. In a military sense his impulsiveness and impetuosity detracted from his ability because it interfered with his judgment. In spite of Roosevelt's undenied enthusiasm and Wood's ability, the troopers in the Arizona column considered Major Brodie to be the real military backbone of the regiment.

Both Colonel Wood and Roosevelt expressed satisfaction with the incongruous group from Arizona. Three days after his arrival and when only the Arizonans and Oklahomans were in camp, Wood wrote his wife: "These men are the best men I have ever seen together, and will make the finest kind of soldiers."[14] Representing every conceivable occupation, with about half of them claiming to be ranchers or cowboys, the Arizonans had a maturity that conflicted with the popular misconception that the regiment was composed of young cowboys. In age they ranged from eighteen-year-old Arthur Tuttle to Sergeant Greenwood, who admitted to forty-four. The average age for the Arizona troops was twenty-eight. Physically they averaged five feet and eight inches in height, with six-foot six-inch Albert Wright of Yuma the tallest, and Frank J. Harner of Prescott the shortest at five-feet two and three-fourths inches. By birth they represented practically every state and territory in the Union. Only eight were natives of Arizona. "We rendezvoused at San Antonio," wrote Wilbur French of C Troop, "twelve hundred as separate, varied, mixed, distinct, grotesque, and peculiar types of men . . . [as were] ever assembled."[15]

It is difficult to evaluate correctly the full particulars of the Arizona boys. Some, like Tuttle and Sol Drachman of Tucson, lied about their ages. Others, like Greenwood and Hodgdon, gave erroneous addresses because they thought that only men from the territories could be enlisted. There were many drifters and gamblers who successfully concealed their social status by claiming to be cowboys or ranchers when they enlisted. Others, for reasons known only to themselves, gave fictitious names and deliberately concealed all other details of their personal lives. They literally came out of obscurity to enlist and dropped into anonymity when the war ended.

The problem of identification is further confused by the errors which have been perpetrated in legend and in print. Edward Marshall's *Story of the Rough Riders* is particularly inaccurate when describing individuals. Even Roosevelt made numerous mistakes in his book, *The Rough Riders*. A typical error concerned Private Walter J. McCann of B Troop, whom

Roosevelt claimed had been a buffalo hunter in his youth.
Because McCann was only thirty years old in 1898, this is
highly unlikely. There were no great herds left by the time
McCann was old enough to hunt. Captain McClintock always
claimed that McCann was a skilled stenographer. Many errors
were inconsequential in nature. Bird of Nogales was listed
by Roosevelt as coming from California; George and Fred
Bugbee from Safford were recorded as being from Lordsburg,
New Mexico; Charles E. Mills of Morenci was on the roster
as coming from Cedar Rapids, Iowa; and Joel Rex Hall of
Bisbee was incorrectly listed as being a resident of Seattle,
Washington.

The question of proper identity is further confused by the
custom of assigning nicknames, a common practice throughout the regiment. Some men became known by half of their
own name with the addition of some descriptive adjective.
Others were divorced entirely from their real names. Such
sobriquets were sometimes given in derision and sometimes
in accurate description. An example of the former was a
private in A Troop, Daniel L. Hogan of Flagstaff, who
became known as the "Admiral of the Hassayamp" because
of his tongue-in-cheek habit of entertaining the easterners
with hair-raising stories of his boating exploits on the Hassayampa River. The Arizona boys, of course, all realized that
the Hassayampa, which rises in the mountains near Prescott
and flows into the Gila River west of Phoenix, contained
water only after a heavy rain or snow fall. There was one
unidentified gambler in the regiment who was unusually
quiet. He became known as "Hell Roarer." Another man, decidedly more boisterous by nature, became "Prayerful James."

The most widely known enlisted man in the regiment
was A Troop's Charles Hodgdon, or "Happy Jack" as he was
universally known. Hodgdon's antics as the regimental clown
made him so well known that many Volunteers never did
learn his real name or know to which troop he was assigned.
He seemed to be everywhere. Some of the New Mexico men

later claimed that "Happy Jack" came from their home territory.

The very nature of the regiment and conditions in general brought many unusual men into the unit. One such trooper was Charles Younger, an ex-fireman from Winslow in A Troop. Younger reputedly was a cousin of the famous Younger brothers who rode with Jesse James. There were several journalists who were anxious to keep their friends and relatives well posted as to their adventures. One was Adelbert D. Webb, a thirty-year-old employee of the Safford *Arizonian*, who agreed to send regular dispatches under the pseudonym, "Trooper Rawhide," for publication in the Solomonville *Arizona Bulletin*. Although cynical and prone to complain, A. D. Webb, as he liked to be called, kept the people of Graham County well informed.

Occasionally Major Brodie was asked to extend special favors to some of the men. One of his troopers, Private George Truman, decided to try for a commission. On June 11 Charles D. Reppy, editor of the Florence *Tribune,* wrote a letter of recommendation for Truman. After commenting on Truman's educational background and pointing out that he had resigned his position as under sheriff of Pinal County to enlist, Reppy concluded: "A man of his ability could do his country much better service with a good command than as a private soldier, hence for the interest of the Government I would urge his early promotion to at least the command of a company."[16] Notwithstanding this fine recommendation, Truman did not get a commission. Another example is classically illustrated by a letter on behalf of Samuel Garrett of Phoenix, which Brodie received from one L. F. Eggers, an attorney in Los Angeles. In a bold, ostentatious hand Eggers wrote:

Sir and Friend. I wish to Congratulate you on your chivalry and I hope and pray you and your dear boys may all safely return. By the way I desire to ask you with all the Kindness and Sincerity of my heart that you take the best of Care and Kindness of a young man in your Command by the name of Mr. Saml H. Garrett. His father a prominent Atty of this City feels the pressure of his youngest son going into the Army and he is a most excellent man and will highly appreciate all Kindness extended to his Son by you.[17]

Although the men officially had joined the First United States Volunteer Cavalry, the San Antonio newspapers soon began calling them "Rough Riders." Tradition holds that this term developed from a remark made by Roosevelt that he was going west to join a group of "rough riding men." Actually, however, the expression first appeared in print on April 21 when the editor of the Tucson *Arizona Weekly Star* quoted Governor McCord in reference to "Colonel Brodie's regiment of Arizona Rough Riders." This occurred before the Volunteer Bill was passed and before Roosevelt knew what his assignment would be. The expression did not immediately catch on, and the Arizona papers used such designations as "Cowboy Cavalry," or "Colonel Wood's Cavalry Regiment" until the end of May. The Eastern and Texas papers, however, adopted the popular name Rough Riders from the beginning. The Arizona troopers at first resented being called this because they considered it an aspersion on their riding ability. Later they started using it themselves. The regimental officers soon adopted it and the official title was almost forgotten except in the preparation of official reports and records.

The public always associated the regiment with Lieutenant Colonel Roosevelt rather than with Colonel Wood. Before long a sign appeared at the San Antonio railroad depot pointing the way to the camp of "Roosevelt's Rough Riders." This did not appear to bother Colonel Wood, who permitted the sign to remain.

From the San Antonio newspapers the Arizona boys learned of the proposed mission of the regiment. On May 7 the San Antonio *Express* announced that the Rough Riders would operate as an independent command in conjunction with the insurgents south of Havana. Their objective would be to sever the supply lines that entered that city and other northern ports from the south. A few days later, Brodie issued a statement that the command would be assigned the mission of tracking down Spanish guerrilla bands in the interior of Cuba. In order to prepare for this unique assignment, the officers did not plan to follow the Regular Army cavalry drill because time limitations prevented the transformation of the Volunteers into cavalrymen trained according to regulations. The drill selected to replace the regular exercises was designed to enable the regiment to accomplish its predicted role in anti-guerrilla activities. This proved to be only the beginning, and the press, with complete disregard for any resemblance of security, continued to report and speculate on military plans, troop movements and embarkation sites and dates.

As the Volunteers settled down to their first week of army life, the ability of Brodie to organize and train men became apparent. He believed in discipline as well as hard work and, under his direct supervision, the first squadron rapidly began to develop military proficiency. The presence of seven old line sergeants from the Regular Army was no small asset to Brodie as he worked to whip his men into shape. Turning raw recruits into fighting men had been their business. The Arizona squadron benefited by their "know how." As little equipment had been received until the end of the first week, the men drilled long hours on foot in civilian clothing, with its obvious individual differences. Carrying broom sticks instead of rifles, the Arizonans presented a ludicrous and pathetic sight as they solemnly paraded. Corporal French wrote:

[We were] garbed in the various habiliments of the fashions of the time. The aesthetic in their dude rags, standing collars and patent leather shoes, as well as hard-boiled hats. The millionaires in Fifth Avenue duds. . . . The cowboys in chaps, high-heeled boots and spurs. The miners and down-and-outers in soiled and ragged blue denim overalls and jumpers.[18]

Major Brodie kept his men at drill all day. Reveille sounded each morning at 5:30, and taps did not end the

activities until 9:00. The schedule called for two hours of
platoon drill and one hour of troop drill daily. It was a
demanding schedule.

The greatest problem Brodie faced in training his squadron concerned supplies and equipment. In spite of Roosevelt's
efforts in Washington, the equipment arrived slowly and in
small quantities. Fortunately, sufficient stockpiles of those
items necessary for everyday life, such as mess kits and blankets, to equip Brodie's men were located at nearby Fort Sam
Houston. The officers there cooperated fully, for the post
quartermaster had been ordered to support the Volunteers
with rations and equipment. The supply of material was
limited, however, and most equipment had to come from
depots in the East. This included tents, saddles, 30-40 caliber
Krag-Jorgensen carbines, .45 caliber Colt revolvers, uniforms
and the multitude of small accouterments necessary to equip
fully the regiment.

The Arizonans considered the selection and procurement
of the six-shot Krag carbine the outstanding example of the
foresight Wood and Roosevelt used in planning for their
regiment. Of Danish design, the Krags first had been issued
in this country in 1894 to the Fourth Infantry. In 1898 only
14,875 of these weapons were available. All field commanders
wanted them. The finely machined bolt action and flanged
cartridge case with a round nosed two hundred and twenty
grain bullet provided both a speed of fire and impact needed
to even up the odds when the action began. The Spaniards
were known to be armed with the new Mauser magazine rifle.
Moreover, Colonel Wood was determined to get the Krag
because he knew it would ensure that his men would be
brigaded with the Regular Cavalry.

In response to Roosevelt's prodding, the supplies finally
began to arrive and were issued according to seniority. Consequently, the Arizonans donned uniforms before the remainder of the regiment. The standard issue consisted of cheap
cotton underwear. socks, one pair of rugged, high-topped

shoes, tough canvas leggings, a heavy, blue flannel shirt, trousers and jacket of brown canvas and topped by a gray campaign hat.

Again, the selection of the uniform reflected Colonel Wood's foresight. The canvas jacket and trousers selected by Wood actually composed the stable uniform of the Regular Army. Wood chose it for his duty uniform because of his experiences in Mexico. While on the trail of Geronimo in 1886, Wood had compared the stable uniform with the standard field issue of blue trousers and shirt of light wool. He found the canvas material to be cooler and more comfortable. It also had proven more resistant to the tearing effects of thorns and brush. Actually, the old blues were already on the way out. In March, 1898, regulations had been published prescribing a new khaki uniform. The new issue did not become available for general use, however, until after the war with Spain was over.

The San Antonio used clothes dealers, realizing the opportunity to buy good clothing at a cheap price when the uniforms arrived, attended every uniform issue. In his weekly letter Trooper Webb described one such individual "with a pronounced Roman nose" who offered a Volunteer from Phoenix twenty-five cents for a thirty dollar suit. The angry soldier summoned his friends, and they decided to make an example of the huckster. Placing the offender on a blanket, the outraged troopers bounced him high in the air until he begged for mercy. "It is unnecessary to state," Webb concluded, "that he never came back."[19]

For new men, untrained in military procedures, the clothing and equipment issue proved confusing. Troopers with prior service eased it somewhat by showing the recruits how to adjust sizes by trading around with others and thereby avoiding the almost impossible task of getting a quartermaster sergeant to reverse his decision, once he had tossed a size 38 short blouse to a six-footer with a forty-four inch chest. But the real chaos attended the issue of weapons and saddle equipment. The pleasure of receiving the new, bolt action carbines and the familiar single action Colt revolvers was almost negated by the chore of removing the protective cosmoline in which they were shipped. Soap and water, rags and muscle finally got that job done and the troopers had their weapons ready for inspection.

Then came saddle equipment, but in such fashion as to baffle western cowboy or eastern polo player. In this particular field the quartermaster corps had methods all its own. To further compound the situation, the equipment arrived piecemeal. Even the regimental officers did not know what each day would bring in the way of supplies and equipment. Regardless of sequence or need, the equipment was issued as fast as it arrived. To the recruits, marched to a point of issue with no warning as to what they would receive, it was unbelievable.

The quartermaster sergeant would identify each item as he tossed it in front of the perplexed trooper. To the uninitiated, such items as browbands and headstalls mixed together looked like so much junk leather, but they knew better than to argue or ask questions. They gathered everything up that was thrown in front of them and moved on down the line. The remainder followed, piece by piece, either that day or the next. Gradually they got it all: A McClellan saddle, size 11, 12 or 14 inch seat, according to the sergeant's estimate of the heft of the soldier's hips, stirrups, rifle boot, saddle bags, grooming kit, surcingle, latigo cinch straps, halter shank, saddle blanket and various other items of necessary gear. Most of the leather required saddle soap and oil and lots of hard work before it could be used. But it was accomplished. By May 12 Brodie's squadron was completely equipped. Ten more days were required to outfit the rest of the regiment.

The horses arrived and were issued in the same fashion. Purchased locally by the remount service, the horses in theory qualified for service according to standards of the Regular Cavalry. Each mount was to be four years old or older, sound, fifteen and a half hands high, or a little more, and weigh approximately 1100 to 1250 pounds. Some horses did not meet these requirements. The regimental adjutant later complained that many of the horses seemed too small. Another specification was that the horses had been saddled and ridden. The troopers found that this regulation had been circumvented. Many of the new mounts had either never been ridden, or at least, not very far. "Some of the damn horses bucked like hell!" recalled Private Tuttle.[20]

Gathered at Fort Sam Houston, the horses were driven to Camp Wood by details sent for that purpose. Standard procedure called for the troopers to bring the animals to camp by riding one and leading eight or ten others by ropes. This proved monotonous and the Arizona boys found it easier, and much more exciting, to haze them along like range cattle. Sometimes, to the consternation of the inhabitants, the men drove their herds right through the streets of San Antonio. One prospective Rough Rider, A. L. Bradford, changed his mind about joining after being frightened away from the enlistment table at a drugstore downtown by a thundering herd of horses being driven by a band of yelling soldiers.

The genuine cowboys in the regiment, men such as Sam Rhodes of the Tonto Basin and Frank Van Siclin of Safford, thoroughly enjoyed working with these unbroken "broncs." In addition to providing an excuse for them to demonstrate their exhilaration by turning every water call into a wild west show of bucking, plunging and rearing horses, they earned welcome pocket money by breaking the mounts of the more timorous or less experienced troopers. The standard rate for this service amounted to ten dollars, which the cowboy usually transferred to the nearest bartender at the earliest opportunity.

As if by mutual agreement, the men of each troop decided to outfit their units with horses of the same color. O'Neill's men decided to provide themselves with bays; McClintock's boys selected sorrels; and Alexander's troopers chose to ride browns. To secure this uniformity the Volunteers raided the picket lines of neighboring troops each night to exchange their own undesired horses for those which had the proper characteristics. Unfortunately, some of the eastern recruits had been granted permission to bring their own mounts. One morning McClintock found an unusually fine thoroughbred sorrel tied to his picket line. A few hours later Hallett A. Barrowe, an eastern recruit in I Troop, showed up angrily claiming that the sorrel was his own personal property and that "B Troop was a troop of damned horse thieves."[21] Much to McClintock's regret, he had to return the magnificent steed to its rightful owner.

Colonel Wood originally had intended to quarter the men in tents, but the shortage of canvas forced him to use the exposition building and grandstand. After two weeks, however, the tents finally arrived, and the Arizonans moved under canvas on May 20. These "dog tents," consisting of two shelter-halves buttoned together and suspended from a cross pole, measured four feet high, four feet wide and six and a half feet long. The two men who occupied each tent made it as comfortable as possible by covering the ground with straw.

Colonel Wood insisted that the troop areas be arranged in military fashion with the enlisted quarters lined on both sides of the troop "street." The officers' tents were to be at the end of the street. The members of A Troop named the space between their tents "O'Neill Avenue" in honor of their commander; while the B Troop street became "Arizona Avenue." Captain Alexander's men, perhaps more versed in national affairs, named theirs "Manila Avenue." The first squadron moved into the area behind the exposition building, and the other two squadrons established themselves closer to the river on the east.

Brodie led his squadron, the only one then equipped with horses, out for mounted drill on May 12. It is a reflection of Brodie's background in the Regular Army that only five days after he led his squadron into the fairgrounds at San Antonio, tired, disheveled and in civilian clothes, he had them uniformed, armed, in the saddle and out for mounted drill. Brodie drilled them daily thereafter. Columns of dry Texas dust rose from the area where he and his veteran non-coms worked to turn green officers and men and equally green horses into a smooth-working cavalry unit. Making full use of their early start, the Arizonans were attaining a semblance of order and efficiency when the regiment was ready to take the field for the first time.

On May 23 the regiment first drilled as a unit. By that time the carbines and revolvers had been issued to all, which helped promote the military appearance of the men. On this particular day selected troopers with blank cartridges galloped around the regiment firing their pistols to teach the horses to stand gunfire. Some mounts accepted this treatment, but most balked, bucked or tried to run away. Their riders soundly cursed their "postage stamp" McClellan saddles as they tried to control their plunging horses. O'Neill's troop suffered one minor casualty when Fred Bugbee accidently discharged his pistol, and the flaming muzzle-flash burned his foot and shoe. Sergeant Greenwood, thoroughly disgusted with these untamed mounts, made a notation in the morning report: "Horses totally unfit for service."[22]

During the last week in May, Wood ordered a substantial increase in drill. This was because he had received a telegram asking him to report when his regiment would be ready for combat. He felt this indicated that his unit was being considered for marching orders. Wood changed the time of morning drill call to an hour before sunrise and kept the men at their tasks until sunset. Cavalry drill occupied a minimum of six hours a day, while care of the horses, guard mount, drill in the manual of arms and other duties consumed the remaining hours. The long brown lines showed the beneficial effects of the increased training, as the men became more familiar with drill formations. In spite of some adverse effects of the

The First Volunteer Cavalry Regiment as it appeared at San Antonio, prior to departure for Tampa and thence to Cuba, where it served dismounted. (*Courtesy Sharlot Hall Museum.*)

increased work load, morale remained high. Webb reported: "Troopers have fallen from their saddles and sentries have fainted while patrolling their posts or standing in line, from heat prostration, but there is no grumbling and the man who would openly give expression to the wish that he had stayed home would speedily become the laughing stock of the regiment."[23]

The official records of the United States Weather Bureau at San Antonio support Webb's complaint about the heat. On May 31 the monthly high of ninety-seven degrees was recorded. On that same day humidity registered eighty-two per cent at 6:26 A.M. and fifty per cent at 6:26 P.M.

On Sundays all drill stopped to enable the men to take care of their personal needs. In the morning Chaplain Brown conducted services. To assist him he selected three members of C Troop, Thomas Grindell and Wesley Hill from Tempe, and Arthur Perry from Phoenix, to form a choir. In the afternoon the troopers boiled their clothes to kill body lice, wrote letters and gossiped with the crowds of visiting townspeople. These civilians swarmed into the bivouac every Sunday to take pictures and investigate every facet of camp life. At first, Colonel Wood allowed these civilians to come at any time, but later he found it necessary to restrict their visitations to Sunday.

At first, in consideration for the spirit of independence which prevailed among the westerners, Wood applied a minimum of discipline. Later, he gradually increased it until Regular Army standards had been met. Much of the responsibility for this fell on the regimental adjutant, Lieutenant Tom Hall of New Jersey, a graduate of West Point. He soon became the most unpopular officer in the regiment. When the men found it increasingly difficult to obtain passes, they resorted to the expedient of slipping through the holes in the fence to enjoy themselves in the local bars. The Arizonans boasted of the skill with which they eluded the sentinels on these nocturnal excursions, and noted with satisfaction that the guard house contained many less adept recruits from New Mexico. In an attempt to eliminate these operations, the number of guard posts was increased twice.

The technique used by some of the troopers from New Mexico to avoid arrest became a favorite joke. One night the first sergeant of F Troop, Horace E. "Kid" Sherman, was returning to the camp with a large group of drunken comrades who were all A.W.O.L. Rather than attempting to slip all the men past the guards by having them crawl through holes in the fence, Sherman formed his friends into military formation and marched them boldly up to the main gate. Halted by the sentry, who could not see the true condition of the inebriated troopers in the darkness, Sherman masterfully berated the confused soldier and informed him that a guard was not permitted to stop a work party that was approaching in military formation. The puzzled sentry, completely demoralized by this dressing down, opened the gate and admitted the group to camp. Once inside, of course, the troopers quickly scattered to their respective tents.

Most of the men understood the value of discipline and even the "hard characters," as Roosevelt called them, gave little trouble once they understood what their officers expected. As in any military group, however, there were some who got into trouble. Shortly after arrival, an Arizonan was fined one hundred dollars for being drunk and disorderly. He had allegedly chased everybody off the main street of San Antonio with a butcher knife and, after escaping from six policemen who had arrested him, tried to upset a buggy containing two ladies. Two other Rough Riders used their horses to smash a cart carrying an elderly man under the pretense they were demonstrating how they intended to kill Spaniards in Cuba. William A. Owens, a member of B Troop from Globe, acquired the nickname "Smoke-em-up-Bill" for shooting out the lights on a San Antonio street car. Some of the men also had minor squabbles in bars and other places which were not reported in the newspapers.

The most widely publicized breach of propriety occurred during a concert held at the park by Professor Carl Beck's band. Beck had given many such performances for the Rough Riders and, for this particular occasion, had composed a special number called "The Cavalry Charge." As usual, the concert was held after dark and many townspeople came to listen and enjoy the social hour which was to follow. At the appropriate place in the concert a band member fired a revolver loaded with blanks for emphasis. What followed is not clear, but a voice shouted: "Help him out boys." Several pistols blazed. Someone, perhaps a rowdy from town, threw a switch and plunged the pavilion into darkness. Women screamed, officers shouted "fall in," more pistols roared and the large crowd made a dash for the waiting street cars and private vehicles.

The next day the San Antonio *Light* blistered the Rough Riders in print under the headline: "Prof. Beck's Band played the CAVALRY CHARGE and Rough Riders Played Hell."[24] This incident resulted in much unfavorable publicity for the regiment, which, up until that time, had enjoyed good relations with the San Antonio newsmen.

The regimental adjutant, Lieutenant Tom Hall, later claimed that the Rough Riders could not have fired their revolvers because all weapons and ammunition were kept under lock and key. Private Tuttle, however, later admitted that some of the Arizona men had brought their own revolvers with them. He also gave a possible motive for the incident by pointing out that all the barrels of beer mysteriously vanished in the darkness, only to reappear in the Rough Rider camp.

Toward the end of May, the Arizonans began to speculate on their departure from San Antonio. Tuttle wrote his mother: "From the indications, I think we will leave in a few days, but if we don't we will probably stay here all summer."[25] Both local newspapers reported on the gathering of a large force at Tampa, Florida, reportedly for the purpose of invading Cuba, and predicted that the Rough Riders would soon join it. Even Colonel Wood shared their optimism and prepared to strike camp. After he had received the telegram on May 23 asking when he could move, Wood secured marching rations, extra horseshoes and other supplies necessary for a change in station. The Arizona boys, aware of these activities, began to ship their superfluous belongings home.

On May 28 orders directing the Rough Riders to move to Tampa finally arrived. After reading the telegram, Wood quietly handed it to Roosevelt and shook his hand. The emotional Roosevelt threw his hat into the air and let out a yell of jubilation. The men correctly interpreted this display, and the camp went wild with demonstrations of joy. Hats, blankets, clothing and other material sailed high in the air as the excited Volunteers cheered and danced with pleasure. Not until the melancholy notes of taps spread through the camp did the men quiet down. The officers, meanwhile, worked late into the night to enable the Arizona column to entrain early the next morning.

The boys from Arizona had come a long way in the month they had been in the army. Thirty days after gathering at Prescott, they were prepared to board a train for the East — and perhaps Cuba. For the past three weeks they had undergone intensive training in all those facets of military life that their commanders deemed necessary. They had drilled long hours in the hot, choking dust on horses they had to break themselves; they had endured sleepless nights in little tents infested with mosquitoes, chiggers and centipedes; they had lost their individualism in drab uniforms and accepted military customs they neither liked nor understood. Their stay at San Antonio had been a memorable one, but now they were looking forward with eager anticipation for a hot fight in the Caribbean.

CHAPTER 3

On To Cuba

THE LEADING ELEMENTS OF THE ROUGH RIDERS arrived at Tampa, Florida, on June 1. They found a state of absolute confusion. Different regiments, Regular and Volunteer, had been gathering there for a month, but the problems of personnel and logistics had not been solved. Many of the Volunteers arrived without equipment, and the single-track railroad from the north proved incapable of transporting the necessary supplies. Adequate camping grounds had not even been established. To make matters worse, the War Department kept urging Major-General William Rufus Shafter, commander of the troops at Tampa, to embark his corps for Cuba as soon as possible. Final orders arrived on May 31, but General Shafter was unable to get the ships loaded until June 7. This delay proved to be beneficial to the Rough Riders, because it gave them time to get to Tampa and secure a place in the expeditionary force.

At 3:00 P.M. on May 29, some five hours behind schedule, the Arizona squadron, at the head of the Rough Riders, marched out of San Antonio. The railroad officials had agreed to have the troop train made up and waiting, but when the dusty Volunteers rode into the Union Stockyards that morning, they found that this promise had not been kept. All the passenger cars had not arrived, and those for the stock had come without adequate loading facilities. All that morning, while the trainmen shuffled cars along the sidings, the sweating soldiers hazed their recalcitrant horses aboard. After the equipment had been loaded, the men climbed into the passenger cars. The accommodations turned out to be reasonably comfortable. Two double cane-backed seats had been provided for the soldiers who, in groups of three, stacked their blankets, packs, weapons and personal belongings in the extra seat. The Arizonans took great pride in the fact that they, the first territorial group to be organized, also became the first to entrain. The remaining eight troops under Lieutenant Colonel Roosevelt did not leave until the next day.

The trip through the heartland of the former Confederacy proved to be an exciting experience for the blue-shirted Volunteers. At every stop from Texas to Florida large crowds waited to greet the Rough Riders. New Orleans proved especially memorable because of the preponderance of winsome and flirtatious young belles, who provided a welcome distraction from the onerous duties of furnishing feed and water to the horses. Many of the men took advantage of the long delay to exchange names and addresses with the young women. According to Webb, some of the Arizonans had difficulty communicating with the slow-talking Southerners: "Some of the boys have a hard time understanding English 'as she is spoke' down here. The following is an example: 'Dy you all have to carry yo' hosses way down heah and tote yo' watah to camp?' "[1]

Notified that his squadron would be in Florida within seventy-two hours, Brodie had drawn travel rations for three days. But by the time the train had crossed the Mississippi and entered the pine forests of the deep South, the men were out of food. Fortunately, civilians provided welcome baskets of fruit, sandwiches and fried chicken. With outstretched hands the Arizonans leaned out of the train windows to accept the offerings. Webb, in his weekly letter, recorded their appreciation when he wrote:

At a small station in Mississippi an old colored 'Aunty' came out to our train and presented my partner with a Spring chicken, which she had prepared herself. We smuggled the chicken into our roll of blankets and after we had turned in for the night we had our first meal for that day. The old 'Aunty' will always be remembered with loving thoughts.[2]

Many members of the Arizona squadron did not wait for provisions to be given to them. At every stop hungry Volunteers, often with the connivance of their officers, slipped off the train in search of unattended chickens, pigs and geese. Later, after the train had started again, the troopers butchered their stolen fowl and swine, kindled small fires and cooked hot meals on the moving train. At Tallahassee, Florida, some enterprising foragers from McClintock's troop appropriated several hogs found rooting in the feeding pens next to the tracks. The station agent, and owner of the animals, happened to see the theft. He complained to Major Brodie, who ordered the men to release the pigs. As fast as the troopers threw them off one side of the car, the animals ran underneath the train and out the other side where, hidden from the agent, eager hands waited to throw them right back on again. "It sure was comical then," Lieutenant Rynning recalled, "to see that station agent strutting up and down the platform and telling his friends: 'Those sonsofbitches ain't going to get away with no hogs of mine.' "[3]

During the journey to Tampa many of the Arizona boys found that the Spanish-American War had served to heal the bitterness left by the greater conflict of thirty-five years before. Southerners, young and old, extended every courtesy to the Rough Riders. Captain McClintock personally experienced this shortly after arriving in Florida. He was in charge of the horse train, and at Tallahassee he found that there were no facilities for watering at the station. He ordered the men to unload the animals and take them into the town square where there were several hydrants. When the citizens realized that the horses still could not drink because there were no troughs, they voluntarily had their servants bring out wooden and zinc tubs to emplace by each hydrant. McClintock was surprised to find everyone so extremely helpful and coopera- tive — but he was particularly impressed by the charm of the Southern ladies.

Late in the afternoon of June 1, Brodie's section arrived in Tampa. Here the men encountered still more of the inor- dinate confusion that characterized the entire trip. Halted at Ybor City, a suburb of Tampa, the troopers realized that no one seemed to know what to do. Colonel Wood, who had accompanied the first section, finally walked into town in an effort to find someone who could direct him to his bivouac. During his absence General Joseph Wheeler rode by and directed Major Brodie to detrain and camp there for the night. The Arizonans quickly unloaded their equipment, established a picket line by a nearby corral and prepared to get what sleep they could. It turned out to be very little, as the remaining sections continued to arrive and unload their baggage near them all night.

Everyone was exasperated at the endless confusion and evidence of poor preparation, but Lieutenant Colonel Roose- velt was particularly vehement. Before the so-called "Dodge Commission," a group of military experts impaneled by Presi- dent McKinley after the war to investigate the conduct of the War Department during the conflict with Spain, he later testified: "When we reached Tampa we had twenty-four hours of utter and absolute confusion. There was no one to show us where we were to camp. The railway system there was in a condition of absolute congestion."[4]

The next morning, in a column of fours, the Rough Riders marched to their bivouac area south of the city near the Fifth Corps Headquarters in the Plant Hotel. The route of march passed through Tampa, and the troopers got their first good look at the city. From the suburb of Lakeland on the north to Port Tampa nine miles south, white-canvased cities had blossomed forth to accommodate the army of 30,000 soldiers. The dusty streets and board sidewalks of Tampa, a cigar-making city of 10,000, were jammed with soldiers from every branch of service. In appearances the blue-clad Regulars stood apart from the Volunteers, who had arrived in varying degrees of readiness. Some of the Volunteers had arrived without weapons; some without uniforms; and a few units had no blankets, tents or camp equipment. It was a quarter-master's nightmare. In addition to the soldiers and resident civilians, the area was filling up with the usual assortment of opportunists. Girls, gamblers and itinerant businessmen of various descriptions were arriving in ever-increasing numbers.

The Rough Riders were one of the last units to arrive at Tampa. Orders directing the Regular Army to mobilize had been issued as early as April 15, and the different regiments immediately had started to gather at Tampa, New Orleans and Mobile. With the declaration of war, additional camps to provide for the influx of Volunteers and increased enlistments in the Regulars were established in Georgia, Florida and Virginia.

Plans called for both the Regulars and Volunteers to be organized into eight corps of approximately 27,000 men each. The Fifth Corps was to be assembled at Tampa under the command of Major-General William R. Shafter, a corpulent, three hundred pound veteran of the Union Army. Shafter's appointment to the Fifth Corps came from General Nelson A. Miles, the Commanding General of the Army, who had been impressed by Shafter's combat record in the Civil War. Not only had Shafter served in every rank in the army from private on up, but he had won the Congressional Medal of Honor in so doing. He also had garnered valuable experience while campaigning against Indians in Texas after the Civil War. He had the reputation of being a fighter and he had an excellent military record. Unfortunately, Shafter's bulk and tactless handling of correspondents rendered him vulnerable to much abuse and ridicule at the hands of hostile newsmen. He was blamed for everything that went wrong, although much of what happened was not his fault. His reputation, built over a period of years, was temporarily destroyed in a few short months after being sent to Tampa.

Late in April General Shafter arrived in Tampa to forge his command. He established his headquarters in the Tampa Bay Hotel. This hostelry, a grotesque, Alhambra-type structure complete with gilded minarets and nearly a hundred rooms, had been built in 1888 by Henry B. Plant, a prominent Florida railroad tycoon. Its garish splendor made it easily identified. Soon its halls bustled with activity as harried staff officers and bored war correspondents exchanged the latest gossip. Line officers, fresh from duty on the frontier, were renewing friendships with classmates and acquaintances they hadn't seen in years.

Ordered to follow the triangular concept of military organization, General Shafter planned on forming three infantry divisions and one division of cavalry. Each division was to contain three brigades, and each brigade was to have three regiments. These general commands were formed as fast as the troops arrived in Tampa. To command the First Infantry Division, composed of eight regiments of Regulars and one of Volunteers, General Shafter had Brigadier General J. Ford Kent.[5] Commanding the Second Infantry Division was Colonel Wood's old friend from Fort Huachuca, Brigadier General Henry W. Lawton. A third infantry division was not formed. General Shafter sailed for Cuba before sufficient troops to man it could be located. He did, however, have an independent brigade of three regiments commanded by Brigadier General John C. Bates.[6]

Brigadier General Joseph "Fighting Joe" Wheeler, a diminutive, gray-bearded ex-Confederate, commanded the cavalry division. President McKinley wanted Wheeler to accept a commission because he felt that the appointment of an ex-Southern general to a position of high command would show that the United States once again was a united nation. The ban enacted during Reconstruction on officers of the Confederacy holding federal office in the United States had long since been lifted by Congress.[7]

General Wheeler's subordinates were Brigadier Generals Samuel Storrow Sumner and Samuel Baldwin Marks Young. Both men had been Union generals in the Civil War; both had stayed in the army after the war; and both had been promoted to brigadier general of Volunteers on May 4. Sumner commanded the First Cavalry Brigade, which included the Third, the Sixth and the Negro Ninth regiments.[8] As the commanding officer of the Second Brigade, Young had the First Regular and the Negro Tenth.[9] With only five regiments of Regular Cavalry available to him, Shafter never formed a third brigade of cavalry.

General Shafter relied on the Regular Army to form the backbone of his Fifth Corps. He assigned Volunteer units to his three divisions only when Regulars were not available. He wound up with only one Volunteer regiment in each of his three divisions.

Through late April and early May, while he struggled with the complexities of his new command, General Shafter received several conflicting sets of orders. On April 29 he was instructed to send 5,000 men to Cuba to furnish logistical support to the rebel bands operating in the southern part of the island. The arrival of the Spanish fleet forced the cancellation of this plan. On April 29 Admiral Pascual Cervera, with four cruisers and three destroyers, sailed from the Cape Verde Islands for Cuba. The American naval officers, charged with the responsibility of preventing Cervera's arrival in Cuba, withdrew Shafter's escort vessels to aid in the search for the Spanish fleet. Even with these additional ships, however, the navy was unable to prevent Cervera from slipping into Santiago harbor on May 19.

Meanwhile, the War Department continued to send orders to General Shafter. During the first week in May Shafter was directed to land a force on the northern coast of Cuba to secure and hold a beachhead pending arrival of sufficient troops to capture the entire island. This plan had to be abandoned for lack of transportation. During the next few weeks a fleet of steam transports, reportedly large enough to convoy 25,000 men, was assembled at Tampa. On May 26 Shafter was ordered to prepare for an invasion of Cuba. This looked like the real thing, and orders were sent to Colonel Wood instructing him to join General Young at Tampa with the third regiment for Young's brigade. Within a week the Rough Riders were there.

Shortly after their arrival, the Arizonans were introduced to their division commander, "Fighting Joe" Wheeler. Their first good look at Wheeler was on Sunday, when Chaplain Brown delivered the customary service. Lounging in a palmetto grove close to their bivouac, the Arizonans, complete with cartridge belts and campaign hats, were half-listening to the uninspired address. Corporal French happened to glance to the rear and there stood General Wheeler. In this white-haired little man French saw the same characteristics that had endeared another officer to the Arizona men. No finer compliment could Wheeler have received than that paid him by French who wrote:

He had a remarkably shaped head, and wonderfully expressive eyes. . . . I have known another man with the same shaped head, same eyes and features. Eyes that seemed to be looking a thousand years into the future. That man was Colonel Alex O. Brodie. Joe Wheeler and Alex Brodie were in a class by themselves. Two men out of millions. . . . Others may be more spectacular, but it is the Wheelers and the Brodies that have made and will continue to make us a great nation.[10]

The military and civilian visitors to the camp of the Rough Riders came away with varied reactions. Although many civilians came to see the Volunteers, they lacked the enthusiastic patriotism that had characterized the people of San Antonio. This was because the residents of Tampa already had experienced numerous incidents with the soldiers. During May the Tampa *Morning Tribune* carried many stories of fights and riots involving members of the Fifth Corps. Apparently there was no one particular unit responsible, as the errant soldiers were identified as being from both Regular and Volunteer units. Many of them — but not an unusually high number — were Negroes. Most of the trouble took place in the houses of prostitution, but some incidents occurred on the streets. Consequently, local inhabitants stayed in their houses after dark, coming out only when absolutely necessary. Many had begun carrying firearms for protection. Under such conditions it is not surprising that the reception given the Rough Riders was decidedly cool. The mayor of Tampa, fearful that the Volunteers from the West would attempt to live up to their wild cowboy reputation, made a vain appeal to headquarters that Wood's troopers not be paid until after they had sailed. This, of course, was not feasible.

In contrast to the civilian reaction, praise for the unit came from both the English and German attachés, who told Wood that his regiment had the best kept bivouac in the Fifth Corps. They commented particularly on the efficiency of the soldiers on guard. The German also pointed out that the First Volunteer Cavalry was one of the few regiments that had arrived fully equipped, uniformed and capable of moving with no other transportation facilities than its own organic pack train. The Arizonans also heard General Miles, who had come to inspect the embarkation, compliment them.

The reporters and war correspondents made a beeline for the Rough Riders encampment. Some of them struck up friendly relations with the men; others had a negative reaction to the troopers and to Roosevelt. In both cases the type of relationship established greatly colored the writings of each reporter. It seems that it was impossible for them to remain neutral. Those who got along well with the Volunteers heaped praise upon the regiment. Others, who did not get along quite so well, were extremely critical.

Two influential reporters who liked the regiment were Richard Harding Davis of the New York *Herald,* and Edward Marshall of the New York *Journal.* Marshall in particular was laudatory to the point of being ridiculous. His feelings are adequately covered in his book, *The Story of the Rough Riders,* where he wrote: "It was the greatest fighting machine that any army ever held."[11] Marshall was so impressed by the regiment that he lived in the shadow of it for the rest of his life. During the First World War, while a correspondent in England, he made a trip to Scotland, where he told a hotel clerk that he had been a Rough Rider. This, of course, was a complete falsehood. Davis, on the other hand, tempered his conclusions with a more detached and judicial viewpoint. Nevertheless, Davis was not critical of the unit.

A different stand was taken by Burr McIntosh. Like most of the correspondents, McIntosh first saw the Rough Riders at Tampa. He was not impressed. McIntosh's opinions stemmed largely from his dislike of Roosevelt. In his own book, *The Little I Saw of Cuba,* McIntosh charged that Roosevelt provided "tips" to those correspondents who "were sure to write things in the proper spirit."[12] By his own admission, McIntosh was not a member of this "in" group and therefore did not join the ranks of those who did nothing but extoll the virtues of the newsworthy Rough Riders. To the contrary, as a member of the opposition, McIntosh's comments are pointed barbs of derision which attempted to minimize the effectiveness of the regiment.

As soon as the details of camp organization had been completed, final training of the Rough Riders began. For some unexplained reason this drill did not include practice in firing the new carbines. Ammunition was available, but possibly no suitable range could be located. At any rate, Colonel Wood limited drill to practice in dismounted combat formations until the horses had a chance to recuperate from the trip to Florida. With their troopers deployed as skirmishers, the officers led their men on mock charges through the palmetto scrub

against simulated entrenchments, or supervised defensive maneuvers while the Volunteers, crouching in rifle pits dug along
the beaches, snapped their carbines at hypothetical attackers.
This was hot, dirty work, and the men much preferred the
occasional mounted drill which began a day or two after
arrival. At the end of each day the Arizonans frequently galloped their horses bareback through the shallow surf along the
beach. Sergeant Hughes later recalled that the horses seemed
to enjoy the cool spray as much as the men.

After drilling only three days, the Rough Riders received
their embarkation orders on June 6. To the consternation of
the troopers, however, these orders directed that only two
thirds of them could go. Again, this was a result of poor planning. When the transport vessels, which the navy had promised
would be capable of transporting 25,000 men to Cuba arrived
at Tampa, it was found that they had room for only 17,000
men. Consequently, the decision was made that each cavalry
regiment would embark only eight of its twelve troops. Moreover, all pack trains such as the one with the Rough Riders
would be detached from the parent organization and consolidated under direct control of Fifth Corps.

Colonel Wood decided to leave one troop from each of
the first and second squadrons and two troops from the third
squadron. After careful deliberation he selected Captain Alexander's C Troop, the junior unit in the first squadron, to
remain at Tampa along with H, I and M Troops under Major
Henry Hersey. Tradition holds that Captain Maximiliano
Luna's F Troop originally had been selected to remain, but
Luna appealed to Colonel Wood on the grounds that Luna,
being of Spanish ancestry, should be allowed to go to Cuba to
prove his loyalty to the United States. The petition was well
received and Captain George Curry was directed to remain
with H Troop in place of Luna.

In addition to leaving four troops, the orders also con-
firmed an earlier rumor that because of limited transportation
the cavalrymen would leave their horses and pistols at Tampa.

The Rough Riders were doomed to serve in combat as common infantry! "That almost took the starch out of the boys," recalled Sergeant Hughes. "We had been planning things we would pull off on the Spaniards on our horses, and as a cowboy is almost as helpless on foot as a fish is out of water."[13] Some unknown trooper, upset over turning his horse over to Major Hersey's Tampa detachment, remarked that henceforth the regiment should be known not as "Roosevelt's Rough Riders," but as W. W. W.s for "Wood's Weary Walkers."[14]

Furthermore, each embarking troop was limited to seventy men. This forced each commander to leave a good-sized squad in addition to his horses and pistols. When Captains O'Neill and McClintock selected those to stay, there were outraged protests raised against their decisions. O'Neill had three officers and eighty-three men assigned to his A Troop, and from which he had to leave thirteen. At first he named Sergeant Sam Rhodes of the Tonto Basin the commander of his Tampa detachment, but later he changed his mind and appointed Corporal George Bugbee instead. From the three sets of brothers in A Troop — the Bugbees from Safford, the Azbills from St. Johns and the Wallace boys from Flagstaff — O'Neill ordered that one from each family stay behind. McClintock left eight men under Corporal Charles Heitman of Tucson, and took seventy-one with him. Unlike O'Neill, McClintock took both the Norton boys, the only family that had furnished him with two of its sons. He did leave his two sick troopers, Private Sol Drachman from Tucson, who had contracted malaria, and Frank Roberts, a new recruit from Texas, who fell sick just before embarkation.

Many troopers scheduled to be left did everything possible to secure a place in the invading army. Some of the eastern boys offered as much as five hundred dollars to anyone who would exchange places with them. Private Martin L. Crimmons of B Troop did not have to go quite that high, as five men offered to accept his inducement of fifty dollars. When the young trooper presented himself to McClintock, however, he was told that the embarkation roster was already made up and could not be changed. Crimmons then appealed directly to Lieutenant Colonel Roosevelt, who declined to interfere and told Crimmons there would be no changes. "Two of my best friends," Roosevelt explained, "Elliot Cowden and Hamilton Fish, are being left behind. All cannot go."[15]

In spite of Lieutenant Colonel Roosevelt's promise to Crimmons, several adjustments were made to enable certain selected individuals to get to Cuba. One of these fortunates was Sergeant Hamilton Fish, who was transferred from I to L Troop. Another was the second lieutenant of I Troop, John C. Greenway, who was attached to G Troop. The only Arizonan to be included in this group was Albert P. Wright, the six-foot six-inch trooper in Captain Alexander's command. Wright joined headquarters as the regimental color bearer. He took with him the silk banner of the Arizona squadron — the one that had been made by the ladies of Phoenix — in preference to the beautiful flag brought by the contingent from New Mexico.

It was natural that the men selected to go to Cuba looked upon themselves as being chosen because they were the finest members of the regiment. They felt that those who stayed behind were not up to quality. The passage of time reinforced this opinion. Many years later Private Jesse D. Langdon of K Troop recalled that there was considerable "shuffling" to enable Colonel Wood to take the "cream of the crop."[16] Those who stayed behind had a different story. In later years many of them claimed that those left in Tampa had been selected because of their superior ability to handle horses. In reality, there was very little partiality shown.

The nine-mile move to the docks at Port Tampa for the dismounted Rough Riders proved to be a mass of confusion. It was, according to Roosevelt, more of "the higglety-pigglety business" that had characterized the entire operation at Tampa.[17] Marched from their camp on the evening of June 7 to meet a train at a nearby railroad siding, the Rough

Riders waited until early morning for transportation. It never arrived. About 2:00 A.M. Colonel Wood ordered his sleepy troopers to march to another siding where, he had been told, another train would meet him. Again no transportation appeared, and the first light of day disclosed that the men had spent the last few hours of darkness within rifle shot of their old encampment. They could see their comrades in C, H, I and M Troops preparing breakfast. At this point determined and resourceful Colonel Wood commandeered a train of empty coal cars, which happened to pass headed in the opposite direction, and ordered the engineer to transport his Volunteers to the docks. Tired and black with coal dust — but undaunted in spirit — the troopers chanted their regimental slogan as they rolled into the loading area at Port Tampa:

> Rough, tough we're the stuff
> We want to fight and can't get enough.[18]

While Major Brodie supervised the unloading of the coal train at the port, Colonel Wood and Roosevelt went off to find their transport. After spanking coal dust from their uniforms and equipment, the Arizonans rested on their blanket rolls and studied the colorful spectacle of the Fifth Corps embarkation. In the harbor, swinging slowly at taut anchor chains, lay thirty-four transports. Each one was identified by a large white number painted on the bow. No specific loading plan seemed to exist, and the Volunteers watched regiment after regiment, some accompanied by laden transport wagons, hurry along the beaches and piers in search of a ship which could be boarded. Each unit could be identified as to component by the type of weapon carried. The Regular Infantry had Krag rifles, the Regular Cavalry had short carbines, as did the Rough Riders. Other Volunteers shouldered obsolete .45 caliber Springfields. All marched under full field pack with gleaming, brass-filled cartridge belts.

After a short wait Lieutenant Colonel Roosevelt, obviously excited, returned and told his officers that the regiment could take ship number eight, the *Yucatan* — if they could get it before anyone else. Colonel Wood, after receiving this information from the officer in charge of the loading, had gone aboard to take possession and direct the captain to berth his ship at the wharf. The Arizonans needed only a brief explanation to get them moving. They had not come this far only to be left now! The troopers jumped to their feet, buckled on their cartridge belts, threw their blanket rolls over their shoulders and marched to the pier at double time. They arrived none too soon. Just behind them came the Seventy-First New York Volunteer Infantry, which also had been assigned to the *Yucatan*. Lieutenant Colonel Roosevelt, with his grinning Rough Riders on board and lining the rails to listen, met and turned the New Yorkers back at the gangway.

Both Colonel Wood and Lieutenant Colonel Roosevelt received a great deal of criticism for this act, which Roosevelt later admitted was highly irregular. Be that as it may, however, the fact remains that the Volunteers had their ship.

By late afternoon, June 7, the Rough Riders had loaded and were ready to sail. They had aboard eight troops of seventy men each with their personal equipment and firearms. For support they had two Colt rapid fire guns, presented to the regiment by wealthy New York friends, and a pneumatic dynamite gun which had been assigned to them at Tampa. This latter weapon was described as somewhat of a novelty, but which was capable of executing great destruction. It consisted of two tubes with a superimposed barrel. A charge of guncotton was exploded in one tube, which forced compressed air into the breech by way of the second tube. This was considered sufficient to propel a three-pound dynamite projectile at least two miles. A special squad had been formed to care for the gun. Even with all this equipment, however, the ship was not filled and Colonel Wood permitted four companies of the Second Infantry to come aboard. This brought the total number to forty-three officers and seven hundred

and seventy-three enlisted men. The Rough Riders expected
to sail immediately, but they soon learned that the invasion
had been postponed because a Spanish fleet had been reported
cruising off Key West.

The invasion was delayed one week by the presence of
this mythical Spanish fleet. On June 8, three American ships,
cruising near Cuba, were identified to the Navy Department
as a Spanish cruiser and a destroyer. Shafter immediately was
ordered not to sail with his transports until the navy could
destroy this enemy "ghost fleet."

For the next five days the armada swung at anchor in
Tampa harbor. There was very little that could be done to
keep the men occupied. Cramped in their limited quarters,
the Arizonans played cards, wrote letters home, fished —
mostly without success — and swam in the tepid waters of the
bay. Although disappointed at the delay, they derived some
satisfaction in being part of the impressive martial array.
"The sight in the harbor is a magnificent and impressive
one," wrote Private Hodgdon of A Troop, "and shows what
war means when one sees nothing but big warships with ugly
guns pointing at you."[19] The men considered it fine sport to
swim from ship to ship to visit with friends. On one such
excursion, Sergeant Sam Rhodes fell victim to a stingray.
From that time on his unsympathetic comrades called him
"Stingaree Sam."

On June 13 the question of the Spanish fleet was cleared
up and the flotilla sailed. As bands played and soldiers
cheered, the *Yucatan* weighed anchor and took its place in
the fleet steaming down the bay for the open sea. At this
point disaster almost struck. It is not clear what happened,
but the *Matteawan,* a transport carrying the Twentieth Infantry, was anchored near the main channel. Most of the
ships already had passed when the *Yucatan* appeared. Because
of a faulty steering mechanism or perhaps an error in naviga-
tion, the *Yucatan* veered out of line and headed straight for
the motionless transport on a head-on collision course. It was

a bad moment, for the *Yucatan* had 3,500 pounds of dynamite — ammunition for the dynamite gun — stored in the bow. Everyone was afraid that it would explode on contact. At the last possible moment, however, the crew got the transport under control, with the vessel's bow just scraping the side of the *Matteawan*. Burr McIntosh, on board the *Matteawan*, noted that the ships were so close together that some troopers tried to shake hands with men on the other vessel. The Rough Riders were proud of the equanimity with which they stood on deck waiting for the expected explosion. After avoiding the collision, the crew took the *Yucatan* to the mouth of the harbor where they anchored for the night.

The following afternoon, after the flotilla had been formed, the force started for Cuba. In three divisions of three parallel columns each, the ships steamed south at an average speed of five knots. Naval patrol boats protected the front, the rear and both flanks of the convoy. The significance of the occasion did not escape the Arizonans, who fully realized that they had a place in the largest amphibious operation ever attempted by the United States.

Unaccustomed to life at sea, the men from Arizona found that they had to make adjustments to their new environment. No longer could body lice be controlled by boiling clothing, but the men substituted the simple expedient of dragging their infested uniforms behind the ship. One morning Tuttle, who practiced this technique at night, awoke to find that the propellers had cut the line, and he had lost an irreplaceable pair of trousers and a shirt. Some of Tuttle's friends offered the opinion that his clothes were so covered with vermin that the sharks had taken the uniforms for the sustenance they contained.

Crowded together on the *Yucatan* with no possibility of voluntary isolation, and perhaps psychologically affected by thoughts of approaching combat, an occasional flare of temper disturbed the customary harmony. Corporal "Ed" Doherty, a big, quarrelsome ex-miner from Jerome, made the mistake of selecting Fred Bugbee to ridicule for being seasick. Bugbee put a sudden end to this when he seized his Krag and threatened to shoot his tormentor. Several of the Graham County boys, who recognized that Bugbee's vow was no idle threat, managed to disarm their angry comrade while others hustled Doherty out of sight. From the expression on Doherty's face, it was obvious that he too realized that Bugbee was not a man to be trifled with.

Only the prospects of getting into action enabled the men to tolerate the discomforts aboard ship. At first Captain O'Neill's troop had been quartered on deck, but after several days they had to join B Troop in the multiple tiers of double bunks stacked between decks. No breath of fresh air circulated to these quarters, and the sweltering troopers surreptitiously competed for sleeping room on the deck. To supplement the monotonous diet of coffee, hard-tack and canned meat, the men paid outrageous prices for additional food: a sandwich cost twenty-five cents, lemons went for ten cents apiece, warm beer sold for thirty cents a pint and half a cup of ice water cost ten cents. Some profit-conscious sailors also provided cheap whiskey at twenty dollars a gallon. According to Webb it left much to be desired. "The only thing there seems to be plenty of aboard this ship is whiskey," Webb recorded. "In his young days your correspondent has experimented with some pretty tough bug extract in Arizona, yet he can truthfully say that he has never tackled any red liquor that would come up to the standard of this rat poison sold right here on board this government ship."[20]

These charges, of course, were denied by the crewmen. Three months later Oliver O. Howard, a veteran of the Union Army who had retired with the rank of major-general and who had once conducted peace negotiations with certain Arizona Apaches after the Civil War, spent four days on the *Yucatan*. During this period the crewmen assured Howard that the Rough Riders had received good treatment while they were aboard the vessel. "We had to starve ourselves," a sailor told Howard, "to feed such ravenous soldiers."[21] Another member of the crew told Howard of an unusual incident that happened shortly after the flotilla left Tampa. He related how Shafter had ordered the captain of the *Yucatan* to take his ship alongside the *City of Washington* to provide aid to that transport, which was having trouble. The naval commander of the convoy, who had not been advised of Shafter's order, saw the *Yucatan* pull out of line and signaled a halt. Soon he was alongside the *Yucatan* to censure that transport's captain. The discussion ended, however, when Lieutenant Colonel Roosevelt appeared on deck and was recognized. The naval commander, who did not care to direct a reprimand in the presence of a former Assistant Secretary of the Navy, decided to overlook the breach of discipline.

After all the difficulties encountered in getting to Tampa and on a ship, the Arizona Rough Riders were on their way to war. They missed their comrades in Captain Alexander's C Troop, but they welcomed the New Mexicans in Captain Frederick A. Muller's E Troop, which had been assigned to Brodie's squadron as the fourth troop. The other four embarking units, F, G, L and K, had been assigned to Lieutenant Colonel Roosevelt, who went as the other squadron commander. Major Henry Hersey and Major George Dunn had been ordered to remain at Tampa.

As the convoy steamed farther into the tropics, the Arizonans speculated as to their ultimate destination. Some thought they would go to Puerto Rico, but most predicted that the campaign would take place in Cuba. They agreed that either Havana or Santiago would be the objective. On the morning of June 20 all speculation ended when the convoy changed course. With the trade wind at their backs and land visible to starboard, the men realized they were following the southern coast of Cuba. The army of invasion was headed for Santiago!

CHAPTER 4

A Smell of Powder

Cuba, "the Pearl of the Antilles," lay ninety miles south of the Florida Keys. With a maximum length of seven hundred and sixty miles and an average width of eighty miles, the island somewhat resembled a giant lizard, its head buried in the waves of the Windward Passage. Its backbone was a mountain range which ran the length of the island and reached its highest elevation in the east. The main portion of the island was lush and tropical with an average annual rainfall of fifty-two inches, two thirds of it falling in the rainy season from June to November.

As a military objective in 1898, Cuba posed complex logistical and tactical problems to Shafter's invading forces. Transportation facilities between the widely scattered centers of population were limited to a few primitive roads and inadequately maintained railroads. The only significant cities were the seaports of Havana, on the northwest coast, and Santiago de Cuba on the southeast. Both ports had excellent harbors and large garrisons of Spanish troops. To control the native population of 1,600,000 Spanish-speaking inhabitants, the Spaniards maintained a garrison of 80,000 Regulars and 25,000 volunteers.

Cuba was first seen by the soldiers of the Fifth Corps on June 17, when the high mountains on the northern coast became visible. Two lighthouses also were seen. Later, after the convoy beat its way through the Windward Passage around Cape Maisí and down the southern coast, the Arizona Rough Riders realized that the topography of Cuba was strangely reminiscent of the American Southwest. Between Guantanamo Bay and Santiago, the high mountain range behind the coast looked just like the mountains of Arizona. One noticeable difference being the tropical vegetation which covered the slopes with a brilliant shade of green. General Shafter also was intently studying the shoreline, but he was concerned with the military aspects of the situation.

During the six-day voyage from Tampa to Cuba, Shafter had studied maps and intelligence reports prior to selecting a tentative landing site. Ordered to capture the Spanish garrison at Santiago and cooperate with the navy to destroy the Spanish fleet in the harbor, Shafter carefully surveyed the terrain around Santiago as his ship proceeded slowly along the coast. He knew that Santiago could not be approached from the sea because it lay four miles inland at the head of a narrow channel. Enemy batteries at Morro Castle near the mouth of the harbor, at Scoapa across the bay, and at Punta Gorda farther up toward Santiago effectively protected the inlet. Shafter tentatively decided to land to the east at either Siboney or Daiquiri. Siboney lay fifteen miles from the harbor, and Daiquiri nine miles farther. Disadvantages included the fact that neither of these small hamlets had a harbor, nor did the rocky shoreline offer any protection from the constant trade winds. Before forming a definite plan of operation, Shafter decided to wait until he arrived off Santiago and was able to consult with General Calixto Garcia, leader of the

Insurrectos in the area, and Admiral William T. Sampson, commander of the blockading navy.

In the afternoon of June 20, while the transports rode at anchor off Santiago, Shafter went ashore to meet with Sampson and Garcia. Sampson wanted the army to effect a landing near Morro Castle at the harbor entrance, but Garcia concurred with Shafter that the troops should land at Daiquiri. Although this site lay nine miles farther from Santiago than Siboney, it had landing facilities in the form of an iron pier. Garcia assured the Americans that the Spanish forces in the vicinity numbered 12,000 men, with six hundred at Siboney and three hundred more at Daiquiri. At the conclusion of the conference Shafter issued his orders. On the morning of June 22, following a thirty minute naval bombardment, the Fifth Corps would land at Daiquiri and regroup for the march on Santiago. To keep General Arsenio Linares, commander of the Department of Santiago, from concentrating his forces in opposition, the navy would attempt to conceal the operation by sending several warships and transports west to bombard three coastal villages.

While General Shafter was in conference on June 20, the Rough Riders studied the entrance of Santiago harbor. The city itself could not be seen because of interposed hills, but the ancient guardian of Santiago, Morro Castle, was clearly visible. Sergeant Hughes was particularly impressed. He saw in the Castle a reflection of the architectural style of the old Spanish missions in southern Arizona. "We can see Morro Castle as plainly as you can the [mission of] San Xavier from the school house," he wrote his brother back in Tucson.[1] Like an enormous watchdog, with its formidable stone walls a monument to former Spanish colonial glory, this fortress perched on a high cliff just above the harbor entrance.

After dark the next evening, June 21, the entire flotilla weighed anchor and steamed twenty-four miles eastward toward the small hamlet of Daiquiri. Shafter had returned from his conference with Garcia and Sampson and was ready to put his plan into effect. The men had been told that debarkation would commence at daybreak, and while their ship proceeded through the dark, tropical night, they checked their equipment. Webb took time to write his last letter before the campaign started. He described how the carbines, which had not yet been fired in spite of the obvious opportunity to have had target practice at sea, were carefully stripped, cleaned, oiled and reassembled; how the cartridge belts and canteens were filled; and how each man placed his personal belongings in his long horseshoe roll in order to be able to debark at a moment's notice. "Before this letter reaches its destination," Webb predicted, "the Arizona volunteers will probably have smelled powder for the first time on the field of battle."[2]

General Shafter's plan of debarkation called for the Second Infantry Division to hit the beach first followed by a detachment of four Gatling guns. Brigadier General John C. Bates was to follow with his brigade, and General Wheeler's dismounted cavalry division was to land next. The First Infantry Division and corps artillery units would be the last to go ashore. The transports carrying the Second Division were to position themselves close to the beaches, with the other vessels standing farther out to sea. A thirty minute naval bombardment would precede the landing to drive the Spaniards out of the village.

The troops began going ashore at 9:40 A.M. on June 22. On board the *Yucatan,* which was at anchor behind the troopships of the Second Division, the Rough Riders lined the rails to watch. The preliminary bombardment was spectacular. The smoking guns of the warships fired high explosive shells, which raked the water front and hills behind with impressive accuracy. Several blockhouses took direct hits. Surprisingly enough, there was no response from shore. During this cannonade the infantrymen of the Second Division were climbing down cargo nets into longboats and steam launches. At 9:40 the supporting fire was lifted and the boats headed in toward shore.

Unexpected difficulties arose immediately. The sea was unusually rough; the supply of landing craft was found inadequate; and the pier was too small. In an attempt to speed up the landing, the sailors began running their boats through the pounding surf and onto the beach. As the Rough Riders watched in amazement and disbelief, the debarking soldiers formed by troops on the beach and marched into the underbrush as fast as they landed. It seemed unbelievable, but the Spaniards had decided not to oppose the landing.

As the Volunteers waited to climb into the longboats, someone, perhaps Lieutenant Colonel Roosevelt, decided to send a group ashore to raise the regimental colors over Daiquiri. The logical place seemed to be a blockhouse on Mount Losiltires, a tall hill just east of the landing point. Several naval guns had fired at the fort, but had not been able to hit it. Color-Sergeant Wright, Surgeon Henry La Motte and Chief Trumpeter Clay Platt secured a boat and made an early landing with the infantry. When they reached the top of the hill they found that Edward Marshall, a correspondent for the New York *Journal,* had preceded them. After Wright made several futile efforts to scale the pitched roof, he gave the flag to a sailor who had just joined the group. This man managed to lash the flag to the staff on top of the blockhouse.

The soldiers on the beach and transports below saw the Rough Rider flag as it swelled in the morning breeze and gave it a rousing greeting. According to McClintock, "an Arizona captain" on board the *Yucatan* recognized the satin ribbons and threw his hat to the deck as he shouted: "Howl, ye Arizona men — It's our flag up there!" The invasion turned into a noisy celebration as men cheered, steam whistles shrilled and warships fired a salute. A group of *Insurrectos* on shore even joined in with a ragged volley of their own. "No flag on land or sea ever had a grander salutation," concluded Captain McClintock, "and the flag was the flag of the Arizona squadron."[3] There is no apparent reason for the

failure of McClintock to state whether it was he or Captain
O'Neill who started the demonstration.

The premature debarkation of the Rough Riders, accomplished before the infantrymen were all ashore, was a
result of Roosevelt's political connections. During the morning and early afternoon, while the infantry struggled with
the problems of getting on the beach, the Volunteers waited
impatiently. By mid-afternoon it was obvious that all the
troops could not get ashore before dark. Both Colonel Wood
and Roosevelt were actively searching for a means of getting
their men off the ship before darkness suspended the landing
operation. The coveted opportunity came when a former aide
to Roosevelt from the Navy Department supplied his old
associate with a Cuban pilot. This individual directed the
Yucatan to a new berth much closer to the beach and in
direct path of the longboats and steam launches which were
ferrying the infantrymen ashore. Soon the Rough Riders were
on their way.

The most difficult part of the operation was the transfer
from the longboats to the wharf. Most of the planks had been
removed from the pier, and the heavy surf made it impossible
to lash the boats to it. The heavily laden men waited until
the boat rose on a swell to a height even with the top of the
pier and then jumped to the slippery surface. All of the
Volunteers got ashore safely, but a boatload of Negro troopers
from the Tenth Cavalry capsized. Captain O'Neill, who had
already debarked and who had remained on the pier trying
to bring some order out of existing chaos, realized that two of
the men were in trouble. Fully clothed, O'Neill dove into the
water in a vain effort to rescue Privates Cobb and English,
who were being dragged under by their heavy equipment.
Although this rescue attempt failed, O'Neill did help recover most of the carbines which had been dropped when the
boat went over.

In spite of these and other difficulties, nightfall found
General Lawton's division, General Bates' independent brigade and the Second Cavalry Brigade, a total of 6,000 men,

safely ashore on Cuban soil. There was still no sign of the enemy.

The decision to allow the Fifth Corps to land unopposed reflected the uncertainty that characterized the decisions of the Spanish high command. General Arsenio Linares, commander of the Department of Santiago, had 36,582 men available, but he had scattered them in small garrisons all the way to Guantanamo, one hundred miles to the east. Although numerically strong, these troops suffered from low morale caused by food shortages and tardy distribution of pay. In addition, they had become accustomed to fighting a defensive war in small detachments stationed in stone blockhouses with connecting breastworks. At first Linares planned to hold Siboney and evacuate Daiquiri, but he changed his mind and abandoned Daiquiri on June 22 and Siboney the day after. His troops moved three miles northwest from Siboney down the Santiago road and fortified a naturally strong position near the town of Sevilla. At that location on the morning of June 23 they repulsed a Cuban attack.

As soon as the Rough Riders got ashore they established a small camp behind the Tenth Cavalry on the outskirts of Daiquiri. Although they found many crude buildings which had withstood the bombardment, they had been ordered by Colonel Wood not to enter them. The profuse growth of vegetation, which included palm and mango trees, waist-high grass and a thorny plant somewhat like an Arizona yucca whose spines could pierce a canvas legging, afforded protection for the prolific jungle creatures. The area teemed with colorful tropical birds, large hairy tarantulas and hideous land crabs, which scuttled into the brush and clicked their wicked-looking pincers at the curious onlookers.

The appearance of the Cuban people — both civilian and military — had a profound effect on the Arizonans. Shortly after the men landed, they were besieged by these ragged unfortunates who came streaming into Daiquiri to beg for food and relate their tales of Spanish atrocities. The

Cuban soldiers wore little clothing, but proudly exhibited firearms and edged weapons of every conceivable manufacture and description. They accepted all the hardtack and salt pork they could get, in addition to the extra suits of underwear donated by some of the Arizona troopers. As fighting men they appeared to be of little value. Sergeant Hughes later compared the Cuban *Insurrectos* with the Indians of Mexico when he wrote:

I have traveled among the Yaquis when they were at war with the Mexicans, among the Opitas, Moctezumas, and the Taraumaria Indians, and in all my travels I never saw such a dilapidated, hungry, undressed group of men in my life as these Cuban soldiers were. The only thing they wore was a cartridge belt, mostly empty, to this some of them would arrange a "G" string. Some of the more energetic would fabricate sandals out of the fiber of the Maguay, Spanish dagger, or coca leaves, fastening them to their feet with thin grass cords.[4]

The caustic first sergeant of McClintock's B Troop, Billy Davidson, expressed the opinion of many when he inspected the Cuban allies and concluded: "So that's what we came to free! If the walking wasn't so blankety-blank bad, I'd go home right now."[5]

The first night ashore proved to be an exciting experience. There was considerable confusion as the different regiments sought out their camping grounds and brought up their equipment, but eventually the men settled down for an uneasy night. No one knew where the Spaniards were, and apprehension was increased shortly after dark when the clear notes of a far-off Spanish bugler came in on the night air to remind the troopers that the enemy was not far away. Before long the sudden crash of a carbine brought everyone to his feet. A sentry had mistaken the noise made by a large land crab moving through the brush for an enemy patrol. This incident was repeated frequently all night. The worst came just before daylight. The Rough Riders had been ordered not to pitch their tents, and they had stretched out in the curve of their blanket rolls. In this condition each man had been soaked by a heavy rain that fell just before dawn.

Wet and still tired, the Volunteers were happy to see the sun finally appear over the mountains.

Impatient to move, the Rough Riders had a long waiting period that first day ashore, June 23. Initially, Colonel Wood kept his men together, but as the day progressed and no orders arrived, the troopers began to seek relief from the hot sun. Some bathed in a nearby creek; others constructed shelters with fronds from palm trees. At 1:00 P.M. orders came directing the regiment to march to Siboney. The quartermaster of the regiment immediately took a detail to the waterfront and secured marching rations from the corps supplies, which were being unloaded and stacked near the pier. Each man was issued a three-day supply, which he stored in his haversack.

Early that afternoon Colonel Wood led his regiment in a column of troops down the narrow, rocky trail that led to Siboney. To the correspondents, who had gathered to observe the move, the Rough Riders made an impressive sight as they marched off in a column of fours with packs neatly rolled and carbines sparkling in the midday sun. Colonel Wood and Lieutenant Colonel Roosevelt were both mounted, for their horses had been pushed into the sea earlier in the day and had swum ashore. The other officers marched with their men.

The orders directing the Rough Riders to Siboney came because the changing situation had caused General Shafter to alter his plans. Late in the afternoon of June 22, the day the troops landed, Shafter had been informed by the Cubans that the Spaniards had evacuated Siboney. He immediately ordered General Lawton, whose Second Infantry Division had debarked first, to march to Siboney and secure the town. That afternoon, while the cavalry division and Bates's brigade were coming ashore, Lawton left Daiquiri with two brigades.

After camping along the trail that night, General Lawton's men entered Siboney about 8:00 A.M. the next morning. They arrived just in time to see the last elements of the

Spanish garrison withdraw toward Sevilla. Lawton immediately advised Shafter of the situation, and the Commanding
General changed his plans to take advantage of this opportunity to get his command closer to Santiago. He ordered
General J. Ford Kent, whose First Division was still on the
transports, to sail to Siboney and debark there. At the same
time General Wheeler was directed to march his Second
Cavalry Brigade under General Young to Siboney by way of
the same trail that Lawton had followed. General Sumner
was ordered to remain at Daiquiri with his First Cavalry
Brigade and supervise the landing of supplies. Unfortunately,
the orders were vague as to what should be done when the
troops reached Siboney. Lawton had been instructed to push
a strong force down the Santiago road and intrench there "if
they met no opposition."[6]

The nine mile march from Daiquiri to Siboney introduced the Rough Riders to the difficulties of transporting
men and supplies in Cuba. Because Lawton's infantry had
left the day before, Wood set a fast pace so as to arrive in
time to participate in any possible fighting. He did not know
that the town was secure. Roosevelt led the advance with his
squadron, and Brodie's men followed at the rear of the column
— an unprecedented place for the Arizonans who always
before had marched in the van. The tramp of many feet
churned the trail into a bed of dry dust, which rose in clouds
to envelop the long column. Few trees grew along the route
to provide relief from the hot sun. Each man carried about
sixty pounds of equipment, much of which he soon began
casting away. As the units which had gone before had done
the same thing, the path became so littered that it appeared
to mark the route of an army in retreat rather than one
bent on conquest. As the march continued the column grew
progressively longer as stragglers began to fall behind.

Leading elements of the Rough Riders reached Siboney
at dark and established camp on the outskirts by the glare of
naval searchlights, which attended the debarkation of the

First Division. None of the troops had established a unit mess, and the men paired off to prepare supper. Many of the Arizonans, proficient in the skills of outdoor life, concluded mutually beneficial arrangements with easterners who did not know how to cook. The dude rustled wood and water while the westerner tended the rations. Scarcely had these preparations commenced when the inevitable evening rain put an end to the open fires. Some of the troopers, in open defiance of strict orders, took refuge in the thatched Cuban huts. Tuttle and his friends from Graham County sought shelter under some wrecked railroad cars. Here they kept small fires burning and provided hot coffee to their comrades who straggled into the bivouac until midnight.

While his men prepared their bivouac at Siboney, Colonel Wood rode off to receive his orders from General Young. The origin and interpretation of the orders passed on to Young by General Wheeler created a controversy that lasts to this day. The instructions originally received by General Lawton, authorizing him to push a strong force down the Siboney-Santiago road, had been addressed to Lawton "or Senior Officer at the Front."[7] When Wheeler arrived at Siboney, he superseded Lawton as senior officer and immediately took command of the situation. After conferring with General Castillo, leader of the *Insurrectos* at Siboney, who gave him a map and a description of the Spanish position on the road to Santiago, Wheeler decided to attack the Spaniards with General Young's Second Cavalry Brigade.

Having received verbal orders to make the attack from Wheeler, General Young contacted Castillo to get more information. Castillo cooperated fully, explaining in detail the terrain and Spanish position. According to the Cuban, the enemy had established a line across the Santiago road on a ridge near Sevilla, approximately three miles away. The position was approached by two trails from Siboney, which converged a mile in front of Sevilla at a place known as Las Guasimas. It was here that Castillo's attack had been repulsed

on the morning of June 23. Castillo assured both Wheeler and
Young that the exact location of the Spanish position was
marked by the body of a Cuban who had been killed in the
attack that morning and left on the trail just in front of the
enemy defenses. The guerrilla leader estimated that 2,000
Spanish soldiers were stationed there. He volunteered his
opinion that the Spanish force would withdraw to Santiago
during the night. He went on to add, however, that he had
received information that the enemy was being reinforced.
The Cuban promised General Young that he would support
any offensive action with his own forces. He pointed out that
he had eight hundred soldiers in Siboney.

With this information, General Young decided to probe
the Spanish position with two converging columns. He ordered
Colonel Wood to advance at daybreak down a tortuous path
on top of the ridge just north of town, while he took eight
troops of Regulars along an easier route down in the valley.
These two trails were supposed to converge near the reported
Spanish defenses. General Young instructed Colonel Wood to
proceed with caution and to attack any Spaniards he encoun-
tered. He also instructed two personal aides, First Lieutenant
T. R. Rivers of the Third Cavalry and Second Lieutenant
W. R. Smedberg of the Fourth Cavalry, to accompany the
Rough Riders.

General Lawton, who did not realize what was happening
until he saw the cavalry moving out the next morning, later
claimed that Wheeler had exceeded his authority in bypassing
the Second Infantry Division. This was corroborated by General Shafter, who later stated that his intent had been to have
Lawton's division stay in the advance. But Wheeler had not
been named "Fighting Joe" for nothing. As the senior officer
at Siboney, he had "determined to make an attack."[8]

It was about midnight when Wood returned from the
conference with General Young. Most of the Rough Riders
had already turned in, but Captain Capron and the junior
officers of L Troop were gathered around a small fire drink-

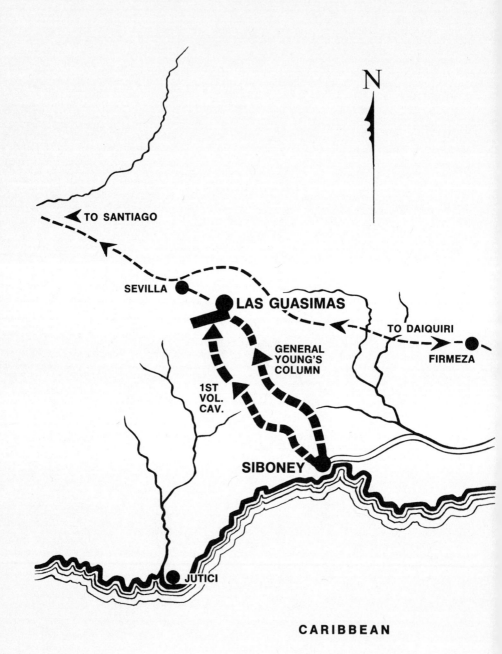

BATTLE MAP OF LAS GUASIMAS

ing coffee. Wood joined them and briefly outlined his plans
for the coming morning. After agreeing to Capron's request
that L Troop be allowed to take the advance, Wood left the
group with Capron's last comment ringing in his ears: "Well,
tomorrow at this time the long sleep will be on many of us."[9]
Ironically enough, this young captain, who was hailed by
Roosevelt as "the ideal of what an American regular army
officer should be," was destined to be among the first to fall.[10]
There was a Spanish rifle bullet waiting for him in the hills
above Siboney.

At 5:40 A.M. on June 24, the Rough Riders started up
the steep trail to the top of the long ridge that led to Sevilla.
Colonel Wood, riding ahead of the first squadron led by
Roosevelt, set a fast pace in order to arrive at the crossroads
near Sevilla concurrently with the Regulars, who followed an
easier road in the valley to the right. Behind Roosevelt's
squadron marched the two Arizona troops with Captain Huston's D Troop and Captain Muller's E Troop. All four units
were under the command of Major Brodie. Each man carried
a blanket roll, with his belongings packed in the ends to
make it ride comfortably on the shoulder, a full cartridge belt
and a canvas-covered canteen which swung from the shoulder
at the end of a long strap. Each trooper also carried rations of
canned meat, green coffee beans, hard tack and canned
tomatoes. Before long the weight of the packs and steepness
of the trail began to take effect. The Arizonans came across
stragglers who could not hold up under the fast pace. By the
time the regiment halted on top of the ridge, half a mile from
Siboney, a total of fifty-two men had dropped behind the
column. While his men rested at the first halt on top of the
ridge, Wood instructed Captain Capron to deploy L Troop
as an advance guard.

Captain Capron sent Sergeant Hamilton Fish and three
men forward as a point. A support of twenty men followed
the point, and Capron marched behind them at the head of
the rest of the troop. The main body was about two hundred

and fifty yards behind the point. No flankers were deployed because of the extremely thick jungle. Flankers could not have kept up with the column marching on the trail. When Capron completed these arrangements, the march was resumed. It was ironic that Sergeant Fish, whose grandfather of the same name, as secretary of state under President Grant, thirty years before, had prevented a war over Cuba, should now be probing for the first contact in this invasion of the island.

The crest of the ridge above Siboney had a slight down-hill slope toward Sevilla, and the Rough Riders made good time once they reached the top. Dense jungle foliage grew like green walls along both sides of the trail. It reflected no sign of human life. Only the chirping of birds and noise made by the men broke the morning stillness. In spite of repeated warnings, the Volunteers seemed unconvinced that they would soon encounter Spaniards. The officers found it difficult to control the incessant chatter. Some of the men in B Troop, after they had recovered from the effects of the climb, even began singing the favorite song of the regiment, "There'll Be a Hot Time in the Old Town Tonight." Another halt was called and the men sat down along the sides of the trail to pull at their canteens. Suddenly the order came down the line for silence, quickly followed by a report that enemy outposts had been located.

When Colonel Wood received a report from L Troop that the enemy had been located, he halted the regiment and moved forward to check with Capron. During his absence one of the three newspaper correspondents who had accompanied the Rough Riders, Edward Marshall of the New York *Journal,* took this opportunity to walk down the line of waiting troopers. He noted that the men were still talking and apparently unconcerned over the whole situation. As he passed one group he heard one soldier quietly comment to a comrade: "By God! How would you like a glass of cold beer?"[11]

Meanwhile, another correspondent, Richard Harding Davis of the New York *Herald,* was taking pictures of the men in the main body of L Troop. When Colonel Wood returned, Davis heard Roosevelt complain to the Colonel that the pace was too fast for the men. "I have no time to bother with sick men now," Wood replied. A moment later he added an explanation: "I have no time for them now; I mean that we are in sight of the enemy."[12]

It is not clear whether Captain Capron actually saw the Spanish positions or surmised their presence by discovering the dead Cuban. But Colonel Wood began deploying the regiment. He ordered Lieutenant Colonel Roosevelt to form G, K and A Troops into a skirmish line to the right of L Troop, which was directed to remain on the trail. Major Brodie was ordered to extend the left flank of the line into the more open terrain to the left utilizing E, F and D Troops. Captain McClintock's B Troop was to remain on the trail behind L Troop in reserve. Colonel Wood expected his right wing, with O'Neill's Arizonans located at the extreme end, to extend along the north slope of the ridge and down into a small valley to link up with General Young's Regulars. They were advancing up a ridge which paralleled the Rough Riders' position to the right.

Colonel Wood had partially deployed his Rough Riders when Spanish riflemen, crouching in concealed positions along the trail in front of the Volunteers, began raking L Troop. When the first shots were fired, the mules carrying the Colt machine guns bolted to the rear. Because the dynamite gun had been left at Siboney, this defection left the regiment without supporting weapons.

The opening shots of the battle of Las Guasimas found O'Neill's troopers moving forward in a skirmish line along the north slope of the ridge. To their immediate left front K Troop was coming up on line next to G Troop, which had been the first to deploy and was already in position to the

right of L Troop. To the left of L Troop, and on the other
side of a barbed wire fence, F Troop was on line, with D and
E Troops coming up behind it. The Arizonans in A Troop,
following the example set by those who had preceded them,
left their packs on the ridge before plunging after K Troop
into the matted tangle of brush along the side of the hill. This
vegetation made the advance extremely difficult and restricted
observation to the extent that each man could see only his
immediate neighbor. O'Neill, recognizing the difficulty that
he would have in retaining control, ran up and down his skirmish line in an attempt to preserve some semblance of troop
formation. His men had advanced one hundred and fifty yards
along the slope, and had not yet come up even with K Troop,
when a few scattered shots, followed by the thunder-roll of a
heavy volley, served notice that the battle had started.

As the men in Captain O'Neill's troop plunged forward
to take their position to the right of K Troop, they soon
found themselves in a direct line of enemy fire. The first
shots directed at A Troop came from the thick brush on a
ridge at the end of the valley to their direct front. They were
too high and the bullets cracked through the trees overhead.
O'Neill continued to move calmly along the skirmish line
encouraging his men to stay low and keep moving. He
radiated confidence and personal disregard for the Spanish
fire. At one point he directed several volleys at the hill mass
at the end of the valley, but immediately countermanded the
order when a squad from K Troop, crouching in a shielding
ravine in front of A Troop, sent up a howl of protest.

It was difficult going and most of the Arizona men did
not return the enemy fire. They were too busy trying to work
their way through the tangles of brush which tore at their
clothing and tripped them up. The Spaniards were very well
camouflaged, and most of the men could not locate the enemy.
They did not see much point in shooting at what they could
not see. Some, however, according to Private Webb, were
"popping away in true Arizona style" whenever they thought
they saw a target.[13]

The dense underbrush soon gave way to more open terrain. The Spanish fire became more accurate as the Arizonans closed in. By that time most of the men had discovered that it was easier to move through the brush by walking upright, and were doing so in spite of O'Neill's efforts to make them stay low. Although the troopers made good targets as they came out of the brush, there were only two casualties. Both happened to be from Jerome. Corporal George Doherty, the man who had quarreled with Bugbee enroute to Cuba, was shot in the head, and Private Edward Liggett in the chest. Others had narrow escapes. Private Tuttle, crouching by a tree while trying to locate the enemy, had dirt thrown on him by a bullet which struck between his legs. Still another man, struck on the head by a bullet-sheared tree limb, provided comic relief as he rolled down the hill under the impression that he had been shot. Then, for no apparent reason, the Arizonans realized that the enemy fire had begun to slacken.

The slackening of the Spanish fire came when Linares' men began to abandon their positions on their own left flank. With Captain O'Neill's Arizonans coming up the ravine in front of them, and with General Young's Regulars turning their left by advancing up the ridge which paralleled the Rough Rider attack, the Spaniards decided to pull back. In small groups they began running down the ridge to join their comrades intrenched along the main trail. O'Neill's men, still tied up in the brush down in the ravine, could not see this activity, but the men in K and G Troops, located higher up on the slope to the left, had some clear shooting. Langdon of K Troop recalled that he had one good shot at a Spaniard who ran out of a thicket in plain view just across a small draw. The man was so close that Langdon could see the sweat stains on his light uniform.

As some of the fleeing Spaniards approached the main trail, they were met by a heavy fire from the men in G Troop. The New Mexicans cheerfully took advantage of this opportunity to fire at an exposed enemy. Lieutenant Colonel Roosevelt, however, who was with G Troop, considered the

possibility that the running men were Cubans and ordered
the soldiers to cease fire until it was certain that the targets
were Spaniards. By the time the angry troopers had convinced
their Lieutenant Colonel that it was the enemy, the Spaniards
had disappeared into the brush. This evacuation ended the
fighting for O'Neill's men, but the struggle continued on
their left for a little while longer.

Fighting on the left of A Troop swirled around the trail
where L Troop had first opened the engagement. There are
certain points still not clear, but most accounts agree that
Private Thomas J. Isbell, a Cherokee Indian from Vinita,
Indian Territory, fired the first shot in the battle of Las
Guasimas. A member of L Troop's point, Isbell was easing
his way down the trail when he spotted a Spaniard in the
brush ahead and shot him. The enemy reply was instan-
taneous and disastrous. A volley of rifle fire ripped into L
Troop's point. The four men went down almost together.
Isbell was wounded seven times, but still managed to walk
to the rear for treatment. Another Cherokee from Muskogee,
Private Edward Culver, was wounded in the chest. Sergeant
Fish, physically one of the most powerful men in the regiment
and who had transferred from I Troop so he could go to
Cuba, was killed almost immediately, his body falling across
the trail. The other man in the point also was hit.

Meanwhile, Captain Capron personally was deploying
the rest of L Troop along the trail. Moments later, while
lying down trying to locate the Spanish positions, Capron
was shot in the shoulder, the bullet coming out through his
abdomen. He died about an hour later. First Lieutenant John
R. Thomas from Muskogee took command of the troop when
Capron was shot, but twenty minutes later was himself
wounded in the leg. Leadership then devolved on Second
Lieutenant Richard C. Day from Vinita.

L Troop had become fully engaged and needed help.
The deployment of three troops to the left and three more
to the right had not succeeded in taking the pressure off

Captain James H. McClintock, commanding B Troop, taken in Cuba the day before he was wounded in action at Las Guasimas. (*Courtesy Los Angeles County Museum of Natural History.*)

Capron's men. There seemed to be a gap in the center of the line next to L Troop. Colonel Wood, who originally had planned on holding B Troop in reserve, ordered McClintock to advance and relieve the hard-pressed troopers from the Indian Territory by deploying his Arizonans between L and F Troop to the immediate left of the trail.

Captain McClintock received his orders to move forward with enthusiasm. He had been anxious to get into the fight and, like everyone else in B Troop, was afraid that the battle would be over before he got into it. When McClintock's Arizonans did reach the firing line, they found themselves in the busiest part of the field — deploying under a hail of bullets from the well-executed Spanish volleys. Showered by leaves and twigs cut by the heavy fire, McClintock had just placed his men in a line of skirmishers when he crashed to the earth with two bullet wounds just above his ankle. "I saw you fall," Private Thomas Wiggins from Bisbee later wrote him. "You first staggered and caught your Ballance and then fell Waveing your Revolver over your hiad as you went down."[14] The stunned captain called for First Lieutenant George Wilcox, turned the troop over to him, and was carried back to the aid station on the broad shoulders of Private Bruce Proffitt, a husky ex-rancher from Phoenix. The other two casualties in B Troop, Private Wiggins who had been shot in the hip, and Private Norman Orme from Phoenix, who had a serious lung wound, came in later. So rapidly had the fight developed that B Troop reached the firing line only ten minutes after the first shot was fired.

With one exception B Troop came forward and deployed in good order. In compliance with McClintock's instructions, the men had paused to remove their packs and pile them by squads along the trail before going forward. The squad led by Sergeant Hughes was a little slow in doing this, and the rest of the troop went off and left them. In trying to catch up, Hughes mistakenly led his men down the wrong fork in the footpath and wound up between L and G Troops to the right of the trail. Consequently, nine men fought an independent action without benefit of their troop officers. In addition to Hughes they were: Corporal Thomas "Will" Pemberton and Dick Stanton from Phoenix, Bill Owens and Clifton "Ed" Middleton from Globe, Jesse Toland from Bisbee, George Truman from Florence, Will Chester from Oakwell, Texas, and John Hammer from San Antonio. The other member of the squad, Frank "Barney" Harmson from Tucson, had been left at Siboney.

In addition to being out of position, Hughes had difficulty with one of the officers of an adjacent troop. It is not clear what happened, but evidently there was some argument as to how the men were to be deployed. Hughes wrote his brother: "I cannot write as I would like to in this letter of a little disagreement I had with a lieutenant on the firing line. I told him what to do with his troop and told him to do it dam quick. That I did not want to get my men butchered like his were."[15] A few years later and without further elaboration, Hughes identified the officer as Second Lieutenant Richard Day of L Troop.

Meanwhile, as B Troop was coming up on the firing line, Major Brodie was preparing to mount an attack on the Spanish right flank. To protect his own left, which he felt was vulnerable to a possible counterattack, Brodie ordered Muller's E Troop to position itself immediately behind Huston's D Troop, which was on the extreme left. This arrangement gave Brodie a squadron reserve — a sound tactical maneuver that had been completely overlooked by Roosevelt, who had placed all of his troops on line.

With his left secure, Major Brodie ordered an advance on the Spaniards entrenched near a ruined house to his direct front. The squadron was just getting started when an enemy bullet shattered Brodie's right wrist. Stunned by the impact, the major sat down in a small clearing and calmly smoked a cigar that Sergeant Charles Utling, a member of B Troop from Phoenix, had paused to light for him. At first he refused to leave the firing line, but pain and loss of blood so weakened him that he finally consented to go to the aid station in the rear. Meanwhile, the entire left wing continued to press forward.

While Brodie walked back to the aid station, his squadron was rallied by Roosevelt, who came over from the right to take command of the left wing. This in itself was the result of a unique maneuver. When the firing had died down on the right, Roosevelt, who "knew it could not be wrong to go forward," took G Troop and crossed to the left of the trail in search of Colonel Wood.[16] This rearrangement in the order of battle, of course, was made without the consent or knowledge of the commander. It also left K and A Troops on their own without any support. Shortly after Roosevelt reached the center, where he reported to Wood and got G Troop back on the firing line, word was received that Brodie had been wounded. Roosevelt was immediately ordered to assume command of Brodie's squadron and bring it forward. He quickly joined Huston's D Troop and soon was busily firing a carbine he had taken off a wounded Rough Rider. Second Lieutenant David Goodrich of Akron, Ohio, who had originally been in B Troop, but who had been transferred to D Troop to accept a commission on May 19, mistook Roosevelt for one of his own soldiers. Goodrich told the colonel: "Keep your interval, sir; keep your interval and go forward."[17]

The final charge was made through dense brush against several red-tiled buildings which were part of a large, abandoned ranch. Most of the enemy fire was too high and casualties were relatively light. "That was the trouble with them," Sergeant Hughes wrote his brother, "they always shoot too high. If we had been in their position they would never have lived to tell the story."[18] On the last leg of the assault the troopers withheld their fire until they had approached within three hundred yards of the Spanish positions. At that point they opened a heavy fire as they emerged from the brush into a more open field. The Spaniards, now under orders to withdraw, fired a few parting volleys and then retreated down the road toward Santiago with most of their dead and wounded. Lieutenant Wilcox led his B troopers forward until he reached an impenetrable thicket backed by a barbed wire fence just short of the ranch house. Here the troop halted and took no further part in the closing actions of the day. According to Lieutenant Rynning, B Troop had been engaged two hours and forty minutes.

With his exhausted Rough Riders in possession of the Spanish entrenchments, Wood considered his men to be incapable of further pursuit and decided to camp there and wait for orders. The first sergeants rounded up their men. The members of A Troop took great pride when every man that had left Siboney that morning — except for the two who were dead — responded to roll call. McClintock's troop had lost three wounded, but no one had been killed. Thirty minutes later three troops of the Negro Ninth Cavalry arrived on the field and went on picket duty eight hundred yards to the front. These soldiers had hurried up from Siboney to save the regiment from a reported ambush and they expressed great disappointment that the fight had ended. One Negro cavalryman accosted Sergeant Hughes with the excited plea: "Show me a Spaniard. I am rarin' to go."[19] Hughes could do nothing more than point to a body lying in the nearby grass. The Negro troops had arrived too late; the fighting was over.

The tale of ambush and disaster, that had brought the Ninth Cavalry forward in relief, also became the basis of the premature battle descriptions released by the press. These reports started when Edward Marshall was shot in the back while standing quite close to Colonel Wood. The regimental adjutant, First Lieutenant Tom Hall of New Jersey, saw Marshall fall and assumed that Wood had been shot. What happened next is not exactly clear.

It seems that Lieutenant Hall seized a nearby mule and rode toward Siboney spreading his belief that Colonel Wood had been shot. The story quickly spread and soon the word reached Siboney that the Rough Riders had walked into an ambush and were being cut to pieces. The eager correspondents in Siboney, somewhat miffed at having missed the first battle and anxious to get their stories filed, flashed the report home that the Volunteer Cavalry had been ambushed and wiped out. This report seemed entirely plausible to General Lawton, in command at Siboney, because he already had received a request for reinforcements from General Wheeler, who had observed the actions of the Regulars along the valley road. As a result, three troops of the Ninth had been ordered to reinforce the Rough Riders.

Another result of the adjutant's behavior was the loss of his reputation. He never had been popular, and most of the troopers considered his actions at Las Guasimas a sign of cowardice. He resigned from the regiment a few days later.

The Arizonans left in Siboney reacted immediately to the news of the purported massacre. When Chaplain Brown, who had gone aboard the *Yucatan* to secure some important papers left there, returned to Siboney, he found that the Rough Riders had already left for Sevilla. Anxious to find out what was happening, Brown started up the trail with John Fox, a correspondent for *Harper's Weekly*. The Chaplain had just flourished his six-shooter with the boast that he could "settle a Spaniard at fifty paces" when they learned of the "ambush."[20] Brown showed considerable distress at the news and insisted on joining the command as quickly as possible. A similar reaction came from Farrier "Barney" Harmsen of B Troop, who had been left at Siboney because of rheumatism. Harmsen supposedly met Hall on the trail and was told that his troop had been annihilated and that his captain was dead. Taking a firm grip on his carbine, Harmsen started up the slope with the expostulation: "If the good old troop is gone, by God, it's my place to go with it."[21]

After they had consolidated their position along the ridge, the Rough Riders sent details in to the brush to locate

the dead and wounded. Unfortunately, vultures had found
some of the fallen first. After inspecting the mutilated body
of Corporal Doherty, the big miner from Jerome who had
quarreled with Bugbee, O'Neill turned to Roosevelt and
asked: "Colonel, isn't it Whitman who says of the vultures
that 'they pluck the eyes of princes and tear the flesh of
kings'?"[22] Roosevelt, surprised at the inquiry, replied that
he did not know the quotation. Early the next morning
Chaplain Brown, in the presence of most of the regiment,
committed the bodies of seven dead Rough Riders to their
graves in the little basin where they had fought and died.

For two days after the engagement the Volunteers
camped on the battlefield. A lack of equipment rendered the
camp uncomfortable. When the details which had been sent
back to secure the haversacks cached along the trail before the
battle returned, they reported that the Cubans had rifled
the packs of all blankets, rations, and extra clothing. "We
was the worst starved-out bunch for three days after the
Guasimas run-in that ever happened," wrote Lieutenant
Rynning. "When we went into action at Guasimas we piled
all our haversacks in a heap, and while we was fighting the
Spaniards, the lousy Cuban soldiers came along and stole
every bit of grub out of them."[23] This shortage of food became so acute that Roosevelt personally led a detail to Siboney
in search of rations. The most valuable man in this endeavor,
however, proved to be the chaplain. Not only did Brown
acquire bacon, coffee and hardtack, but he also located a
stray mule and brought up the regimental mail from Siboney.
By this time the Arizona boys had come to appreciate the
versatility of their Prescott chaplain.

Based on the performance of their allies on June 24, the
Arizonans concluded that in the future they could expect no
help from the Cuban *Insurrectos*. Two Cubans had accompanied Wood's regiment to Guasimas. One, a guide, disappeared into the brush at the first volley and was not seen
again. Scarcely had the fight commenced when the other, a

major in the revolutionary forces who had bragged of his
proficiency with a machete, had been seen using the flat
side of that same machete to whip his mule as he galloped
back down the trail. General Castillo's group of eight hundred, which had been scheduled to participate in the battle,
did not arrive on the scene until long after the Spaniards had
withdrawn. Here the Cubans quickly and irreparably strained
Anglo-Cuban relations by stealing the food and blankets the
Rough Riders had left along the trail before going into action.

With their camp established, the Arizonans found time
to compare notes on their battle experiences. It had been
a hot little fight, but the troopers thought they had done
well. Reportedly not impressed by the Spanish technique of
firing by volley, the men did have considerable respect for
the rapidity with which the enemy had fired. In a letter
to his brother, Henry B. Fox, a member of A Troop from
Jerome, described the enemy fire: "Great heavens! how
those bullets did fly; they plinked us thicker than a swarm
of bees."[24]

Two Rough Riders could not face this enemy fire and
ran. One was the regimental adjutant and the other, according to the diary of Private Roger S. Fitch of G Troop, was
an unnamed New Mexican in G Troop who "showed the
white feather." The Arizonans could report with pride that
everyone in A and B Troops had stayed on the field. With
characteristic exaggeration and flair for the dramatic, Captain
McClintock wrote Governor McCord: "Not an Arizonan
has flinched, although scores have fallen on the battlefield."[25]
Little John Foster, B Troop's Trumpeter, also had his
favorite story to relate. He told how he had been with Colonel
Wood and, after the skirmish, overheard Wood sharply
reprimand Roosevelt for the latter's failure to advance pickets
in front of the left wing after the Spaniards withdrew.

Two days later, June 26, the Rough Riders moved
three miles closer to Santiago. They established a new camp
in a brushy glen beside a mountain stream, buttoning their

shelter halves together to form little tents for protection against the daily rains. Rations continued in short supply, but Chaplain Brown continued to bring up more from Siboney. A few cases of malaria now appeared, and Adjutant Hall received a report that Private Leroy Tomlinson, a member of B Troop who had enlisted at Prescott but about whom little else is known, had died of fever aboard the hospital ship *Olivette*. As the days passed the Arizonans watched regiment after regiment move into bivouac along the Santiago road. This troop concentration, augmented by growing stockpiles of ammunition brought up by mule train over roads made almost impassable by rain and mud, convinced the men that some type of offensive action had been planned. In his weekly letter Webb concluded: "I think a big battle is eminent."[26]

Meanwhile, as the Rough Riders made ready to march on Santiago, their performance at Guasimas was receiving wide-spread attention at home. Only three correspondents — Marshall, Davis and Stephan Crane of the New York *World* — had accompanied the Volunteers. It was their colleagues who had waited at Siboney, and none of whom had seen as much as one shot fired in the battle, who were the ones to file the first reports. These accounts, based largely on the adjutant's tale of disaster and somewhat verified by General Wheeler's request for reinforcements, had been sent before clear knowledge was gained of what had really transpired on that brush-choked ridge in front of Sevilla. It was not until the injured Marshall and out-spoken Davis returned to Siboney that the truth was learned. By that time it was too late. Newspapers all over the country had carried the ambush story. Most people in the United States were convinced that there had been a disaster and there was some talk of court-martialing both Wood and Roosevelt for negligence. Some of the correspondents later admitted their mistake and filed amended reports. Others did not.

Burr McIntosh and Edward Bonsal were two of the correspondents who refused to retract their reports of the

Rough Riders being ambushed. McIntosh later claimed that Davis, Crane and Marshall were selected to accompany the Rough Riders to Las Guasimas because they could be counted upon to write favorable accounts of what happened. McIntosh's version of Las Guasimas is particularly critical, although he implied much more than he actually stated. He left his readers to conclude that the Volunteers were ambushed when he stated complacently: "Someday the truth will be known." Then, with an obvious reference to Roosevelt, McIntosh continued: "Those men on that hill tonight [the dead Rough Riders] are lying there, sacrificed on the altar of a showman's greed."[27]

McIntosh knew better than to write such drivel. He knew full well that the Rough Riders were commanded by Colonel Leonard Wood at Las Guasimas. Roosevelt was a squadron commander and merely followed the orders given to him by his regimental commander. He was not responsible for what happened to the regiment. Both Marshall and Davis denied flatly that the Rough Riders were ambushed, although they did disagree as to the disposition of the various troops when the opening shots came.

By a strange coincidence, one Rough Rider later evened the score with McIntosh. A few days after the fighting ended in Cuba, McIntosh fell ill and was taken to a hospital at Siboney. One night, while he was delirious with fever, a Rough Rider slipped in and stole his beautiful and expensive pair of hand-crafted yellow boots. The trooper probably needed them much more than McIntosh, but the correspondent was incensed.

There was also some disagreement among the Arizonans about the battle. In their letters home they generally agreed that the Spaniards were waiting in ambush, but they were not in agreement that the ambush was successful. Most of the men in A Troop either stated or implied that A Troop was in the process of deploying when the firing began. Because at least four troops had preceded O'Neill's men, this would substantiate Wood's report that he had deployed five troops before the first shot. A member of B Troop, Corporal Thomas W. Pemberton from Phoenix, stated flatly that they had been ambushed. In a letter to his mother, Pemberton reported that the Spaniards were not only in front of the Rough Riders but along both sides of the trail as well. In these positions they let Capron's advance guard "march right into their midst." Pemberton went on to add, however, that it was a member of L Troop who fired the first shot and then "all hell broke loose."[28] Sergeant Hughes also reported that they had been ambushed.

Four days after the battle on June 28 Hughes described the engagement in a long letter to his brother. Greatly over-estimating the number of Spanish defenders and incorrectly positioning his squad ahead of L Troop, Hughes revealed his typical Rough Rider pride by writing:

We surely had it good and hot. We were lead into a trap and a good one by being too anxious to fight, and we were not only lucky to lick them but to get out alive. The boys did finely. We went through them like a dose of salts. We were marching along a path in single file when we were ambushed by between 4,000 and 5,000 Spaniards. They cut Troop L all to pieces. They killed and wounded 15 or 20 in the first fire. My squad was just ahead of them.[29]

Twenty-five years later Hughes described the battle of Las Guasimas to Hermann Hagedorn. Selecting his words with care, the veteran avoided the word ambush and stated clearly that L Troop had been deployed as an advance guard before the fight was joined. He also made it clear that his squad was somewhere behind L Troop. Hughes claimed that the first shots of the engagement came from the ridge to the right of the Rough Riders where the Regulars were advancing.

In the final analysis, there are several significant factors which should not be overlooked. General Wheeler knew that the Spaniards had fortified a position near Sevilla. Not only had the Cubans provided him with a verbal description, but they also had given him a map. Wheeler's instructions to General Young specifically authorized Young to make an attack. General Young had passed the information about the enemy's position on to Colonel Wood and, in turn, had instructed Wood to attack the Spaniards. In short, the Rough Riders knew where the enemy was and they went up the trail with every intention of finding him and launching an attack. This is exactly what they did. They were looking for a fight and they found one.

Colonel Wood took normal precautions against surprise. Every eyewitness account agrees that L Troop was deployed as an advance guard with a point preceding the troop. Exactly what happened to the point is a matter of conjecture. Men such as Sergeant Hughes, Corporal Pemberton or Corporal Fox could not speak with unquestioned accuracy because they were not with L Troop. One of the men who should have known what happened was First Lieutenant John R. Thomas of L Troop. In an interview with Trumball White after the war, he described the action, pointing out that Isbell had fired the first shot and denying that there had been an ambush.

Additional evidence is found in the casualty list. Out of the seventy-three officers and men in L Troop who went to Cuba, three were killed and seven were wounded at Las Guasimas. This included the four men in the point. Although heavy, this casualty rate indicates the troop could not have been in much of an ambush.

The ranking officers of the Fifth Corps expressed satisfaction with the performance of Wood's untested Volunteers. In his official report, General Young praised both officers and men. After describing the actions of the Regulars along the valley road, he pointed out that the Rough Riders had exceeded expectation for Volunteers. He wrote: "The fighting on the left flank was equally creditable and was remarkable, and I believe unprecedented in volunteer troops so quickly raised, armed and equipped." Later on he extended unqualified praise when he added:

I cannot speak too highly of the efficient manner in which Colonel Wood handled his regiment, and of his magnificent behavior on the field. The conduct of Lieutenant-Colonel Roosevelt, as reported to me by my two aids, deserves my highest commendation. Both Colonel Wood and Lieutenant-Colonel Roosevelt disdained to take advantage of shelter or cover from the enemy's fire while any of their men remained exposed to it — an error of judgment, but happily on the heroic side. I beg leave to repeat that the behavior of all men of the regular and volunteer forces engaged in this action was simply superb, and I feel highly honored in the command of such troops.[30]

This was strong praise from a man who had seen much combat in the Civil War and who had been a colonel in the Regular Army until the outbreak of the Spanish-American War. Obviously, General Young did not believe that the Rough Riders had been ambushed.

Even the ambush controversy failed to detract from the demonstrated ability of the Rough Riders to withstand the pressures of combat. Their performance refuted the vociferous clamors of the skeptics and lent substance to the most ardent supporters of the regiment. It had been a difficult battle for Colonel Wood to conduct. His sole experienced squadron commander had received an early wound; his regiment had by luck escaped a tragedy when his lieutenant colonel had rearranged the order of battle without his knowledge or consent; and a rumor of his own death had spread through the command. Nevertheless, some five hundred Volunteers, together with an equal number of Regulars, had driven 1,500 Spaniards from prepared defenses. Although their attackers did not know it, the Spaniards had received orders to withdraw before the action began — their stand at Las Guasimas amounted to little more than a rear-guard skirmish.

The victory gave the Fifth Corps a new staging area five miles closer to Santiago with ample space for camping grounds and an adequate supply of good water. General Shafter quickly began assembling his troops and supplies for the coming attack on Santiago.

CHAPTER 5

The Crowded Hour

WAITING IN THEIR RAIN-SOAKED BIVOUAC near Sevilla after the battle of Las Guasimas, the Arizonans soon learned that their next objective would be Santiago. The route to this Spanish citadel, five miles west of their positions, crossed the valley of the San Juan River. In anticipation of an attack down this road, the Spaniards had fortified a long ridge called San Juan Heights which blocked the road as it came out of the valley. Here the Rough Riders were to participate in two gallant charges, successfully overrunning the Spanish trenches and opening the road for final victory. Although the attack would center on this mile-long ridge, it would become known as the battle of San Juan Hill.

General Shafter delayed any forward movement after Las Guasimas until his supply lines were functioning. This became a matter of top priority and Shafter ordered General Bates to use elements of his independent brigade to repair the main supply route, which was the Siboney-Santiago road. The corps engineers were kept busy building docks until June

27, when they relieved General Bates of the responsibility of repairing the road. Initially, all supplies were brought up by pack train, but wagons were brought ashore as soon as possible. Both were kept under corps control. It was slow going, but gradually a supply depot of rations and ammunition began to appear at the bivouac near Sevilla.

Toward the end of the month word was received that a large body of Spanish reinforcements was approaching Santiago from the west. Although General Shafter felt that he was not yet ready, he decided to move before these reinforcements entered the city.

The road that ran from Siboney to Santiago appeared to make an excellent axis of advance, but General Shafter wanted to take a good look at it before making his final decision. On the morning of June 30, he took his staff on a route reconnaissance as far as a small hill just above an abandoned ranch named El Poso. He was approximately a mile and a half west of the Rough Riders' bivouac.

Looking west from the hill at El Poso, the Commanding General saw a green, basin-like valley, covered with jungle and bisected by two muddy little rivers which intersected after crossing the Santiago road. Grim fortifications crowned the long hill, called San Juan Heights or San Juan Ridge, which rose above the jungle at the far end of the valley. The road to Santiago passed through El Poso, crossed the Aquadores and San Juan Rivers in the valley, and passed over the ridge to the immediate right of the highest point on the escarpment. This apex was called San Juan Hill. Santiago was a mile beyond. Three miles to the north General Shafter could see the small village of El Caney, reportedly garrisoned by a strong body of Spaniards. At that same time, General Henry Lawton, Commander of the Second Infantry Division, and General Adna R. Chaffee, commanding officer of the Third Brigade under Lawton, were making a detailed reconnaissance toward El Caney.

In the afternoon, and after his reconnaissance, Shafter called in his division commanders. When he stated that the success of the operation against the fortifications on San Juan Heights hinged on a speedy reduction of the garrison at El Caney, he was assured by Lawton, who considered the weak Spanish defense at Las Guasimas, that the Second Division could take the village in two hours. With this assurance Shafter drew up his operations order. At daybreak on July 1 Lawton's division would attack and take El Caney, then march south to the San Juan River at the base of San Juan Heights and form part of the right flank of the assault line. The cavalry division, which included the Rough Riders, upon hearing that El Caney had fallen, would move from El Poso down the Santiago road to the ford on the Aquadores River, then deploy to the right of the road and join Lawton's division coming down from El Caney so as to form a continuous line along the San Juan River. Kent's First Division would follow the cavalry, but deploy to the left of the road. For support Grimes's battery of four Hotchkiss mountain guns at El Poso would provide covering fire.

Before this plan could be implemented, unexpected sickness altered the high command in the cavalry division. "Fighting Joe" Wheeler, flat on his back with fever and unable to attend the council of war, sent Brigadier General Sumner to take charge of the division. The commander of the Second Brigade, General Young, had also fallen ill and Colonel Wood, the senior regimental commander, was entrusted with the leadership of his brigade. This left Roosevelt to head the Rough Riders. When Roosevelt had been offered the regiment by President McKinley back in April, he had expressed the opinion that he could learn to command it within a month. Now, after being in the service twice that long, he had his big opportunity. The Rough Riders were on the eve of their biggest battle and Roosevelt, who was already the commander in the eyes of the public, was going to lead them. A chance for glory that Roosevelt did not intend to miss.

On June 30 the Fifth Corps began moving into position for the coming assault. Late that afternoon the Rough Riders drew rations for three days from the stockpiles near Sevilla, formed by troops and marched west to El Poso. There, the men had been told, they were to bivouac that night and move on San Juan Heights the following morning. Other organizations already had started forward. The troopers found the trail to El Poso choked with soldiers from many different units. At one point the Rough Riders were separated from their brigade when an infantry unit broke into their ranks, but they found an unused bypass which enabled them to double the column and rejoin their unit. Shortly after dark the Rough Riders reached El Poso and encamped alongside the road. After they had eaten, many of the Arizonans, aware that the next day would find them in battle, wrote letters home by the light of flickering campfires. For some strange reason, nobody seemed to object to campfires kindled in plain view of the enemy!

Meanwhile, General Arsenio Linares, who was made aware of the deployment of the Fifth Corps on the evening of June 30 by the campfires burning brightly across the valley, was making his preparations. He arranged his command in three defensive positions across the Santiago road. He established his first line, composed of five hundred and twenty-one men with two rapid fire guns, on San Juan Heights. On the hills to their rear four hundred and eleven men formed the second line, while one hundred and forty were placed in reserve. He also deployed a handful of Spanish irregulars or guerrillas in the valley. As at Guasimas Linares failed to commit all available troops. Consequently, he faced the Americans with numerical inferiority. He also failed to reinforce or withdraw the small garrison at El Caney. This left five hundred Spaniards at El Caney, totally isolated without support or hope of relief, to oppose Lawton's 6,000 infantrymen.

Dawn, of July 1, found the Rough Rider encampment at El Poso bustling with activity. Before daybreak the Arizonans gathered dew-soaked wood and nurtured small fires that sputtered in the morning gloom like so many tiny fireflies. A nearby stream furnished water for cooking as well as washing, and the aroma of frying bacon and simmering coffee soon permeated the crisp, morning air.

After breakfast some of the men climbed the ridge above El Poso to gaze at the Spanish lines across the valley on San Juan Heights. From this vantage point the basin was shrouded in the inevitable morning mist which rose from the humid valley. Ghost-like tree tops swayed above this vapor which partially obscured the base of the heights, but dissipated at the top to reveal fresh earth from recently dug trenches. The apprehension of the soldiers combined with the calm stillness of early dawn to spread an atmosphere of hushed expectancy over the entire regiment.

The members of A Troop had scarcely rolled from their blankets when Captain O'Neill received orders to move his men from El Poso down the ridge toward Santiago harbor. He was to protect the remainder of the regiment from a surprise attack. Some of the troopers had not finished breakfast when Sergeant Greenwood moved them out. Two men, Privates Fred Champlin from Flagstaff and Alexander Wallace from Pasadena, California, were detailed to guard the haversacks and blanket rolls, which were left behind.

Anxious to avoid a repetition of the disaster that had befallen the four man point of L Troop at Las Guasimas, O'Neill sent ahead a strong force of twelve volunteers under a tough and capable sergeant, Henry W. Nash, from Young, Arizona. The troop advanced behind this screen two miles south toward the harbor without contacting the enemy. Several Spanish guerrillas were seen, but they disappeared into the brush before they could be fired upon. Some of the men also thought they heard the unmistakable flat, brittle cracks of several Mausers, but no bullets fell in their vicinity. At Guasimas the men had learned to recognize the reports of different rifles. The Krags had a deeper, more resonant boom than did the high velocity Mausers used by the Spaniards.

From their new positions on the ridge east of Santiago harbor, O'Neill's men had an excellent view of the surrounding terrain. The rays of the rising sun had penetrated into the valleys, driving away the last vestiges of lingering shadows and giving promise of a beautiful day. Everything stood in bold relief. To their left the troopers could see the deep blue waters of the harbor; to their right front lay the chocolate-colored threads of the San Juan and Aquadores Rivers. San Juan Heights rose sharply from the jungle beyond these streams. The enemy fortifications were clearly visible. Some of the men discussed the feasibility of a flanking movement to avoid a frontal assault on the Spanish trenches. Suddenly the silent valley reverberated to the crash of artillery. A shell arched through the air to explode in a cloud of smoke in the Spanish lines. As the firing increased, O'Neill hurried his troop back down the ridge. He wanted to join the attack on San Juan Heights which he believed to be beginning.

Grimes's battery of four Hotchkiss guns opened the battle for San Juan Hill at 7 o'clock, the morning of July 1. At first the Spaniards did not reply as the battery laid shot after shot on their breastworks. The Rough Riders, who had gathered near the guns at El Poso to watch this spectacle, cheered heartily when several direct hits knocked bricks and other debris from a red blockhouse silhouetted on the skyline. Cynical Dick Stanton of B Troop, seated comfortably on a pile of bricks alongside the road, cast a speculative glance at the puffs of smoke which accompanied each shot from the black powder charged battery and remarked to Sergeant Hughes with pointed reference to the cheering Rough Riders:

"In a few minutes you are going to hear some cheering on the other side."[1] His words proved prophetic. Within a few seconds the men heard a peculiar hissing sound high in the air, followed by an ear-splitting roar. The first Spanish shell exploded harmlessly high above the Volunteers. Seconds later the boom of the gun was heard.

Although the first Spanish shot was too high, their successive rounds were more accurate. The pall of smoke hanging over Grimes's battery gave them a convenient aiming point, and they had accurately computed the range. They had no difficulty in placing their shots directly over El Poso, raking the entire hill with shrapnel. Moreover, the Spanish artillery used smokeless powder which concealed the location of their guns from counter-battery fire. One shell exploded directly above the Rough Riders, ripping Champlin's right arm and both legs with jagged shrapnel. Two pieces from the same projectile struck Wallace. One chunk tore harmlessly through his hat brim, but the other struck him on the cartridge belt and knocked him down. Wallace was not hurt, but Champlin died thirty-two hours later. In a vain effort to save him, the surgeons amputated his right leg and left foot. Another shot struck a building and killed several Cubans hiding there. Grimes's battery also received an apparent direct hit which put one gun and its crew out of action.

The waiting Rough Riders reacted immediately to this Spanish fire. Concluding that the safest place seemed to be on the enemy side of the ridge, the Volunteers, without orders, plunged over the crest and down the forward slope toward the San Juan River. Some of the men had climbed on the red tile roof of a nearby building to observe the bombardment. When the enemy artillery began returning the American fire, these troopers kicked down a shower of broken tile in their frantic haste to scramble off the roof and join their comrades seeking shelter from the flying shrapnel.

In testifying before the Dodge Commission after the war, Roosevelt admitted that he lost control of the regiment at

El Poso. He stated that his men went "over the crest of the hill into the brush; and I found it difficult getting the regiment together again."[2] In his published account, however, he evidently reconsidered the situation because he stated that he had sent the men over the ridge to avoid the artillery. It is obvious that the Rough Riders had not been concerned with orders. They just wanted to get off that ridge.

The Arizonans had learned to expect a certain amount of confusion in their forward movements. The march to the ford was no exception. Several infantry units had preceded the Rough Riders, but they had been halted along the narrow road to let the cavalrymen pass. The road became a sweltering mass of men as the Volunteers picked their way over tangled, slippery tree roots and halted infantrymen. Fortunately the troopers were traveling light, having left their haversacks and blanket rolls at El Poso. The Colt machine guns also had been left, for there were no mules available to carry them. Roosevelt's men had not gone far when they heard an ominous humming and snapping in the trees overhead. Even those who had never been under fire recognized the sound of rifle bullets. The Rough Riders, who had been battle tested at Las Guasimas, joked about their untried comrades in other units who instinctively ducked when bullets rattled through the tree tops. All of the Spanish fire did not prove high. As the men pressed on, they passed several blue-clad bodies crumpled along the road.

As he had received no definite instructions, Lieutenant Colonel Roosevelt halted his column when he reached the ford at the Aquadores River. By this time it was mid-morning and the valley, warmed by the sun and sheltered from cooling breezes by encircling hills and dense forest, had become uncomfortably hot. The Rough Riders welcomed the opportunity to rest. Tired, with their blue shirts dark with perspiration, the Volunteers sank to the ground to pull at their already half empty canteens. They watched Roosevelt, who was anxious to obtain further orders, ride up a small knoll to join

General Sumner. The general, mounted on a large white horse, and several other officers had gathered there to observe the crossing. After a short wait Roosevelt returned and ordered his men to fall in and follow him across the Aquadores River and into the brush on the other side.

By the time the Rough Riders crossed the river, congestion had become a serious problem at the ford. General Kent's infantrymen were piling up on the road faster than the cavalrymen were crossing the river. The jungle was so thick that troops could not move off to the side of the road. Then came one of the most unbelievable incidents of the entire campaign. Someone had ordered a signal corps observation balloon brought to the ford. By herculean efforts a group of soldiers dragged the balloon, swaying high above the trees, down the road by ground ropes.

As the balloon neared the ford, it seemed to be the target of every Spanish gun on San Juan Heights. Enemy bullets were smacking into it with impressive regularity. They also were ripping into the column of men jammed on the road down below. Colonel Wood, in charge of the Second Cavalry Brigade, wrote in his diary that the arrival of the balloon "caused the loss of lives of a large number of our men. It was one of the most ill judged and idiotic acts that I have witnessed."[3] Just before enemy fire brought the balloon down, the observer, Colonel G. M. Derby of corps engineers who was suspended below the balloon in a wicker basket, located an unused trail to the left. He reported this upon landing, and the infantrymen in General Kent's division were soon moving down the trail. This helped relieve the crowded conditions near the ford. It also enabled the infantry to get into their assigned attack positions to the left of the road and along the San Juan River.

Lieutenant Colonel Roosevelt maintained that his command escaped the fusillade which pelted the troops at the ford because the Rough Riders already had crossed the river before the balloon arrived. Some of the Arizona men did not see it that way. Private Tuttle recalled that A Troop had not yet moved out when the balloon arrived. A group of exasperated soldiers, including Private Frank Van Siclin of Safford, seized the guy ropes and helped drag the bullet-riddled target down. As it neared the ground, Tuttle, lying on the bank of the river a short distance away, heard the observer shout to someone down below: "They are strongly entrenched on your front and on your right."[4] Shortly thereafter A Troop moved out behind the remainder of the regiment.

It was also at this crossing that the Arizonans last saw their luckless adjutant. Many of the men stopped in the ford to fill their canteens. This congestion was viewed with disfavor by General Sumner, who ordered Lieutenant Hall to position himself at the crossing and keep the men moving. As the troopers crossed the river they passed Hall, sitting on his horse in mid-stream and briskly ordering those who tried to fill their canteens to keep on going. As far as the Arizonans were concerned, he never rejoined the regiment. A few days later Hall was on his way back to the states — allegedly because he had come down with malaria. There were few who missed him.

Holding their carbines across their chests to keep them dry, the Arizonans splashed across the hip-deep waters of the Aquadores and marched three-fourths of a mile north. At a sunken road just beyond a small stream they received orders to halt. The thick brush along the river had slowed the rate of march, but it had also shielded them from enemy rifle fire. Now, as the column reached the sunken road, the brush thinned out and a plunging fire began to hit the regiment. Troop and squadron formation, already confused by the movement through the brush, began to dissolve as the men sought shelter along the road and down in the nearby creek bed.

After establishing themselves in what cover they could locate, the Rough Riders studied the enemy positions. Half a mile to the front a small hill, on which sat an abandoned

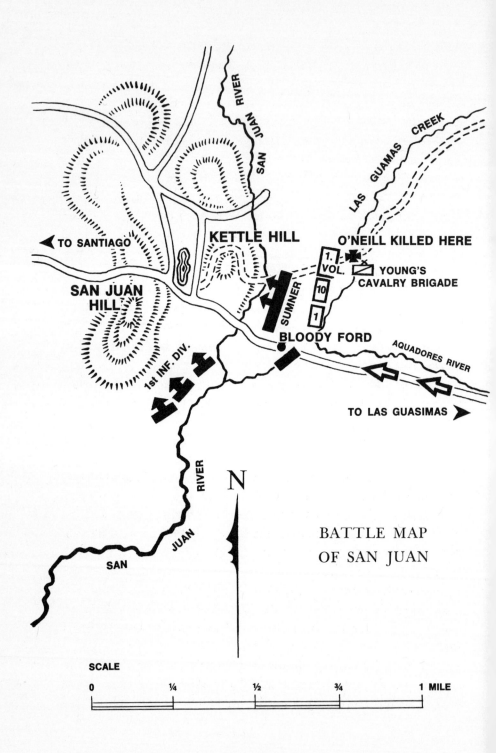

TO SANTIAGO

SAN JUAN RIVER

LAS GUAMAS CREEK

KETTLE HILL

O'NEILL KILLED HERE

1. VOL.

YOUNG'S CAVALRY BRIGADE

10

1

SAN JUAN HILL

SUMNER

BLOODY FORD

AQUADORES RIVER

1st INF. DIV.

TO LAS GUASIMAS

SAN JUAN RIVER

N

BATTLE MAP OF SAN JUAN

SCALE

0   ¼   ½   ¾   1 MILE

mill and two large iron kettles used in refining sugar, rose behind the San Juan River. Five hundred yards behind this knoll, called by the men "Kettle Hill," was the higher mass of San Juan Heights. A narrow, grass-covered valley with a small lake and a few scattered palm trees separated these terrain features.

The sunken road, along which most of the Rough Riders had sought cover, headed straight toward Kettle Hill. Flanked on both sides by barbed wire fences, the road passed over the crest of the hill near the ruins of the sugar mill. The Spaniards occupied these buildings, most of which had brick lined cellars, and it was from here that they were firing at the Rough Riders. The troopers wanted to shoot back, but the officers forbade it, knowing that the black Regulars of the Ninth Cavalry had moved into positions in the grassy field between the Volunteers and Kettle Hill. Unable to reply to the Spanish fire or escape the stifling heat, the Rough Riders could do nothing else but huddle along the road and wait.

For an hour the Rough Riders clung to their exposed position below Kettle Hill. The range was too great for accuracy, but the Spaniards poured a steady hail of bullets down the road. They could not fail to inflict some casualties. A few Volunteers were killed outright, their bodies being left where they fell. Others, wounded, soon formed a steady file to the rear in search of medical attention. Some of them walked unaided; others had to be helped along. This slow but steady accumulation of casualties had a depressing effect on the Arizonans, but they were quick to react to any situation which released their tension and gave them some comic relief. Several of their comrades provided the opportunity. One was A Troop's Emilio Cassi, an excellent trumpeter who had been born in Monaco and who prided himself on his musical ability. In the confusion Cassi had lost his hat, his carbine and his instrument. He gave everyone who saw him a hearty laugh as he ran up and down the road in front of his comrades, with enemy bullets slapping the ground about him, repeating over and over in uncontrolled excitement: "I lose my bugle! I lose my bugle!"[5]

Another was Private Henry "Shorty" Sellers, a member of A Troop from Williams, Arizona. While lying under partial cover alongside the road, Sellers had his hat brim painfully doubled into his eye by a spent rifle bullet. To the amusement of his comrades, Sellers jumped to his feet shouting: "I'm kilt — I'm kilt."[6] After his friends had calmed him down and he realized what had happened, Sellers picked up the small, steel-jacketed Mauser bullet to carry as a souvenir.

Captain O'Neill realized that his troopers needed something to steady them. The Arizona men were, he knew, Volunteers and not seasoned troops. In order to reassure his men and keep their spirits high, O'Neill walked calmly up and down the road in front of his troop, showing disdain for the Spanish bullets churning the road about him with little spurts of dried mud. He had done the same thing at Las Guasimas. His opinion, forcibly expressed on several occasions, was that an officer never should take cover. He also seemed to believe in a joking remark he had made earlier that "the Spanish bullet has never been molded that will kill Buckey O'Neill."[7] Several of his subordinates, as well as Lieutenant Woodbury Kane, who had deployed K Troop close by, implored O'Neill to take cover. What happened next is not exactly clear.

Smoking the inevitable cigarette and pausing here and there to joke with his men, Captain O'Neill continued to walk up and down the line. Later he strolled over to confer with Captain Robert D. Howze, an aide to General Sumner. Private Tuttle, who had just stood up to help Sergeant Greenwood, who had been shot in the foot, heard the murmur of their conversation. He glanced to his right and saw the two officers talking about fifteen feet away. While the young private was looking right at him, O'Neill suddenly stiffened and then collapsed without a sound. He had been shot squarely in the open mouth by a rifle bullet. "I heard the bullet," Tuttle recalled. "You usually can if you're close enough, you know.

Capt. Buckey O'Neill, commanding A Troop, pictured in
San Antonio before leaving for Cuba where he was killed
in action while deploying his troop to attack Kettle Hill.
(*Courtesy Sharlot Hall Museum.*)

It makes a sort of 'spat.' He was dead before he hit the ground."[8]

O'Neill's death was a severe blow not only to the Arizona squadron but to the regiment as well. He had molded his troop somewhat in the image of his own remarkable personality, and his men were badly shaken when they saw his body lying before them in the blood-stained dust of an obscure Cuban road. Everyone in the immediate vicinity ran to O'Neill, but most got back under cover when they realized that there was nothing to be done. Two troopers did pause long enough to drag their captain's body into a small depression underneath the shade of some trees and cover the officer's face with his campaign hat. There was no opportunity to do more at that time, for the regiment was preparing to move forward.

Unfortunately, A Troop ceased to exist as an organized unit when Captain O'Neill fell. Immediately after the fatal shot struck, Lieutenant Frank Frantz, who naturally succeeded to the command, rushed to his friend's body. He then ran down the creek bed past B Troop in search of a doctor. He had not even paused to wash his bloody hands. The logical man to restore confidence, experienced Sergeant Greenwood, whose foot had been badly shattered, already had been dragged to the rear. Privates Webb and Tuttle had lowered him into the creek bed where he was shielded by the embankment. With no one in control the troopers drifted off to fight with other units. Even Second Lieutenant Carter failed to assert himself. "The death of Captain O'Neill," Webb wrote, "seemed to paralyze the troop as no one appeared to know what to do . . . each man in the troop started out to do a little fighting on his own account to get even with the Spaniards."[9]

Although the lack of effective leadership in A Troop afforded an opportunity for the men to retire from the firing line, they stayed to fight on their own initiative. Private Henry Bardshar, an ex-miner from Prescott, attached himself

to Lieutenant Colonel Roosevelt and remained at his commander's side throughout the rest of the campaign. He stayed
even closer to Roosevelt than did Albert Wright, the color-
sergeant.

B Troop, deployed behind O'Neill's men, was also suffering from the Spanish fire and oppressive heat. Lieutenant
Wilcox was anxious to maintain control and he repeatedly
walked up and down the line to supervise the deployment.
But the hot sun and exertion of movement soon forced him to
lie down in the shade after turning the troop over to Second
Lieutenant Rynning. A short time later Rynning also became
ill and First Sergeant William Davidson took over from Rynning. This capable old veteran of Regular Cavalry personally
took charge of the first platoon and entrusted Sergeant John
E. Campbell, an ex-cavalryman from Phoenix, with command
of the second one. This change of command was always denied
by Rynning, who claimed that he was not sick and that he
stayed with his troop all day. In reply to Roosevelt's statement that Rynning was sick, the Arizona Lieutenant retorted
in his own book, *Gun Notches,* that Roosevelt "got just about
everything wrong."[10] The official records of B Troop, however, specifically state that Davidson and Campbell were leading the two platoons. Moreover, these records show that
Rynning was sick from the first to the third of July. In addition to the two officers, several enlisted men either became
incapacitated by heat or suffered wounds which removed
them from further action.

While the Volunteers were waiting at the foot of Kettle
Hill, other units moved into attack positions to their left.
The cavalry division formed two overlapping lines to the
right of the Santiago road. General Sumner's brigade, composed of the Third, the Sixth and the Ninth Cavalry regiments, formed the forward line. The Third Cavalry was on
the left and anchored on the Santiago road. The Sixth was
next to it, and the Ninth was on the right, extending as far
as the sunken road which led up Kettle Hill. General Young's

brigade, now commanded by Colonel Wood, was deployed behind and slightly to the right of Sumner's brigade. The Rough Riders were on the extreme right flank of the second line, their left overlapping the right flank of the Ninth Cavalry. The Tenth Cavalry was next to the Rough Riders and generally behind the Ninth. The First Regular Cavalry was on the brigade left and behind the Sixth regiment.

On the left of the Santiago Road and in front of San Juan Hill, General Kent had five infantry regiments on line. General Lawton's division was theoretically to be on Lieutenant Colonel Roosevelt's right, but it had run into a hornet's nest at El Caney and had not been able to secure that village in the time allotted. Lawton was unable to join the cavalry as planned. By 12:00 o'clock Wheeler's cavalrymen and Kent's infantry occupied a mile-long front just east of the San Juan River. From these positions the entire force began moving forward shortly after noon.

The Rough Riders were tired of waiting. Lieutenant Colonel Roosevelt, impatient, and of the opinion that his position along the sunken road had become untenable, finally received orders from General Sumner to support the Regulars in a general forward movement on the Spanish lines. Upon being given these instructions by a staff officer, Roosevelt immediately sprang on his horse and, as he later put it, "my crowded hour began."[11]

Forming his men in a column of troops deployed as skirmishers, the excited Roosevelt ordered his Rough Riders forward. His right flank was anchored on the barbed wire fence to the left of the road. Initially there was some hesitation on the part of the men, but Roosevelt personally rode back and forth exhorting his troopers to get moving. He joked with some and swore at others. Momentum quickened and soon the entire regiment was moving forward on the double. Roosevelt stationed himself with the rear of the column at first, but quickly rode to the front when the rear troops, cheering and moving rapidly, began to pile up on those in the lead. All pretense of military formation dissolved in a universal desire to be first on the hill. A few soldiers were struck down as they swept forward — one was right beside Roosevelt — but the others kept right on going.

When they reached the troops occupying the field below Kettle Hill, the Rough Riders found that the Regulars of the First Cavalry Brigade had not yet received orders to advance. Privates Dudley Dean and Henry Bardshar, two of the Arizonans who had joined Lieutenant Colonel Roosevelt as a "fighting tail" when the officer leadership of their own troop faltered, heard a sharp exchange between their commander and the officers of the Ninth. The Regulars declined Roosevelt's invitation to join the assault without orders from their own commander. Roosevelt, determined to continue with or without support, brusquely replied: "Then let my men through, sir."[12] The sight of the grinning Volunteers rushing by proved too much for the Regulars and small groups of them began to get up and edge forward. Their officers, realizing that they were powerless to stop this spontaneous reaction, soon began to move forward themselves. The movement spread to the Third and Sixth regiments to the left.

When General Sumner's First Cavalry Brigade joined the attack, the entire cavalry division became badly mixed. The Rough Riders and Tenth Cavalry, following the road which angled slightly to the left, became intermingled with elements of the First Regular Cavalry, which was moving slightly to the right. All three of these units became mixed together and with the Ninth regiment which they overran. At this point the assault north of the Santiago road had become general. Military organization had almost disappeared. The Spaniards faced a heterogeneous mixture of Regulars and Volunteers — black men and white.

As the Volunteers approached the San Juan River at the base of Kettle Hill, they found the enemy fire becoming more accurate. Rifle and machine gun bullets snapped cleanly overhead, but some slugs popped in the air and the Arizonans thought the Spaniards were using explosive bullets. Later they learned that the enemy guerrillas, firing from leafy positions high in the trees, were armed with .45 caliber weapons instead of Mausers. The bullets for these older rifles had a brass jacket which had a tendency to strip off with an audible popping sound.[13] The guerrillas could not be seen, but the Spanish Regulars, volley firing in small groups from the buildings on Kettle Hill, were clearly visible. Most of them wore peculiar straw hats which, the Arizonans soon found, made good targets as they bobbed up and down behind the window sills and earthen parapets of a few rifle pits. The excitement of the charge affected the entire command and compounded the spreading confusion. Trumpeter John Foster of B Troop, finding that no one paid any attention to his bugle calls, finally threw the instrument into the brush and went to work with his carbine.

Splashing across the shallow, muddy waters of the San Juan, the Rough Riders scurried up the lower slopes of Kettle Hill on the final leg of the charge. On the west bank of the river they encountered a thick, hedge-like growth backed by two barbed wire fences. The first arrivals cut lanes through the hedges with machetes, enabling the rest of the group to pass on through. The barbed wire proved to be a more formidable obstacle — especially to Roosevelt, who was still mounted on his horse "Little Texas." The Arizonans with him, however, enlisted the aid of several Negro troopers of the Tenth Cavalry and lifted the posts out of the soft, mushy ground.

The Spaniards, ordered to avoid a hand to hand fight, clung to their positions until the line of advancing cavalrymen swarmed over the second fence and then began to withdraw. This gave the Arizona boys their best opportunity of the day and Bardshar, in the presence of Roosevelt, who had to dismount at the second fence, dropped two who ran out of a blockhouse in front of him. The rest of the Arizonans were scattered all over the slope, but most of them had similar

opportunities. Practically everyone stopped to empty his magazine at the enemy as they withdrew. A moment later the first
Spanish fortifications to be captured in the battle of San Juan
were occupied by Roosevelt's Rough Riders.

The controversy as to who was first on Kettle Hill has
never been solved. The New Mexicans in G and E Troops
claimed that they had this distinction because their guidons
were the first to be planted on the crest. Two troops of the
Ninth Cavalry also claimed the honor. They had swung to
the right across the road during the charge and had come up
on the opposite end of the hill from the Rough Riders. There
were also some troopers from the Tenth and First Regular
Cavalry present. One of the strongest bids came from the
Arizonans. In his official report to Colonel Wood, Lieutenant
Colonel Roosevelt, after admitting that the guidons of G
and E Troops were the first, went on to add: "But some of
the men of A and B Troops who were with me personally
got in ahead of them."[14]

The crest of Kettle Hill offered no sanctuary from enemy
fire. The Spanish defenders had withdrawn five hundred
yards to the west and joined their comrades entrenched on
San Juan Heights. Realizing that the American cavalrymen
would attempt to occupy their old positions, the Spaniards
plastered Kettle Hill with everything they had. They sprayed
the crest with rifle and machine gun bullets fired from the
fortifications on San Juan Heights and with shrapnel from
the artillery located to the rear.

In the face of this galling fire, Lieutenant Colonel Roosevelt found it difficult to get his men organized. His troopers
were coming up in small groups with no regard for formation
and exhausted to the point that few had the energy to do more
than flop down among the rocks and clumps of grass. Roosevelt could see General Kent's infantrymen, three quarters of
a mile to the left, starting up the lower slopes of San Juan
Hill. As fast as he could get the cavalrymen organized, Roosevelt ordered them to form a skirmish line and support the

attack by firing on the Spanish trenches across the valley. By
this time elements of General Sumner's cavalry brigade,
located between Kettle Hill and the Santiago road, had
started to move onto that portion of the ridge to the right
of San Juan Hill. They were accompanied by several Arizona
Rough Riders who had drifted to the left and had skirted
Kettle Hill with General Sumner's men. Mute testimony to
the intensity of the fire these men faced was offered by the
silent blue figures that studded the valley.

The occupation of Kettle Hill by the Rough Riders on
the afternoon of July 1 signaled the end of the first phase
of the battle for the high ground in front of Santiago. Accompanied by part of the First Regular, the Ninth and Tenth
Cavalry regiments, the Rough Riders had taken the first
Spanish positions in the battle. In spite of having lost three
of their five officers, the Arizona troops had fought well. Both
Lieutenant Wilcox and Rynning later returned to duty, but
the death of O'Neill was, according to Roosevelt, "one of
the severest that could have befallen the regiment. He was
a man of cool head, great executive capacity and literally
dauntless courage."[15] Casualties among the enlisted men also
had been heavy, but Roosevelt's unwavering confidence in
his regiment was unshaken. He already had determined to
continue the attack on that part of San Juan Heights to his
front as soon as he could regroup his force.

Although no longer advancing over open terrain, the
Rough Riders suffered more casualties on Kettle Hill than
they had during the charge. Enemy artillery proved to be
particularly effective. Using fuses timed for air bursts, the
Spanish gunners placed a devastating barrage of shrapnel on
the cavalrymen, who were utilizing all available cover. Some
of the men occupied Spanish rifle pits, while others crouched
behind natural obstacles. Three or four sought refuge behind
the iron kettles, which rang like bells when struck by pro-
jectiles. One trooper, firing his carbine over the rim of one
kettle, inadvertently depressed the muzzle slightly and his

bullet, striking below the opposite rim, ricocheted around and around inside the kettle with a clanging noise clearly audible above the din of battle.

Captain McClintock's B Troop, which had lost few men in the assault, now paid a heavy price for its role in the engagement. One of the first to fall was Private John W. Swetman, a twenty-four-year-old cowboy from Globe. Swetman, who had established a reputation as a crack shot among his fellow Arizonans, was encouraging his comrades to take careful aim before they fired. As he knelt on one knee to steady his carbine in conformity with his own exhortation, he suddenly toppled over. He had been shot in the center of the forehead. Moments later a burst of shrapnel fatally wounded Private Oliver B. Norton, a young recruit who had enlisted at San Antonio on May 27. When Norton fell, his brother, Sergeant Edward Norton, a native of Mississippi who was working at a nursery in Phoenix when the war started, immediately picked up the badly shattered body of his brother and carried it to the aid station. This temporary facility had been established just behind the old sugar mill. Here another artillery shell killed Private David Logue, a twenty-six-year-old copper miner from Globe, and Corporal Joel Rex Hall from Bisbee.

The Norton situation was what Captain O'Neill had avoided by refusing to permit brothers to go to Cuba. He knew that in the heat of battle the older brother would tend to look after the younger. If one happened to be a noncommissioned officer, family ties might interfere with performance of military duty. Captain O'Neill also did not want to be responsible for one family losing two of its sons.

In addition to the four Arizona men who died on Kettle Hill, several others received disabling wounds — but they refused to leave the firing line. Sergeant Hughes, who had suffered a bad scalp injury from a piece of shrapnel just after crossing the river, stayed at the front until the regiment began moving off Kettle Hill. Charles B. Jackson and Wag-

oner John H. Waller, in A Troop, also were wounded but
refused to withdraw. Jackson, a twenty-six-year-old rancher
from Prescott, was shot in the neck, and Waller in the arm.
A veteran of the Civil War, "Henry" Waller as he liked to
be called, was virtually illiterate, but he had a reputation
among his comrades as being a fine soldier. With so many
injured and bloody men on the firing line, Roosevelt became
concerned about morale and personally ordered several to the
rear for treatment. One of them, Private Fred Bugbee, his
face covered with blood from a gash on his head, was ever
remembered by the Arizona men because of his reply to
Roosevelt: "You go to hell. We are not going back."[16] With
an understanding smile, Roosevelt turned and walked away.

While the Rough Riders were establishing a base of fire
on Kettle Hill, the balance of Shafter's force was moving forward. Kent's division, which was deployed to the left of the
Santiago road, already had broken out of the canebreaks
along the banks of the San Juan River. Its leading files were
starting up the lower slopes of San Juan Hill. To the immediate right of the road and to the left of Kettle Hill, the
Regular Cavalry under Colonel Henry Carroll had joined in.
The entire valley floor was covered with Shafter's men who
were moving right into the muzzles of the Spanish guns. All
the attacking regiments were taking heavy casualties. The
critical moment of the battle had arrived.

Lieutenant Colonel Roosevelt was beside himself with
excitement. The events transpiring on his left were clearly
visible, and he was anxious to get into the action. His opportunity came when he identified a peculiar drumming sound
as originating with the three Gatling guns Lieutenant John
H. "Blackie" Parker had pushed forward to support the attack.
Parker had a theory that rapid fire guns such as his Gatlings
could best support an assault by advancing with the attacking
elements. This was a novel approach and a departure from
standard tactical doctrine then in use. Parker was anxious to
test his theory in combat. By hard work he had managed to

extricate his guns from the confused throng back at the ford and get them up on the firing line.

By the time the Gatling guns had come up, the infantrymen were approaching the top of San Juan Hill. Lieutenant Colonel Roosevelt decided to charge the enemy on that portion of San Juan Ridge to his immediate front. Shouting for his men to follow, he jumped over a barbed wire fence and ran down the slope. He had covered approximately one hundred yards when he realized that only five men from F Troop were with him.

Leaving those five men where they were, Roosevelt returned to the crest of Kettle Hill to round up the rest of the regiment. His men apologized for not having followed, claiming that they had not heard the order to charge. Before Roosevelt could get his men moving, someone told him that General Sumner had arrived on the hill. Roosevelt was no longer the ranking officer. Sumner, however, apparently had the same idea as Roosevelt, for when the excited Rough Rider reported to him and requested permission to lead a charge, Sumner told him to go ahead. This time it was different. Except for the equivalent of several troops left on Kettle Hill in reserve, Roosevelt led his Rough Riders and elements of the First Regular and Ninth Cavalry regiments.

From their positions near the sugar mill, the first platoon of Wilcox's B Troop watched the charge. Under Sergeant Davidson they had been ordered to remain on Kettle Hill with the reserve force. They never forgot the colorful spectacle which they witnessed. The troopers noted that there was little military formation during the charge — in fact it was made in the same wild disorder as the assault on Kettle Hill. The Rough Riders, accompanied by elements of the First Regular and Ninth Cavalry with a few stray infantrymen, followed individual tactics of sprinting forward in short rushes. At each stop they paused to fire their carbines and then dashed to the next spot of cover. The Rough Riders were distinguishable because of their brown trousers. The

Regulars and Volunteer infantry wore shirts and trousers of regulation blue. Both ends of the line became crowded when some troopers swerved to the flanks to avoid the small lake in the center of the grass-covered valley. The pond proved to be quite shallow, however, and many waded through it.

Throughout the entire attack Parker's drumming Gatlings provided excellent fire support. The black-bearded young lieutenant kept pushing his guns forward to the closest possible range. All along the Spanish parapets ahead of the Volunteers spurts of dust indicated the accuracy of this steady fire.

To the spectators at El Poso the charge appeared no less impressive. This hill was the best vantage point available, and many correspondents and foreign observers had gathered there to watch. Although their accounts differed in minor points, they agreed that the charge on San Juan Heights was an example of gallantry that exceeded all expectations. The troopers seemed to be exposed for the most part, and the smoke and din of battle made many observers fear that the Spanish fire was so hot that the charge could not succeed. One correspondent wrote that the sight of General Shafter's men running across the valley was "a glorious, almost incredible sight."[17]

Everyone saw Roosevelt. Those who watched from El Poso could not recognize him at that distance, but with the aid of field glasses they could see a man running well ahead of the right flank of the assault line. Those who were close enough recognized Roosevelt. In his soiled brown trousers and white suspenders crossed over his blue shirt, he was the most conspicuous man on the field. With a typical, Rooseveltian flair for the dramatic, he had tied a blue bandanna to his hat which streamed behind him like a banner. He did not have his saber — he never carried it in battle again after it had tripped him at Guasimas — but he punctuated his shouts of encouragement by waving his revolver over his head. The Arizona men never forgot this performance.

Those who participated in the charge also remembered it for a lack of organization. Years later Sergeant Thomas P. Ledwidge described it to Hermann Hagedorn:

My place in the line carried me over the very top of Kettle Hill, and for a moment I saw the entire line of the Cavalry Division as it moved ahead. The formation was very irregular and I must confess that it presented none of the spectacular elements that I always previously associated with great battles. There were no great masses of troops charging with waving flags and sword-pointing officers in the lead. Instead there were a succession of squads of men hurrying towards the hills, pausing to shoot and then rushing on again. Very little noise, and no dust, that I could see. Neither was there any shouting. There was great animation on the part of the men, and I noticed how everyone seemed to be smiling. If any one had fear in his heart, he was sufficiently an actor to hide it with a smile.[18]

The ferocity and determination of the attack, coupled with Parker's accurate fire, caused the Spaniards to withdraw before the cheering cavalrymen overran their trenches. Only a few resolute individuals clung to their posts — and there they died. With his revolver Roosevelt himself killed one who ran out of a blockhouse. Another fell to Bill Page, a private in A Troop from Richenbar. As Page and Tuttle ran up the ridge, they saw a Spaniard jump out of the trench right in front of them. With no time to stop and too close to shoot, Page swung his carbine by the stock and clubbed the man down. Several other Spaniards fell victim to close range rifle fire, a few surrendered, but most withdrew to the low hills behind San Juan Heights to take up positions in the second line of defense. Roosevelt's panting troopers swarmed into the double set of enemy trenches and planted their guidons on the ramparts. Kent's infantrymen occupied San Juan Hill to the left — and the entire ridge had fallen. It was only 2:30 P.M.

The remainder of the afternoon proved uneventful. Ordered not to advance farther, Roosevelt directed his men to dig in and hold the ground they occupied. Lying in the grass along the crest of the ridge, the Rough Riders traded shots with the Spanish second line all afternoon. They were aided by Parker's Gatlings, which had come up on line to their right. The officers found they could move on the reverse slope with safety and by later afternoon they had partially restored military organization. As night came on the firing began to slacken.

A shortage of ammunition was one contributing factor to the slackening of fire by the Arizonans. During the course of the day some of them had fired as much as three hundred rounds. Moreover, the peculiar construction of the Krag led to the loss of much ammunition. To load the weapon a hinged, box-type magazine on the right side of the receiver was opened and the cartridges dropped one at a time into the magazine. This worked fine in a stationary position, but the Arizonans found that the weapon was extremely difficult to load while running. Between the sunken road below Kettle Hill and the top of San Juan Heights there were hundreds of cartridges that had been dropped by men attempting to load while running. A few of the troopers tried to retrieve some of these cartridges, but since they did not have time to properly secure them in their "thimble" belts, they dropped them into their shirt fronts. This worked well until the weight of the cartridges forced the shirt tail to come out of the trousers, allowing the ammunition to fall back on the ground. Consequently, many of the men arrived on San Juan with only a few rounds left.

Consolidation of the hard-won position on San Juan Heights took place under the cover of darkness. After repelling an abortive Spanish counterattack with rifle fire at dusk, the Rough Riders began digging trenches and rifle pits on the military crest overlooking Santiago. With shovels and picks abandoned by the Spaniards they worked all night. Private Stanton of B Troop furnished hot coffee to those digging the trenches. Private Oscar Wager, a young trooper in A Troop from Jerome, and several others obtained drinking water from the San Juan River behind their positions. Several times they were fired upon by Spanish guerrillas hiding in the tall trees along the river. No pack train arrived with rations, but quantities of rice, peas and a large kettle of simmering stew left by the Spaniards were carefully rationed among the Rough Riders. This was the first food the men had eaten since 4:00 A.M. and, together with the coffee and hardtack a few managed to carry through the day-long battle, it made a satisfactory supper. It had been a hard day and the Volunteers needed to rest.

The performance of Roosevelt's Rough Riders in the battle for San Juan Heights on July 1 speaks for itself. Just sixty-seven days before the men had been civilians, reading in the morning papers that war had been declared on Spain. Now they were combat veterans, having been enlisted, organized, trained, transported to Cuba and thrown against an experienced enemy entrenched in good positions and armed with modern weapons. These rough-hewn Volunteers had been foremost in the fighting and had a long casualty list to bear gory testimony. Of the four hundred and ninety Rough Riders who answered reveille at El Poso on July 1, eleven were dead and sixty-five wounded by nightfall. Four of these wounds would prove to be fatal. Approximately forty had been overcome by heat. Moreover, two more men would be killed and eleven wounded the next day, July 2.

In spite of this, Roosevelt's enemies circulated the malicious rumor that the first Volunteer Cavalry participated in no hard fighting before Santiago. Technically, their charge that the Volunteers did not even get on San Juan Hill is correct, but, ironically enough, this does not in any way detract from the troopers' performance both on Kettle Hill and in charging San Juan Heights. The confusion stems in part from the fact that Kettle Hill was a separate terrain feature and not an integral part of San Juan Heights proper; and that San Juan Hill was merely the apex of a longer land mass called San Juan Heights or San Juan Ridge. The fifteen per cent casualty rate taken by the Rough Riders on the first day of July was the highest in the cavalry division and compares very favorably with the casualty rate suffered by the infantry. It shows that the fighting on the right flank was just as vicious as it was on the left or at El Caney.

The Arizonans were proud of the record they made at San Juan. Composed of five officers and one hundred and thirty-six men on the morning of July 1, the two Arizona troops made up approximately one fourth of the effective fighting force of the Regiment. Yet, out of the fifteen Rough Riders who died from wounds received that day — eight were in the Arizona troops.

In addition to Captain O'Neill, the only regimental officer killed, Privates James Boyle of Prescott, Fred Champlin from Flagstaff and Lewis Reynolds from Kingman made up the roster of those killed in A Troop. In B Troop Corporal Joel R. Hall and Privates David Logue, Oliver Norton and John Swetman were all killed. Out of sixty-five wounded Rough Riders, thirteen were in A and B troops. In addition, there were several men in each of the two troops who passed out from heat just before the charge on Kettle Hill. One man turned up missing. Albert C. McMillan, a recent enlistee in B Troop from New York City, disappeared during the battle and later turned up claiming to have been sick. Sergeant Davidson obviously didn't believe this story, for he recorded in the muster rolls that on July 1 McMillan was "absent, whereabouts not known. Supposed to have been sick."[19]

In addition to having sustained a fatal casualty rate in excess of their proportional numbers, the Arizonans also garnered the lion's share of the plaudits and commendations. In his report to Colonel Wood, written on July 4, Roosevelt selected the names of twenty-eight men to commend for their performance. Eleven of them were in A and B Troops. Troopers Bugbee, Jackson and Waller of A Troop along with Sergeant Hughes of B Troop were commended for continuing to fight after being wounded. Private Norton of B Troop was mentioned for "fighting with marked gallantry";

while troopers Richard Goodwin, Dudley Dean, John Foster and Sergeant Campbell of B Troop, as well as Samuel Greenwald of A, were "all worthy of special mention for coolness and gallantry."[20] Roosevelt also complimented "Bardelas of A," but here he must have been confused, for the muster rolls reflect no such name. The only Arizona officer to be mentioned was Frank Frantz. Later, Roosevelt went over the list of names again and selected seven Rough Riders to recommend for a "medal of honor." This revised roster included John Waller and Fred Bugbee.

Although all units that participated in the attack on San Juan did so in varied degrees of confusion, few of them rivaled the lack of command that characterized the Rough Rider advance. In spite of having promoted Captain Micah Jenkins, a graduate of West Point, to squadron commander to replace Brodie, Roosevelt made no effort to deploy his regiment by squadrons. At one point in the advance Jenkins halted his men to straighten their lines. Noting the movement Roosevelt snapped at Jenkins: "Let the formation take care of itself. The thing to do just now is to take the hill. Lead your men forward."[21] This lack of command became quite evident after Colonel Wood's promotion and transfer. It reflected the inexperience Roosevelt had in military procedure. A case in point was the abortive first attempt to charge San Juan Heights from Kettle Hill. How the Regular officers must have stared in disbelief upon seeing a lieutenant colonel in command of a regiment running down a hill to "charge" the enemy with only five of the four hundred odd men available to him.

Lieutenant Colonel Roosevelt obviously did not consult with his squadron and troop commanders either before or after he made his decisions. Behaving like a platoon leader or, at best, a troop commander, Roosevelt set the example with his own personal courage. The Rough Riders were gallantly led — but they were not commanded! Jesse Langdon of K Troop accurately described the situation involving the

Rough Riders when he wrote that the battle was fought "by a heterogeneous mob, composed mostly of Rough Riders with a mixture of First and Third white Regulars and Ninth Cavalry."[22]

Nevertheless, the record made by the First United States Volunteer Cavalry at San Juan is still impressive. In the fighting on July 1 the troopers had actually participated in two separate charges. In the first, which they had initiated up the sunken road toward Kettle Hill, they had been joined by elements of the Ninth, the Tenth and the First Regular Cavalry regiments. From Kettle Hill they had joined the extreme right flank of the line assaulting San Juan Heights. This second charge had been started by General Kent's infantry division to the left. During both actions the Rough Riders had become badly mixed with soldiers from other units. With three of their five officers incapacitated by death or illness, the Arizonans had followed any officer, Regular or Volunteer, who happened to be close by and imbued with an offensive spirit. Although badly disorganized — all but one had stayed on the field. Webb proudly reported: "Wherever the fighting was the hottest that day there could be found the men from Arizona in the forefront of battle."[23]

CHAPTER 6

A Devil of A Country

THE CESSATION OF HOSTILITIES after the battle of San Juan forced the Rough Riders in Cuba to prepare for still another campaign — the adversities of the tropical climate. Despite cheering news of the fall of Santiago on July 15, the Volunteers remained in bivouac outside the city where mud, rain and fever soon began to take their toll. During this trying period the Volunteers lost more men from the natural elements and inadequate supply than they had on the battlefield. Morale deteriorated as sickness increased and few supplies came forward. By mid-July, as fear of yellow fever grew, both the officers of the Fifth Corps and public opinion in general began exerting pressure on the War Department to withdraw the United States troops from Cuba.

The morning of July 2 found the Rough Riders in the trenches dug along the crest of San Juan Heights. The enemy opened the day with a heavy bombardment and pushed their skirmishers forward. This tactic failed as the Arizonans, along with the other troopers behind the crest, tumbled hurriedly into their trenches to stop the attack with rifle fire. Throughout the remainder of the day intermittent exchanges between the two armies continued. In A Troop Emilio Cassi from Prescott, Edward O'Brien from Jerome, Corporal Harry G. White from Richenbar, Charles Perry from Perry's Landing, Texas, and Stanley Hollister from Santa Barbara, California, were wounded. The only casualty in B Troop was Race Smith from San Antonio. Smith's wound was the only one which proved to be fatal, but Hollister later died of typhoid.

The Arizonans also took their turn in the sharpshooter trench which had been dug in front of the main line. Here Private William Snodderly, a member of B Troop from Bisbee, established his reputation. Snodderly spotted a mounted Spanish officer at what Lieutenant Rynning estimated to be 1,000 yards and managed to put a bullet into the horse. Rynning later stated that the officer "went up in the air with all four legs and his saber waving."[1] That evening after dark the Arizonans continued preparing trenches and machine gun emplacements. Even then the sound of a scraping shovel usually brought in a Spanish volley.

With their position on San Juan Heights secured, the Rough Riders turned their attention to guerrilla snipers lurking in their rear. Supplied with brown sugar and with hollow bamboo shoots filled with drinking water tied above them, these riflemen hid in the protective foliage of high trees overlooking the trails and fords. Armed with .45 caliber rifles instead of Mausers, they fired at any convenient target — including medical personnel, wounded men headed for the rear, couriers and water details. Some of the Arizonans had drawn fire while getting water from the stream behind their lines and there was a rumor that the guerrillas were ex-convicts, released with promises of amnesty if they performed this bloody work. The cowboys from Arizona devoted their particular skills to ridding their area of the sniper menace.

When Colonel Roosevelt took command of the Rough Riders, he extended the cult of "personal" command which Colonel Wood had started. L Troop, for example, was designated "Capron's Troop" after the death of the troop commander at Las Guasimas. In doing this Colonels Wood and Roosevelt followed an old custom, used extensively in the Civil War and later, in the post war years, in the cavalry regiments of the Indian fighting army.

This trait of personal control was shown again in the manner in which Colonel Roosevelt picked thirty sharpshooters to track down and eliminate the Spanish snipers who were taking a painful toll of the regiment in killed and wounded. He chose, by name, men whom he knew to be experienced hunters and riflemen, merely telling his troop commanders to provide them. This was a natural thing for him to do, for he consistently referred to the Rough Riders as "my men" or "my regiment." Such expressions were commonly used in those days when an officer might stay with one command for years, but Roosevelt carried it beyond the normal, even using it in his official reports and correspondence. Other officers used such terms only informally.

At least two of the men Colonel Roosevelt selected for his sniper-hunting detail came from B Troop. One was Private William Proffitt, a taciturn rancher from Prescott who was born in Texas. The other was Private Richard Goodwin, a miner from Phoenix and a crack shot with both rifle and revolver. The first day out this detail killed eleven Spanish guerrillas without any casualties of their own. At the same time other men, hunting on their own initiative, shot several found hiding in trees along the banks of the San Juan River.

The Rough Riders from the West excelled at this type of warfare. Private Arthur Stockbridge of F Troop explained how the men worked out a technique of hunting in pairs. Locating a suspected sniper position, one man, with all due caution, would circle the position, briefly exposing himself from time to time until the sniper moved to take aim at the decoy. The other soldier, hiding in a position affording good observation, waited until the sniper's movement pinpointed his exact location and then simply shot him down.

The Arizonans gave little quarter to the guerrillas. With orders to take no prisoners, Goodwin and his partner, a Negro soldier from the Tenth Cavalry, located two snipers hidden in twin palm trees behind the lines. They were firing toward the Rough Riders on the ridge. Shooting together at the same time, the two cavalrymen brought one sniper down from his lofty perch like a squirrel. The other dropped his rifle and, armed only with a machete, climbed down to plead for his life in broken English. When Goodwin later reported the action to Roosevelt, he displayed two Spanish rifles and two straw hats. In reply to Roosevelt's query as to what had happened to the sniper who had surrendered, Goodwin calmly replied: "Sir, you said not to take any prisoners, so the nigger cut his throat."[2]

After his command occupied San Juan Heights on July 1, General Shafter paused to evaluate his precarious position. His corps stretched in a long, thin line from the El Caney road to a mile south of the El Poso road. He had no reserve and his supply lines were overextended. At first Shafter seriously considered retreating from the field, but after a conference with his division commanders and encouragement from the War Department, he finally decided to hold his position. On the morning of July 3 Shafter formally demanded that the Spaniards either surrender Santiago or evacuate the noncombatants, for he planned to begin shelling the city at 10:00 A.M. the following morning. General Jose Toral, who had replaced the wounded Linares as the Spanish commander, refused to surrender. After additional negotiation, however, a truce was worked out to extend from July 3 to July 10 in order that all refugees could evacuate Santiago. At noon, July 3, the guns fell silent all along the front.

By the time the truce went into effect on July 3, General Shafter had invested Santiago from the east and from the north. His corps was arranged in a fishhook-shaped line five miles long. The cavalry division occupied the center of the line, their guns covering the mile-long ridge between the El Poso and El Caney roads. To the left General Kent's infantry held the heights to the south, with Bates' independent brigade coming from the coast to secure the extreme left flank. General Lawton's exhausted division, not yet recovered from the hard fighting at El Caney, marched up on the morning of July 2 and was ordered to extend the right flank across the northern approaches to the city. General Garcia's Cubans were given the mission of blockading Santiago from the west. Although the firing had been suspended, the officers of all the units kept their men busy preparing fortifications. They realized that if surrender negotiations failed the city would have to be taken by siege.

The truce gave the Arizona boys an opportunity to write letters home describing their role in the battle. These communiques were well received and widely read. The Rough Riders as a regiment figured prominently in most news dispatches, but the newspaper accounts of the battle of San Juan gave no particulars on the Arizonans. Consequently, private letters from Cuba were quickly printed in the local papers. Occasionally those of special merit were reprinted in other territorial publications. The general feeling was that the Arizona men had done well and the people of the territory took great pride in their accomplishments. On August 15 Cornelius Cronin, who had returned from San Antonio with his discharge, described the effects of the battle of San Juan on the populace of Yuma in a letter to McClintock. Cronin wrote in part:

I returned to Arizona before the boys opened the ball in Cuba, and I can assure you the pride and enthusiasm of our people over your achievements was something grand. When the news arrived that "we" had met the enemy and the enemy was "ours" — golly! There was more powder burned and whiskey drank in old Yuma than was ever before known. The news arrived sometime after midnight, and some of the rail-road boys started in to fittingly celebrate the occasion by turning loose about a hundred sticks of giant powder on Main Street, resulting in about every pain of glass in the block being broken.

Cronin went on to assure McClintock that when the captain returned home he would find the people ready "to show you how our heroes are appreciated."[3]

The death of Captain O'Neill caused a sensation in Arizona. Condolences from his many friends and acquaintances throughout the territory were received by his widow in Prescott. One of the most unusual expressions of regret came from Phoenix. Motivated perhaps by the well-publicized attempt by O'Neill to save the two Negro cavalrymen in the surf at Daiquiri — or possibly for some unrecorded action back in Arizona before the war — the Negro citizens of Phoenix sent a resolution to Mrs. O'Neill. They expressed their sorrow over learning of the loss of a "true and tried friend, the territory one of its foremost citizens, the Army of the United States a gallant officer, and his family a devoted husband and indulgent father."[4]

The details of O'Neill's death were sought avidly in Arizona. They became the basis of a never-resolved controversy. The first reports of the battle stated simply that O'Neill had been killed at the head of his troop below Kettle Hill. Later, the commonly accepted version came to be that as the captain walked up and down the road in front of his troop one of his sergeants implored him to get under cover. O'Neill blew out a cloud of cigarette smoke and replied: "The Spanish bullet has never been molded that will kill Buckey O'Neill." It was at that very moment, so the story goes, that the fatal shot struck. The origin of this version is not clear. Roosevelt, McClintock and Marshall all related it in their published accounts, but McClintock, in a radio address in 1930, implied that he never quite believed the story. The regimental adjutant, Lieutenant Hall, stated in his account, *The Fun and Fighting of the Rough Riders,* that O'Neill made his often quoted statement in a joking manner several

days before the battle. This was supported to a certain extent
by O'Neill's second lieutenant, Joshua D. Carter, who wrote
a long letter from Cuba that was published in the Prescott
Journal Miner on July 27. Carter wrote:

Captain O'Neill was constitutionally opposed to getting under cover,
and remarked that he didn't think the Spanish bullet was moulded that
could kill him. That is what cost the brave fellow his life. Other officers
would see their men under cover, and then take to cover themselves,
while Buckey would light a cigarette and walk around in a hail of
bullets. It was inevitable.

Private A. D. Webb, one of the most reliable reporters
of the entire campaign and an eyewitness to the death of
O'Neill, made no mention of the famous statement. Certainly
Tuttle, who was close enough to hear the smack of the bullet
as it struck O'Neill, would have remembered any such remark
if, as the story goes, it was offered in reply to an admonish-
ment to get under cover.

In later years the incident became embedded in the folk-
lore of Yavapai County and traditions of the Rough Riders to
the extent that the exact truth will probably never be known.
After the war countless members of the regiment — most of
whom were not even in A Troop — claimed to have been eye-
witnesses. Their versions are characterized by the fact that
they are all practically identical. Perhaps the explanation of
one former Rough Rider accurately explains why the popular
version has enjoyed such widespread circulation. This veteran,
after admitting that he was not even near A Troop at Kettle
Hill, explained that he too, on many occasions, had claimed
to have been present when O'Neill fell. The classical account
remains a highly dramatic story that pleases the listener and
surrounds O'Neill with an air of cocky braggadocio.

It is unfortunate that such melodrama has come to be
associated with the death of Captain O'Neill. It obscures the
true effect of his personality on the Arizona Rough Riders.
He was immensely popular with his men, who would follow

him anywhere. They felt a deep personal loss when he was killed. Trooper Webb, verging on hero worship, reflected this feeling when he wrote from Cuba:

We have suffered heavy loss, the worst being in the death of Capt. "Buckey" O'Neill, than whom a braver man never led soldiers to battle. Standing erect, midst a storm of bullets, laughing and joking with his men, he met his death as other heroes have met theirs before him. He was buried near the spot where he fell by his own men, two of whom had stood guard over his remains from the moment he was shot until his body was tenderly laid to rest. No parson was there to tell of the nobleness of his character and his funeral dirge was the whistle of bullets and scream of shells. "Buckey" is dead, but death will close the eyes of the last trooper who fought under him 'ere he is forgotten.[5]

Colonel Roosevelt, whose own promotion came through on July 11, took advantage of the lull in the fighting to award promotions and commendations to those who had distinguished themselves during the action. Many changes had occurred in A Troop, with the captain killed and first sergeant wounded. Although he failed to exert control over the troop after O'Neill's death, Lieutenant Frank Frantz won a set of captain's bars for the personal courage he exhibited during the charge on San Juan Heights. Roosevelt also had been impressed with Samuel Greenwald, a young private in A Troop from Prescott. Roosevelt promoted the trooper to second lieutenant. When Greenwald's commission came through a few weeks later, he was transferred to I Troop. Sergeant Henry B. Fox from Prescott replaced Greenwood as first sergeant. In B Troop Lieutenant Wilcox was not promoted because McClintock was still carried on the records as the troop commander. Wilcox did begin receiving captain's pay dating back to the time he took command of the troop on June 24.

The selection of a first lieutenant' to replace Frantz in A Troop briefly posed a problem. Roosevelt solved it by promoting to first lieutenant and transferring John C. Greenway from G Troop. Greenway had unusual ability and proved to be an asset. Born in Alabama in 1872 and a graduate of

Lt. Col. Theodore Roosevelt (left) and Lieut. John C. Greenway, eastern college man who served with the Rough Riders in Cuba and returned to become a noted mining man in Arizona. (*Courtesy Arizona Pioneers' Historical Society*.)

Yale, he was one of the ex-college athletes recruited by Roosevelt. He joined the regiment at San Antonio. Originally assigned to I Troop, Greenway, then a second lieutenant, had been attached to G Troop as an extra officer so that he could go to Cuba. There he quickly established a reputation as being one of the finest and most aggressive officers in the regiment. Testimonies as to his ability came not only from Roosevelt, but from many of the enlisted men as well. It was his platoon of G Troop — he took over Lieutenant David J. Leahy's command when that officer was wounded — which had advanced the farthest toward Santiago at the battle of San Juan. When Greenway joined them, the Arizonans had no premonition that after the war the popular young officer would become a prominent Arizona mining man. His sculptured likeness would represent his adopted state in statuary hall in Washington.

Everyone expected that the truce would soon end, and the Rough Riders prepared their positions in anticipation. There was much to be done and the Volunteers were kept hard at work improving existing trenches and constructing new ones. Communication with the men in the sharpshooter trench, which ran parallel to the main line of fortification and on the Santiago side of the ridge, was a necessity. Several access trenches were dug to that position. All such fortifications had to be constantly cleaned as their soft sides sloughed in the heavy rain. The Arizonans, who were particularly concerned about enemy artillery which had been so effective on July 1 and 2, constructed shelters on the forward side of the trenches to protect them from shrapnel. These "shrapnel proofs," as the Arizonans called them, merely consisted of shallow depressions covered with logs and boards with several feet of earth heaped on that. Lieutenant Carter was confident that these shelters would protect the men "so that bombs bursting overhead might not throw small pieces of iron" on them.[6]

The Arizona boys found that watching the Spaniards, who were plainly visible in and before Santiago, proved a welcome diversion from the hot work in the trenches. The city was only a mile away, and grim-looking fortifications contrasted with the serenity of the whitewashed walls and red tiled roofs. Nevertheless, the troopers confidently predicted that they could take the city. Carter wrote: "Well, I can see the Dons standing over there in the trenches. We expect to fix them as soon as they take down that white flag."[7] Every day Spanish work parties appeared to string barbed wire, dig trenches and emplace batteries. Several of these guns, it was noted with contempt, were located close to well-marked hospitals. Unarmed enemy search parties prowled between the lines, occasionally building fires over the unrecovered bodies of their comrades who had died in the evacuation of San Juan Heights.

The Rough Riders also had a fine view of the truce parties which met daily beneath a large tree between the lines to negotiate the surrender, or "make medicine" as the Arizonans called it. On July 6 the Volunteers gathered on the parapets to cheer the prisoner exchange which returned Commodore Hobson and his crew from the *Merrimac.*

The story of Hobson and his crew of seven volunteers was well known to the Arizona men. At 3:30 A.M. on June 3 Assistant Naval Constructor Richard Pearson Hobson steamed into Santiago harbor on a large collier, the *Merrimac.* His objective was to blockade Cervera's fleet by scuttling his vessel in the narrow channel opposite Estrella Point, half a mile from the harbor entrance. In the face of an intense bombardment, the *Merrimac* was sunk according to plan, but strong tides pulled her to one side of the channel where the derelict offered little obstruction to the harbor. Hobson and his crew were fished out of the bay and made prisoner shortly after daybreak. They remained prisoners until the afternoon of July 6 when they were exchanged. The triumphant return of Hobson and his men took place right in front of A Troop.

Although the front remained quiet during the day, sporadic rifle fire disturbed tranquility after dark. Duty on the outposts was on a rotating basis, and the different troops took turns on the unpopular "cossack posts." Several men occupied each listening post at the same time under the assumption that some would sleep while others stood guard. Most of the Arizonans did not sleep during this duty, for the dark, stormy tropical nights made the pickets on both sides uneasy. In addition, the men found the rifle pits uncomfortable because the nightly rains often filled them waist deep.

The Negro troops of the Tenth Cavalry occupied the lines adjacent to the Volunteers for a time. The Arizonans disliked having these soldiers on duty so close. They felt that the Negroes were prone to begin firing at unidentified sounds in the darkness. Such firing, once started, frequently spread to other units and the officers, in spite of the truce, had difficulty in restoring order. On one such occasion, in a brief flash of lightning, the Rough Riders saw a cloaked Spanish officer walking along the trenches to quiet his men. His success reflected the high state of discipline that existed in the Spanish Army.

Hostilities flared again briefly on July 10, with the artillery on both sides signaling the end of the truce by bombarding the opposing lines. The dynamite gun of the Rough Riders, located behind the trenches, also opened up during this exchange. This lasted only one day, for the truce went back into effect late that same afternoon. The Arizona troopers, some of whom had been temporarily assigned to the dynamite gun squad, found the weapon to be largely ineffectual. The projectile, fired at low velocity by compressed air, traversed a high, wobbly trajectory which could be traced with the bare eye. This gave the Spaniards ample time to seek cover before the shell struck. To make matters worse, the breech mechanism jammed after every second or third shot. The Volunteers kept the gun in action only with assistance from Lieutenant Parker's Gatling gun detachment.

One shot from the dynamite gun did achieve some success. It exploded on a suspected enemy gun emplacement,

and the Rough Riders cheered as their Colt machine guns
shot down a number of Spaniards fleeing the explosion. The
Arizona men were not impressed by these machine guns
either. They found that they jammed when fired enough to
become hot. According to the Arizona Rough Riders, the
only reliable support weapons throughout the entire campaign were the Gatlings.

That same day, July 10, or perhaps one of the other
brief periods when the truce was not in effect, Tuttle and a
man he identified only as "my partner" were standing guard
in the trenches. The other soldier was standing high in the
trench, needlessly exposing himself to fire at a typical, tiled-
roof building across a ravine. The two Rough Riders thought
they had spotted a sniper inside the building who was shooting at them through a window. Suddenly a rifle bullet slapped
into the earthen parapet a few inches below the exposed
chest of Tuttle's comrade.

"By God," the man exclaimed. "I think that sonovabitch
is ashootin' at me."

"Of course he is, you damn fool. Keep your head down."
Tuttle replied.

Both men then proceeded to open rapid fire at the window. Spurts of dust from the walls marked near misses. The
troopers assumed that a lack of this visible impact indicated
that the shots had gone inside. After placing several bullets
through the window the two Arizonans noted that there was
no longer any return fire from the building. Tuttle's partner
confidently announced that they had "got him."[8]

On July 11 peace was restored and Roosevelt received
orders to move his command a mile to the north and place
it in bivouac along the Santiago-El Caney road. Here the
Rough Riders found themselves directly in the path of Cuban
refugees fleeing Santiago. In contrast to their expressed
contempt for the Cuban soldiers, the Arizonans felt great
compassion for the thousands of ragged, impoverished and

undernourished civilians who fled the city. When his troopers began sharing their reduced rations with these unfortunates, Roosevelt, fearful of contagious disease and anxious to maintain the combat readiness of his regiment, ordered his men to stop aiding the Cubans. The order proved difficult to enforce. Learning of these instructions Charles Hodgdon of A Troop protested: "The Almighty would never let a man catch a disease while he was doing a good favor."[9] Roosevelt was not impressed by such logic and insisted that his order be obeyed.

Most of the Arizona men took every opportunity to express their contempt of the Cuban soldiers. Their grievances were many. The Cuban forces had not supported the landing at Daiquiri; they had refused to get out of their ragged blankets on the morning of June 24 to accompany the Rough Riders to Las Guasimas; they had stolen the blankets and rations left unguarded on the trail just in front of Sevilla; they had failed to prevent a column of Spanish reinforcements from entering Santiago on July 1; and in general they appeared to be unreliable and totally lacking in aggressiveness. Perhaps the opinion held by the Arizonans was best reflected by Chaplain Brown who wrote: "I haven't found a man in the entire army who has any use for the Cubans. . . . Those I have seen which number several thousand, are lazy, ignorant, cowardly and worthless creatures."[10] To a certain extent the high command shared these opinions. General Shafter admitted in his battle reports that the Cuban soldiers were not reliable. Shafter confided that he had ceased to rely on the *Insurrectos* to participate in any serious fighting.

After numerous conferences between the lines, Generals Shafter and Toral finally agreed on July 15 to end the struggle for Santiago. This decision had been made after several alternating periods of truce and fighting. Little blood had been shed, however, as the firing had been limited mostly to artillery. The only prerequisite to the surrender was

Toral's face-saving request that a token bombardment by the Americans precede what the Spanish general preferred to call a "capitulation." That night a battery of Regular artillery fired the last ill-aimed shots over Santiago. By coincidence it was commanded by Captain Allyn Capron Sr., the father of Captain Capron of the Rough Riders who had died at Las Guasimas. Two days later, July 17, the Volunteers gathered on their sandbagged parapets to watch the Ninth Infantry march into the Spanish citadel. Cheers rolled up and down the line as the stars and stripes appeared over the city. Santiago de Cuba had fallen — but the Spaniards still occupied Havana. There was some apprehension that the troops would move immediately to invest that city.

Speculation of an immediate advance on Havana ended the next day when the cavalry division received orders to march five miles to the north toward El Caney. They were to locate camp in a healthier area up in the hills. In 1898 the role played by mosquitoes in the transmission of yellow fever and malaria had not been discovered, but the association of such diseases with low, tropical areas led the army high command and the War Department to assume that locating troops at higher elevations would preclude an epidemic.

The cavalry division was one of the first to be affected by this decision. The Rough Riders began moving in the heat of the day and the men, already weakened by fever and lack of food, reached their destination in a state of exhaustion. A lack of transportation was the biggest problem. Chief Packer Tom Horn, a fellow Arizonan who had come to the territory in 1875 as an employee of the Overland Mail Company and who had packed for Lawton and Wood during the pursuit of Geronimo in 1886, provided a mule train, but it proved to be inadequate and much equipment had to be left in the trenches. Some of the squads in B Troop had rounded up a few stray mules on their own. They were able to make the march with comparative ease. Other groups, less fortunate in their ability to locate stray animals, had to carry their possessions in their own packs.

Upon arrival at their new location, named Camp Hamilton in honor of the commander of the Ninth Cavalry who had fallen at San Juan, the Volunteers made it as comfortable as possible. They quickly removed the brush that covered much of the hill on which they were to bivouac, laid out neat company streets, and pitched their tents — all in conformity with Roosevelt's instructions. In nearby Spanish blockhouses they found wood for tent floors, over which green boughs were laid for beds. A clear stream below the hill provided fresh drinking water and also the first opportunity to bathe in two weeks. In time field kitchens were established along its banks. With a shortage of dry fire wood making cooking difficult, some enterprising foragers from A Troop broke into the nearby summer home of a French consul and removed the mahogany stairs. This wood made a hot but expensive fire — as the United States government later paid for damages. In spite of the healthier location at Camp Hamilton away from the stinking, sodden trenches, the Arizonans, disheartened by their tropical environment, expressed dissatisfaction with their surroundings. "It rains every day here," Webb wrote, "and we are wet all the time. It is a devil of a country to live out doors in."[11]

Weakened by inadequate food and tropical heat, the Volunteers found that the arduous march from San Juan to El Caney destroyed the combat effectiveness of the regiment. The morning after the move one hundred and twenty-three men reported on sick call. This virtually eliminated the First Volunteer Cavalry as an effective fighting force. The Arizonans of A and B Troops suffered a great deal from the effects of wounds and disease. From the fall of Santiago on July 17 to the end of the month, A Troop averaged thirteen men on sick report every day. A similar condition existed in B Troop as shown by roll call on July 15, when only twenty-two of the

(Courtesy Los Angeles County Museum of Natural History)

Three unidentified
Arizona Rough Riders
use Colt revolver butts
to "grind" coffee beans
in iron skillets
in Cuba.

original seventy-one men who went to Cuba answered muster
as present for duty. "I now have but half of the six hundred
men with which I landed four weeks ago fit for duty,"
Colonel Roosevelt wrote Colonel Wood on July 20, "and
these are not fit to do anything like the work they could do
then."[12]

Many of the sick Rough Riders, aware of the persistent
rumors that treatment in division hospitals offered little
change from conditions on line, preferred to stay with their
regiment and refused to be evacuated. The serious fever and
gunshot cases, however, did not have this option and many
were soon berthed on a hospital ship headed for the United
States. On July 3 Major Brodie, Captain McClintock and
other invalids on the hospital ship *Olivette* had the memorable experience of watching Admiral Cervera's barnacle-
encrusted fleet steam out of Santiago harbor to meet destruction under the flaming guns of Admiral Sampson's blockading
squadron. McClintock was particularly impressed by the running battle which ended several miles east of the harbor.

Many of the men absent from the bivouac at El Caney
had been detached to perform some specific service at a different location. One was Nelson A. Bartoo, a member of A
Troop from Williams, who had been an engineer on the
Santa Fe railroad before the war. Bartoo was sent to help
repair and operate the railroad which ran from Daiquiri
to Santiago and over which Shafter tried without success to
transport most of his supplies before the surrender of Santiago. Another was George McCarter from Safford who was
placed on detached service for a time working in a printer's
shop in Santiago. There was much work to be done on the
wharfs both at Santiago and Daiquiri, and many Rough
Riders pulled details unloading or sorting supplies brought
by ship. On one such detail Corporal McCarter was working
on the docks at Santiago with C. E. Mills, the ex-superinten-
dent of the Detroit Copper Company. McCarter recalled that
"while we were bucking flour and grain sacks along the

wharf" he asked Mills why, in view of his obvious qualifications, the husky private had never tried to secure a commission. Mills replied that he "was too good a private to be
spoiled by a commission."[13] Other Arizonans were sent to
help establish a refugee camp near El Caney. Rynning related
that he and several others occupied themselves for a time
issuing salt pork and South American dried beef to the
refugees.

Throughout their campaign in Cuba the Volunteers suffered from insufficient and unappetizing rations. Instead of
the canned corn beef which the troopers preferred, the meat
ration usually consisted of limited quantities of canned roast
beef. This insipid and saltless meat became the object of much
derision among the Arizonans, who called it "canned horse."
In an attempt to make it palatable, the men cooked it with
mangoes, hardtack or any available vegetable to make a stew
called "mulligan" or "slumgullian." Even then they did not
like it. Sergeant Nash of A Troop forcibly expressed the
sentiments of all when he later testified that the roast beef,
"or, as the boys called it, 'canned horse,' was as near devoid
of any wholesomeness or appetizing qualities as it was possible
for beef to be."[14] McClintock considered the meat so bad
that he left "a couple of hundred cans" on the *Yucatan* when
he landed his men at Daiquiri at the beginning of the
campaign.

The rations sent forward at regular intervals after the
fighting ended around San Juan were so inadequate that
Colonel Roosevelt sent details to Siboney and Daiquiri to
acquire more. In fact, the Colonel led some of these foraging
expeditions in person. One Rough Rider in particular, however, was so resourceful that Roosevelt made it a point to call
on him when additional food was needed. In spite of a lack
of transportation, Chaplain Brown never failed to find a
loose horse, wagon or mule and return to camp with a load
of provisions. Brown used the money given to him by the
officers to buy canned tomatoes, beans and sugar to supple-

ment the normal rations of bacon, hardtack and coffee. The chaplain took great pride in his uncommon ability to "rustle" supplies and later related with pride how he rode sixteen miles on three successive days to secure additional food.

In spite of these efforts, the Volunteers continued to suffer from a shortage of rations until July 23. On that day Lieutenant Rynning returned from Santiago with a load of fresh beef. The Arizona boys had the impression that much of the fresh beef was purchased by Colonel Roosevelt. The Regulars had their own version of an attempt by Roosevelt to secure unauthorized supplies. According to their account, Roosevelt made the mistake of putting too much pressure on a young lieutenant of Irish descent in the commissary department. The discussion reputedly ended with Roosevelt sitting on the seat of his pants on the floor.

In spite of the efforts of the Rough Riders to maintain their battle effectiveness, conditions in their camp grew steadily worse. Few cases of yellow fever appeared, but malaria, dengue fever and dysentery affected practically every member of the command at one time or another. The constant tramp of many feet combined with the daily rain to convert the streets into quagmires of black, foul-smelling mud, which forced the men to lace their canvas leggings with care. Shelter tents, which were carefully and repeatedly ditched for drainage, afforded little protection from the rain because they were too short to cover a prostrate occupant. Shoes and other leather goods as well as the canvas trousers, kept in a state of perpetual dampness, began to deteriorate. As no replacements were to be had, the Volunteers assumed a ragged and unkempt appearance.

Waiting in their steaming pup tents for orders, the Rough Riders came out only to perform the necessary routine camp functions. Because the slightest physical exertion brought an attack of fever, the men vigorously protested all assignments to work details. On these occasions the disgruntled members of B Troop gained new respect for First

Sergeant Davidson, who employed his own brand of diplomacy to secure work parties. To the profane objections which greeted his duty assignments, Davidson invariably listened with a tolerant, half-amused smile. When the troopers had finished, he ended all further discussion with the candid observation: "Cuss, that's one privilege a private has got — but, obey me you must."[15] Hughes stated that this comment always brought forth the necessary detail.

As morale deteriorated the ranks of the chronic complainers began to grow. Soldiers always "gripe," but there is a direct and positive relationship between a decreasing amount of work to be done and an increase in the number of complaints. Trooper Webb reflected this. As soon as the fighting ended, Webb's letters became increasingly critical. On August 4 he wrote:

> We have now been lying in this 'recuperation' camp for 17 days and for a 'healthy' location to go to and rest up it is a selection worthy of the mighty brain and ponderous intellect of even a commanding general of the United States' armies. I don't believe there is a blessed soul among the four hundred and odd 'Rough Riders,' who constitute the remnant of a regiment on this island, but who has been sick for a greater or less period of time since we pitched our tent on this healthy (?) campground; excepting perhaps, a few commissioned officers who go to town, four miles away whenever they please, ride on the bay, eat and drink what they wish and have a 'dog robber' to cook for them while out here in camp. Even some of these gentlemen (by an act of Congress), have over played their hands and are lying in town waiting to get well, or sober, before returning to this sweet scented camp.
>
> Nearly everyone in camp is fairly putrid with dysentery. Chills come around each day to shake the majority of us to see if we are still alive. When the chills get tired along comes a most diabolical kind of fever which is warranted to burn a man up entirely in just three hours, it usually stops a trifle short of that spontaneous combustion point, much to the disappointment of the poor victim. Strange as it may seem, though, very few deaths have occurred from natural causes, among the 'Rough Riders' so far, but I will make a prognostication that a pestilence will sweep the camp before September 15th, if we remain here.[16]

Many rumors circulated through the Rough Rider encampment. Some depressed the troopers while others cheered them up. Every soldier who returned from Santiago or the coast brought a new message. Some led the men to believe that they would participate in the Puerto Rico campaign; others predicted an overland drive on Havana. Another rumor, and one that aroused a great deal of optimism, foretold an early return to the United States.

While his men speculated about their departure from Cuba, Roosevelt took positive action to hasten the withdrawal of his regiment. With the tacit approval of General Shafter, the colorful Rough Rider secured the signatures of all general officers, with the exception of Hawkins and Young who were absent sick, to a "round robin" letter addressed to Secretary of War Alger. This statement strongly requested that the Fifth Corps be withdrawn from Cuba before it was destroyed by an epidemic of yellow fever. Unfortunately, the letter was released to the press before it reached Alger. Both he and President McKinley were outraged.

Roosevelt later added to the controversy when he maintained that the "round robin" letter was necessary because the Secretary of War had ordered the army to move into the interior of Cuba where, according to Roosevelt, the dreaded fever would surely have destroyed it. Alger, however, subsequently denied this accusation, pointing out that he had been concerned about the health of Shafter's force for some time prior to Roosevelt's action. As early as July 26, eight days before the officers in Cuba expressed their opinion, Alger had ordered construction to begin on a camp at Long Island so that the veterans could return to a cooler climate. Alger went on to explain that the day before he received the "round robin" he had actually issued orders for Wheeler's division to move to Long Island. Because of this Alger concluded: "It would be impossible to exaggerate the mischievous and wicked effects of the 'Round Robin.' "[17]

In contrast to criticism from the War Department over the unsolicited advice, Colonel Roosevelt received the gratitude of his unhappy troopers for taking the lead in securing the "round robin." Lieutenant Sherrard Coleman of the regimental staff later wrote: "It was Colonel Roosevelt who got the troops back home from the fever-ladened atmosphere of Santiago. . . . He was the life and support of what was left of us."[18] This feeling increased in later years when it became known that Secretary Alger had refused to submit Roosevelt's name to Congress with the recommendation that he receive the Congressional Medal of Honor.

The Medal of Honor was one thing Colonel Roosevelt wanted and he tried hard to secure it. After the war he sought testimonies from his old comrades to forward in support of the recommendation made by Colonel and later General Wood that Roosevelt receive the coveted award. On January 4, 1899, Roosevelt wrote to Maxwell Keyes, the first lieutenant of F Troop who had replaced Lieutenant Hall as adjutant, requesting that Keyes write a "certificate" to the adjutant general. Keyes was asked to be very specific, giving his name, rank, and stating that he was an eyewitness to the events he described. Roosevelt went on to explain: "The act (leading the two charges, one on horseback, on my own initiative, and going through the regulars and ordering the charge) should be set forth specifically and as much in detail as you are able."[19] In spite of everything that he could do, Roosevelt did not get the medal. The Rough Riders became convinced that this was because the "round robin" and Roosevelt's critical comments about the conduct of the war in general had alienated both Secretary Alger and President McKinley beyond the point of conciliation.

At the time, however, some of the more perceptive individuals were aware of the political implications of the "round robin." On August 4, with a sagacity beyond his age, young Tuttle interpreted Roosevelt's motives in a letter to his brother back in Safford. Tuttle wrote: "Rosy is trying to get us back so he can run for Governor of New York."[20] Unfortunately, it is not known how widespread this interpretation was, for, in contrast to Tuttle's interesting evaluation, it is commonly accepted that Roosevelt did not make the final decision about the gubernatorial candidacy until after the regiment had returned late in August.

Indications that the long-awaited orders would soon arrive came on August 2, when the first sergeants fell their men out to draw new clothing. "We drew new uniforms the other day, and what in the name of the master of ceremonies in the infernal region we are going to do with them I do not know," complained Webb, who added: "When fully 'ragged out' a Rough Rider trooper now looks about like R. Allyn Lewis, Arizona's brave Adjutant General, in full dress, and a drum-major rolled into one."[21] The clothing issue included badly needed boots, underwear and cotton socks, as well as colorful jackets and trousers of khaki. In addition to shiny brass buttons, yellow cloth decorated the pocket flaps, shoulder straps and cuffs of the belted, pleated jacket. Accustomed to their drab, but practical uniforms, the Arizonans received the new issue with resentment. They felt that the government had used its limited transportation facilities to ship "monkey suits" only suitable for parade ground drill.

After they donned their new clothing the Rough Riders burned their ragged, faded combat uniforms. That afternoon the puzzled Volunteers received snappy salutes from several Regular cavalrymen who passed through the camp. Confused and dazzled by the inordinate display of brass and yellow-cloth finery on the special uniforms made up for the Volunteer Cavalry, the Regulars had mistaken each Volunteer for a commissioned officer. Upon returning to their own units, these angry troopers protested that every "damn one of those damn Rough Riders has been made a second lieutenant."[22] At first amused by this unwarranted promotion, several troopers later capitalized on it in Santiago when they found that the military police, under the same erroneous impression, allowed Rough Riders the freedom of movement commensurate with the officers.

Late in the afternoon of August 6 the shrill notes of officers' call summoned the commanders to Roosevelt's tent. For some unexplainable reason the troopers had a strong pre-

monition and gathered in little groups near the tent. When
the meeting broke up, one officer strolled over to a group of
soldiers and calmly remarked: "The orders have come; we
are going home tomorrow noon."[23] The responding thunder
of cheers, soon echoed by the cavalry regiments bivouacked
nearby, surpassed any such ovation heard since the victory
at Guasimas and reflected the universal desire to leave the
fever-ridden island. Any lingering skepticism vanished the following day when the Volunteers received orders to strike
camp. In contrast to the procedure followed on previous
moves, wagons arrived to transport personal baggage and
troop equipment. Surprised by this unexpected consideration, the Arizonans had only their weapons to shoulder as
they marched away without striking their shelter tents. After
a difficult two-mile march characterized by considerable strag-
gling, the long column reached a railroad siding where a line
of dilapidated cars hitched to an old wood-burning locomo-
tive waited to take them to Santiago.

At Santiago the Rough Riders marched directly to the
wharf area and boarded a steel-decked transport, the *Miami*,
for the voyage home. Since the ship, which some troopers
described as a "converted cattle boat," did not sail until the
next day, some of the men drew a month's pay and received
permission to visit the city. A few had been there earlier, but
for most this was their first visit and they found it interesting
to wander the narrow streets and study the ancient city. In
the poor sections the structures were mostly of adobe. Both
houses and streets were cluttered with refuse and swarming
with half-naked children, who studied the *Americanos* with
wide-eyed curiosity. Dwellings in the better sections were of
a more permanent construction. They had stucco walls with
elaborately carved balconies and intricately laced wrought-iron
trellises in the windows. The cathedral stood in the central
plaza near the Governor's Palace where General Wood had
established his offices as military governor. Many of the
troopers noticed the dour looks cast toward them by the priest
in residence at the cathedral. It was commonly assumed that

he was particularly offended by having the streets of his city filled with hated *Yanqui* or *Gringo* Protestants. The opera house and several *cantinas* — the most popular of which was the "Cafe Venas" — also opened onto the central plaza. The plaza itself was typically Spanish. The city was not spoiled by fortifications, most of which had been placed on the outskirts.

Many of the Arizonans had unusual experiences in Santiago. Liquor, women and simple relaxation were the attractions. Border Spanish, acquired in the mines, on the ranches and in the practice of everyday life in Arizona, made it easy for the troopers from the Southwest to communicate with both the inhabitants and the Spanish soldiers still in the city. With this advantage those who sought after feminine companionship had no difficulty in securing their goal — although some of the more discriminating Volunteers changed their minds upon finding that the girls, who waved and smiled from behind barred windows, appeared to be dirty upon close inspection. The troopers who visited the *cantinas* found that their United States currency bought ample quantities of local rum and sweet Spanish wine. In one cafe Tuttle and several comrades came across a group of Spanish officers who, with true Latin courtesy and mistaking the resplendent new uniforms of the Volunteers for the dress of commissioned officers, invited the troopers to be their guests. Now that the fighting had ended, this social contact revealed a Spanish characteristic not perceived on the battlefield. As Tuttle later recalled: "They were real gentlemen."[24]

By early afternoon the troopers began returning to the ship. Many of them came back early because their disease-weakened bodies would not hold up under too much exertion. Some of the men brought tobacco, candy, fruit and other delicacies to supplement their diet on the return voyage. A few bottles of liquor also were brought aboard. According to Lieutenant Royal Prentice of E Troop, several troopers from New Mexico came up the gangway bearing the unmistakable signs of a brawl they had started with a group of United States sailors. With few exceptions the Rough Riders had all returned to the *Miami* by dark.

Early on the morning of August 7 the *Miami,* carrying General Wheeler, a squadron of the Third Cavalry and the Rough Riders, cast off and steamed out of Santiago harbor. With troops lining the rails, the ship passed between the impressive walls of Morro Castle and the silent guns in the fortifications at Scoapa across the bay. The men cheered upon seeing Hobson's ill-fated *Merrimac* and silently noted the exposed decks of the *Reina Mercedes,* a gunboat scuttled by the Spaniards in an abortive attempt to seal the harbor before dawn on July 5. Farther on, as the ship entered the open sea, the troopers saw a riddled and beached derelict of Admiral Cervera's fleet, which had vainly tried to break Sampson's blockade. Objects identified as human bodies still floated in the wreckage. Turning east the *Miami* passed by Siboney and Daiquiri, where the Volunteers had landed forty-seven days before. Late that evening the Rough Riders took their last look at the green hills of Cuba. "Farewell to the land where we have fought and suffered," wrote an elated Roger Fitch in his diary.[25]

The Rough Riders had been looking forward to going home for a long time. They had gone to Cuba to fight — and not to sweat through the malaria season that followed the surrender. Conditions had been bad enough during the fighting, but they had become worse after the fall of Santiago. Tropical storms had converted the primitive roads into quagmires and this, in turn, had made delivery of supplies and rations impossible. The hot, humid climate had reduced the troopers' natural resistance to tropical fevers. Even more disheartening had been the apathy of the Cuban people, who had not rallied to support the campaign. As one trooper told McClintock: "We have seen many a worse place than Arizona in our travels."[26]

CHAPTER 7

Awaiting Orders At Tampa

WHILE MORE THAN HALF OF THE ROUGH RIDERS were winning praise and glory in the skirmish lines in Cuba, an almost equal number fought the frustrating, unrewarding battle of the picket lines in the swamplike, malaria-ridden encampment at Tampa, Florida. Left with the care of the regimental horses and mules, these men had been promised they would quickly follow the rest of the regiment to Cuba, as soon as transport became available. In the meantime, as they waited for orders that never came, they struggled with the twin enemies of boredom and disease. They suffered extensive casualties to both. The hot, humid climate sapped the enthusiasm and energy even of those who were marked fit for duty. Tampa, with its bars and dance halls, afforded the only form of relaxation.

Originally, Major Henry B. Hersey commanded approximately four hundred and seventy-five officers and men. This was only one hundred less than the number Colonel Wood had taken to Cuba. Hersey had four troops of approximately eighty-five men each, and eight detachments of about fifteen men each. Of this group, three officers and one hundred and seven men were of the Arizona squadron. Captain Alexander had three officers and eighty-four men assigned to his own C Troop, and he also had twenty-three men detached from A and B Troops and for whom he was to a certain extent responsible. These two detachments had to rely on Alexander for the use of much organizational equipment, for their parent units had taken most troop property to Cuba. Alexander also handled such routine matters as discipline, pay and other functions requiring the presence or actions of an officer. This procedure was followed by the other detachments. Captain George Curry of H Troop supervised the detached New Mexicans from E, F and G Troops. Captain Robert Bruce of M Troop performed a similar function for the men from the Indian Territory from L Troop.

Left with the understanding that they would take the horses to Cuba as soon as transportation became available, the troopers waited expectantly for orders. On three separate occasions Hersey's squadron received an alert; but each time cancellation orders squelched the premature exultation. Even General Shafter, who realized the need for mounted troops after Las Guasimas, was unable to secure their services. On June 28 Shafter contacted Alger: "Wired yesterday would like First Cavalry horses and Wood's, with squadron of those regiments left at Tampa, but they should come at once. With them I do not think the enemy could escape."[1] Alger refused to act on this request and the great opportunity passed forever. The rank and file, of course, did not know of Shafter's request but, as time passed and no orders arrived, the men began to realize that they were not going to Cuba. Heartsick over the situation, the troopers began to lose confidence in the military.

The camp was in a miserable location. Established on low ground three miles west of Tampa and near the bay, it had inadequate drainage and stagnant pools formed when the summer rains came. Dark, sonorous clouds of mosquitoes rose from these miasmatic breeding places each evening to descend on the Volunteers. During the day these pests were replaced by swarms of flies, which buzzed incessantly around the picket lines of 1,200 horses and mules near the camp. In time the bivouac in the bottom land was abandoned, and the men moved to a sandy ridge, covered with scrub oak, which encircled most of Tampa Bay. The men were now out of the mud, but there was no relief from the winged insects. Fortunately, there was a supply of good water piped from the city, but it arrived warm, for the pipe lay on top of the ground exposed to the sun.

As the hot days of June passed, morale, that invisible backbone of a military unit, began to deteriorate. Whether or not they were aware of an old military axiom that the status of morale in any combat organization is reflected in the appearance of its members is debatable, but the visitors to the Arizona bivouac noted that Captain Alexander's men deplored their forced inactivity. There was little military uniformity. The men wore ill-kept uniforms. Sleeves were rolled up, leggings and suspenders were worn only by a few and hat brims were shaped according to whim. Each man soaked his hat in a pail of water and then rolled the wet brim into any shape he desired. When the hats dried, the results were different and sometimes spectacular. Tom Sloan, a native of Arizona, traveled to Tampa to enlist in C Troop. In a letter home he described some of the men from Phoenix. Sloan wrote: "Phil [Private Philip M.] Herald has a fine crop of whiskers of which he is justly proud. [Corporal Frank A.] Woodin looks like a train robber. [Corporal Charles E.] Heitman is the only respectable looking one of the whole outfit."[2]

In the same letter Sloan also indicated that several officers had made themselves unpopular by their arbitrary behavior. Captain Alexander, it was rumored, was having disciplinary problems with his men. A few days later Tom Davenport, a mule packer from Phoenix stationed at Tampa, refuted this allegation by insisting that Alexander had established good relations with his men.

The Rough Riders forcibly expressed their discontent to the visitors and correspondents who entered the bivouac. They complained that they had enlisted to fight Spaniards and not to perform sham battles in the palmetto groves of Florida. They had expected to find fever and disease in the humid jungles of Cuba, but to contend with similar conditions in their own country far removed from the enemy was another matter. As cavalrymen they appreciated the necessity of caring for their own mounts, but they had not entered the federal service to serve as "horse grooms" for others.[3] Some couldn't take it. On July 9 Private John H. Jackson, a twenty-nine-year-old carpenter from Jerome who had been left at Tampa with A Troop's detachment, deserted rather than face the monotony of garrison duty in Florida. A total of six men in other troops also deserted.

In order to relieve monotony the officers tried their best to keep the men occupied and free from undue harassment. Alexander began drill each morning at daybreak before the day became too hot. Upon completion of the routine camp functions which followed drill, the troopers retired to their tents to seek protection from the burning sun. As part of the July 4 celebration H Troop, led by the popular bronco buster Tom Darnell, issued a challenge for a "roping, riding, and shooting match" to any cavalry troop for a purse of $100.00 to $500.00.[4] The New Mexicans had great faith in the outcome, largely because of the riding ability of Darnell, who had worked many years on the "Upper A Outfit" near Deming, New Mexico. He was reputed to be the best rider in H Troop, which was supposed to contain the best equestrians in the entire regiment. One troop from the Second Cavalry, whose members were eager to take on the famous Rough Riders, accepted the challenge, but at the last moment the Volunteers withdrew their proposition. There is no explanation as to why the New Mexicans backed down. Late in July, Captain

George Curry of H Troop hired an excursion boat and took
his men for a tour of the bay. Such endeavors were stop-gap
measures only and had no appreciable effect on morale.

Problems also arose over the question of rations. The
Arizonans complained about the quality as well as the quan-
tity of the food issued at Tampa. For example, the troopers
received such unusual meals as grease-covered pork and pota-
toes with coffee for breakfast. Because his squadron received
the Regular Army issue, Captain Curry, who temporarily
succeeded Major Hersey as the squadron commander, concluded that the problem originated within his own command.
Together with the acting post adjutant, Lieutenant Hay Sayre
of C Troop, Curry assembled enough evidence to justify the
arrest of his quartermaster sergeant, charging that he had sold
government rations — particularly fresh vegetables — to civilian merchants. Curry immediately had the man confined,
appointed another quartermaster sergeant and prepared a
court-martial. Before it could be held, however, the regiment
began to prepare for deactivation and the officers decided to
permit the man to resign in order to avoid the delay and
trouble of going through with a trial.

Notwithstanding the adverse conditions at Tampa, Alexander's Arizonans remained in good health at first. During
June and early July only two or three men were absent each
day. Toward the end of July and early August, however, the
number of absentees rose alarmingly. By the middle of August
C Troop averaged over twenty men on sick report every day.
In addition to malaria and dysentery, the two most common
afflictions, typhoid also appeared at Tampa, claiming the lives
of Nathaniel B. Adsit from Buffalo, New York, on August 1,
Thomas M. Newnhome from Phoenix on August 4, Charles
A. Armstrong from San Jose, California, on August 27, and
Frank H. Clearwater from Brownsville, Texas, on September
2. Several others had to be discharged because of disability.
The regimental surgeon, Henry LaMotte, who had returned
to Tampa after Las Guasimas, later testified that the increased

sickness came as a result of lax discipline which permitted the "sinks," or latrines, to go unattended.

Although the three Arizona troops suffered a combined loss of twenty men because of enemy action, disease, transfers or for other reasons during June and July, the squadron actually gained strength because of new enlistments. Even after the battle of San Juan the magical name "Roosevelt's Rough Riders" had a great attraction, and recruits came from all over the country to join. This wave of enlistments was referred to as the "second draft" by Captain McClintock. Between June 13 and August 7, five recruits arrived in Tampa for duty with C Troop. They were: George P. Bowler from New York City; Thomas M. Sloan from Phoenix; Nathaniel B. Adsit from Buffalo, New York; Edward C. Hall from New Haven, Connecticut; and Ashley Pond from Detroit. During the same period fifteen men joined the Tampa detachment of A Troop. They were: Ralph R. Adams from Yonkers, New York; Henry N. Arnold, Paul S. Pearsall, and Henry F. Sewell from New York City; Rufus K. Thomas and Prescott H. Belknap from Boston; Lew W. Brauer and George P. Hawes from Richmond, Virginia; Leroy B. Church from Ithaca, Michigan; William H. Glover from Liberty, Texas; Edward Haymon from Chicago; Joseph E. Thompson from Washington; Henry B. Pierce from Central City, New Mexico; and Thomas L. Freeman and Lawrence Huffman from Santa Fe, New Mexico. Corporal Heitman, in charge of B Troop's detachment, accepted the services of the following: Wallace W. Wilkerson, Robert Day, John C. Peck, and James A. Butler from Santa Fe; Lowell A. Chamberlin from Washington, D.C.; Frank W. Gurney, Conrad F. Goss, and John P. Heywood from Tampa; William W. Merritt from Red Oak, Iowa; Horatio Pollock from Phoenix; Charles M. Tilkie from Chicago; George C. Whittaker from Silver City, New Mexico; and Gould Norton from Tampa.

Some controversy surrounds the enlistment of Gould Norton, who was the third member of his family to join.

When Captain McClintock had formed his troop back in Prescott, he had enlisted Edward Norton, a twenty-two-year-old nurseryman from Phoenix. A few weeks later, on May 27, Edward's younger brother, Oliver B. Norton, came to San Antonio and enlisted in B Troop alongside his brother. The third member of the family, Gould, came to Tampa and enlisted in B Troop's Tampa detachment on June 29. Edward Marshall, in his *Story of the Rough Riders,* related that when Gould arrived at Tampa, he bore a letter from his father to Captain McClintock which stated in part: "This is my third son, I send him to you to take the place of my son Oliver, who was killed."[5] Interestingly enough, McClintock corroborated this story — not in 1916 when he published his most factual account of the Rough Riders — but in 1931 when he delivered a radio address under the auspices of the Union Oil Company of Arizona.

According to the official records of B Troop, the father of the Norton boys could not have written such a letter. Oliver was killed on July 1 at Kettle Hill, while Gould enlisted two days earlier on June 29.

Some of the new recruits found their way to Cuba. Shortly after the fall of Santiago on July 15, Roosevelt replaced Colonel Wood as commander of the Second Cavalry Brigade, Wood having been made Military Governor of Santiago. As this left only one field grade officer, Major Micah Jenkins, to assist him, Roosevelt ordered Major Hersey to Cuba. This gave several troopers an opportunity to get to the island, and Hersey took approximately twenty-five men with him. Of this group at least one, Horatio C. Pollock, who had enlisted on July 3 in B Troop, was from the Arizona contingent. Two others, John D. Hubbell from Boston and Willis McCormick from Salt Lake City, traveled to Cuba on their own initiative and there enlisted in A Troop on July 20. Several newspaper correspondents also enlisted in the regiment. Because most of them came from the East, they joined Woodbury Kane's K Troop.

In addition to caring for 1,200 horses and mules, the Rough Riders also had to provide for their mascots. Now approaching maturity, "Josephine," the puma brought by the Arizonans, succumbed to her natural instinct to prowl at night. One evening she escaped from her cage and slipped among the horses. They stampeded, breaking loose from the picket lines in terror. The next day the Volunteers rounded up their nervous mounts and soundly cursed the nocturnal habits of the young mountain lion. In contrast to the unreliable and ill-tempered Josephine, the golden eagle "Teddy," brought by the New Mexico contingent, wandered the company streets untethered and thoroughly content with his military adventure. The other mascot, "Cuba," a small dog brought by the group from Indian Territory, accompanied Colonel Wood's troops throughout the Santiago campaign and returned to the United States with them.

At first the men were permitted passes into nearby towns. Most of them sought relief from boredom in Tampa, where their own inclinations and soldier's pay led them to congregate in the cheap cafes and houses of the red light district. There a series of near riots soon broke out, causing a quick curtailment in the number of passes issued.

One such incident occurred at a house on Central Avenue near Cass Street operated by a madam named Alice May and referred to locally as a "dive." Such establishments had already experienced some rough evenings in several cases which the somewhat moralistic Tampa papers described as "rape by drunken soldiers." The girls had become wary of entertaining soldiers already obviously inebriated. Shortly after midnight one hot June night, three mule packers and two Rough Riders from the horse detail, left behind by L Troop, sought admission at Alice May's, but were turned back at the door. Angered by the rebuff, they drew pistols and foolishly prepared to shoot their way in.

Indoors, the occupants refused to be intimidated by some drunken soldiers. They armed themselves, rallied around

Alice May and the battle was on. Before the smoke cleared
away and a provost guard from the Fifth Maryland Infantry
hurried up to arrest the soldiers, Alice May was shot in the
leg, and one of the troopers was shot in the arm. All the men
were under various charges facing civilian court action. The
Tampa *Tribune,* in reporting the incident, held strictly to
the old shibboleth that one drunken soldier indicated a
drunken army, and subtitled the incident:

SHOT A WOMAN
PRIVATES AND PACKERS OF THE
ROUGH RIDERS ARE IN JAIL[6]

One of the regimental officers, incorrectly identified as
the "captain of L Troop," attempted to salve public relations
when he announced that the troop was "well rid of such
men." None of the officers in L Troop, of course, could have
been involved in the incident, which happened on June
22. On that day Captain Allyn Capron, First Lieutenant John
Thomas and Second Lieutenant Richard C. Day, whose real
name was supposed to have been Rolla C. Dwinnel, were
in Cuba preparing to guide L Troop into action at Las
Guasimas. The detachment left in Tampa was under the
control of Captain Robert Bruce who commanded M Troop,
the other unit from the Indian Territory.

The troopers from Arizona had other difficulties in
Tampa. One problem involved military courtesy. Corporal
French of C Troop, because of his good behavior and strict
observance of military custom, occasionally received permission to go to town. Once he took Private William Sexsmith,
a cowboy from Yuma, with him. Sexsmith and another inde-
pendent-minded trooper from Yuma, "Al" Neville, had taken
an oath never to salute an officer. This apparently had caused
no trouble until this particular day on the streets of Tampa. A
portly major, offended by Sexsmith's failure to salute and
not appeased by French's snappy attention to military courtesy, accosted the husky private and gave him an opportunity

to correct the oversight. When Sexsmith again refused to salute him, the major summoned military police. Sexsmith decided to resist but, after managing to knock one of the arresting soldiers down, the big private was subdued and placed in the guard house for eleven days. Each day the major turned up to give the cowboy a chance to render the long-overdue salute. "The record shows," recalled French, "that he never did."[7]

Much of the destruction perpetrated in Tampa was by boisterous soldiers from units other than the First Volunteer Cavalry. Apparently these errant soldiers felt that Roosevelt's national stature rendered his men immune to arrest and they all claimed to be Rough Riders when apprehended. Consequently, many incidents came to be erroneously reported. This fact became a matter of public record shortly before the squadron left Tampa when an apology appeared in the Tampa *Tribune*.

Marshal Burke says the Rough Riders have given him less trouble than any organization in either regular or volunteer army that has camped here. Many arrests have been made where the arrested parties claimed to be Rough Riders, and the accounts were published giving the regiment credit for their devilment. When these cases were investigated it would be found that the offenders were wagoners, packmen, or belonged to some other cavalry regiment.[8]

A few days later Marshal Burke held another interview, claiming that "there is no more gentlemanly nor better behaved set of men found anywhere," than the Rough Riders.[9] But by that time the Volunteers had acquired a soiled reputation — a reputation they never quite lived down.

The charge of irresponsibility and lack of discipline that invariably came to be associated with the Rough Riders was always considered to be a grave injustice by the troopers. Many of them spent the rest of their lives stoutly defending their military bearing and record. Even Roosevelt in his book delved into the subject of discipline to the point of being repetitious and somewhat apologetic. The most outspoken proponent of the Arizona squadron in this respect was

McClintock, who expressed the feeling of all the Volunteers when he wrote: "We are proud of our regiment, tho we only wish it known not as a Wild West troupe, but as a body of disciplined American volunteer soldiers."[10]

Disciplined or not, the western miners and cowboys with their athletic eastern comrades made a lasting impression on those who served with them. For example, Kurtz Eppley, a member of Essex Troop of the New Jersey National Guard stationed at Tampa, described vividly the Rough Riders on duty there:

The Riders are the toughest set of men I have ever met. Many of them are outlaws and I might venture to state that 70 per cent of them are 'man killers' of some note in one part or another of the wild and woolly West. They drink, gamble and raise the devil generally. Their language is beyond description and they are always fighting and ready to shoot at the first chance that offers. They all carry 45-calibre six-shooters and knives and when they get in Tampa on a good time they make things howl.

Although awed by these Volunteers, Eppley revealed another facet of western character when he commented on the generous nature of the Rough Riders. "On the other hand," he continued, "they always stand ready to help a fellow out of any difficulty, and will share their last cent with you."[11]

Early in August the order came for the Rough Riders at Tampa to move to Long Island and prepare for discharge. These orders came as no surprise, for different regiments had been leaving Tampa for two weeks. Of course, many rumors had preceded the final orders, but after the surrender of Santiago in July, one story whose persistency rendered it an air of authenticity predicted that Roosevelt's men would move north for discharge. Consequently, everyone at Tampa was expecting the move. A myriad of tasks faced the Volunteers before they could entrain for Long Island. Equipment had to be cleaned and stored on the baggage cars; horses had to be prepared for shipment on stock cars; and the multitude of small details which surrounded the closing of the camp-grounds had to be completed. Although the effective strength of C Troop had been reduced to seventy-nine per cent by fever — one officer and nineteen men were absent out of three officers and eighty-one men assigned — the remaining troopers eagerly fell to their tasks. They were motivated by the knowledge that a quick consolidation of the regiment at one camp was a prerequisite to an early discharge. On August 8 the leading elements of the Florida detachment pulled out in cars provided by the Florida Central and Peninsular Railroad. They were going north at last.

The departure of the Rough Riders from Tampa ended a disappointing period of active duty. Almost forgotten by the press, nearly half of the regiment had remained in anonymity while their comrades had been mentioned for gallantry in Cuba. Although they had not seen combat, the unacclimated troopers had suffered through a difficult summer. Disease and boredom had been relentless enemies. Even though they took great pride in the accomplishments of their comrades in Cuba, the fact remained that they had not done any fighting. Even the attempts of Roosevelt, who complimented them on the way they had followed orders, failed to placate them. For the rest of their lives, especially at the gatherings of the veterans' organizations, many of these men would fear the inevitable question: "Were you left behind with the horse detail?"[12]

CHAPTER 8

Back To Arizona

THE FIGHTING IN CUBA HAD ENDED.

For all practical purposes the Spanish-American War was over.

The United States government now undertook the withdrawal of the Fifth Corps from Cuba. These veterans were to be assembled at a recuperation camp at Montauk Point, Long Island. There they were to recover from the effects of the Santiago campaign and there the Volunteer components were to be disbanded. One of the first elements to gather at Long Island was General Wheeler's cavalry division. This unit came north in two sections, with the Tampa detachment, coming by train, arriving first. It helped prepare the grounds for the veterans then enroute from Cuba. By the middle of September the division was firmly settled, and the Rough Riders, the only Volunteer regiment in the division, was ready to be mustered out.

Secretary Alger selected a site on Long Island because of the mild climate. It was named Camp Wikoff in honor of

Colonel Charles A. Wikoff, killed at the head of his Second Infantry Brigade at San Juan. The camp was located at the eastern end of Long Island near Montauk Point, one hundred and fifty miles from New York City. The post had to be built from scratch. General Young, commander of the Second Cavalry Brigade, who had returned from Cuba early because of illness, started construction on August 5. In addition to the main bivouac area, General Young was ordered to build a yellow fever quarantine station near the wharf where debarkation would take place. The fear of yellow fever was so acute that medical authorities insisted that provisions be made to quarantine all returning soldiers until it could be verified that they did not have the dreaded disease.

Although the civilian employees worked hard, they did not have Camp Wikoff completed when the first units arrived. Part of the difficulty was a lack of transportation. A single-track railroad provided the only means of bringing in tents, lumber and other material. In early August, when it became apparent that the camp could not be completed with the existing labor force, the Tampa detachment of the cavalry division was sent north to help with construction.

The leading elements of the Rough Riders from Florida arrived at Montauk on August 11. Plans called for the Volunteers to come north in sections, with the arrival times of the eight groups staggered, to avoid congestion at the railroad depot in Jersey City where the men had to transfer to the Long Island railroad. The over-taxed transport facilities could not handle even this reduced traffic and congestion developed in spite of all efforts to avoid it. Lieutenant Hal Sayre and the detachment from A Troop were held for two days in the Fourth Regiment's Armory in Jersey City before transportation became available. By the time Sayre's group arrived at Montauk on August 15, their comrades in C and B Troops already had their camp established and were preparing to receive the men arriving from Cuba.

The Arizonans were pleased to find that Alexander O. Brodie was back to take command of the Tampa group at Long Island. After being wounded at Guasimas, Brodie had been evacuated from Cuba and hospitalized for a time at Fort Wadsworth, New York. He had then been on convalescent leave with relatives in New York. On August 11, his shattered right arm still suspended in a black sling and wearing the coveted shoulder straps of a lieutenant colonel, Brodie arrived to take charge of the Rough Riders at Montauk. His promotion was possible because Roosevelt had been advanced to full colonel when Wood became a general.

Lieutenant Colonel Brodie's advancement completed the promotion cycle of the original officers from Arizona. While enroute to Cuba, there had been a ringing toast in the officers' mess: "The officers; may the war last until each is killed, wounded or promoted."[1] The original line officers from Arizona fulfilled this pledge to an extent that exceeded any other territorial group. Both second lieutenants who left Prescott, George Wilcox and Robert Patterson, became first lieutenants to fill vacancies created by the formation of C Troop. Captain McClintock's first lieutenant, Joseph Alexander, became a captain to command the new troop. Frank Frantz, first lieutenant in A Troop, became a captain because of the valor he demonstrated after the untimely death of his commander. Captain Buckey O'Neill, the sole commissioned Arizonan to comply with the more grisly alternative of the toast, found an early grave at San Juan. Only Captain McClintock, doomed to walk with a pronounced limp for the rest of his life, had the same rank upon discharge that he had when he reported for duty at San Antonio.

Under the capable supervision of Lieutenant Colonel Brodie and Captain Alexander, the Arizonans worked hard to organize their new bivouac. They knew that they had only a few days to prepare the camp for their comrades who had already left Cuba and were steaming north somewhere off the Atlantic coast. A sufficient number of four man tents to

Maj. Alexander Brodie, commander of 1st Squadron of
Rough Riders, pictured in San Antonio prior to departure for Cuba. (*Courtesy Sharlot Hall Museum.*)

accommodate the entire regiment had been issued, but they
had to be both pitched and floored. Although lumber and
nails had been provided, there were no carpenter tools. Captain Alexander, who was hailed as a "rustling-son-of-a-gun"
and whose men considered him capable of locating food and
water in the middle of the Sahara desert, immediately presented his case to the camp commander. General Young supplied him with eight saws and an equal number of hatchets.
With this equipment the Arizonans were able to floor their
tents ahead of the other troops, but they had not completed
their quarters when the *Miami* arrived. All work on the camp
stopped as most of the troopers gathered on the long wharf at
Fort Pond Bay to greet the ragged veterans of Santiago.

The home-bound Rough Riders enjoyed the six-day
voyage from Santiago to Long Island. The salt air and fresh
breezes were a welcome relief from the sweltering jungles of
Cuba, and the men spent as much time on deck as possible.
Larger and less crowded than the *Yucatan,* the transport that
had taken them to Cuba, the *Miami* afforded ample room for
the men to stroll about and study the small keys of the Bahama
islands as they passed. At night the troopers gathered in easy
comradeship, smoking and watching the Southern Cross
ride lower in the sky each successive evening until it finally
disappeared below the horizon. Only one incident marred the
voyage for the Arizona men. On August 11 Private George
Walsh, a native of San Francisco who had enlisted in A Troop
at the age of forty-three, died of chronic dysentery. That
night Private Tuttle and Corporal John D. Honeyman of
San Antonio sewed the body in a canvas shroud with four
iron grate bars for ballast. The next morning the soldier was
buried at sea.

Colonel Roosevelt said that Walsh fell sick with dysentery after drinking native rum found at Daiquiri shortly
after landing on June 22. He marched with the regiment to
Siboney the next day before he was entirely sober. "He never
recovered," Roosevelt concluded, "and was useless from that

time on."[2] Nevertheless, the Arizona men thought it tragic that one of their comrades died so close to home after surviving enemy bullets and tropical fevers in a foreign land.

In contrast to the relaxed attitude taken by the men, the officers continued their plans to instigate a vigorous training program on Long Island. They were unaware that peace negotiations were already in progress, and they fully expected to participate as mounted cavalry in an assault on Havana. On August 14, however, when the *Miami* arrived off Long Island, it was learned that an armistice had been declared. This welcome message was delivered by the officer of a gunboat who met the transport as it dropped anchor late in the evening. Word was received that on July 26 Spanish officials formally declared a willingness to give up Cuba, and on August 12, at Washington, they had agreed to relinquish all claim to Cuba and to cede Puerto Rico to the United States. With this cheering news the Rough Riders knew that they had not campaigned in vain; they would do no more fighting in Cuba — or anywhere else.

The next day, August 15, the Rough Riders came ashore at Montauk Point. News of the event brought a large crowd to greet the Volunteers. It was composed of off-duty soldiers from the camp and civilians, who had gathered from as far away as New York City. The Rough Riders at Montauk had requested permission to form the honor guard, but this duty had been delegated to a troop from the First Regular Cavalry. On the ship the cavalrymen formed by troops beneath their tattered guidons, and the Third Cavalry band struck up "Rally Round the Flag" to play the men ashore.

General Wheeler, his staff and Colonel Roosevelt came down the gangway first, followed by the Third Cavalry and then the Volunteers. At first the crowd, cheering and applauding, pushed forward against the restraining line of guards, but fell suddenly silent as the wretched condition of the troopers became obvious. Gaunt and haggard in uniforms that no longer fit their emaciated bodies, the men came

ashore with downcast eyes and the measured tread of sick
men. The correspondent for the *New York Times* commented that the men were too sick to appreciate the welcome
they received. All the troops clearly reflected the ravages
of the campaign, but Frantz's A Troop appeared to have suffered the most. Barely thirty men had strength to march
off the ship. "My God," exclaimed one startled member of
A Troop's Tampa detachment, "there are not half the men
there that left."[3]

The haunting specter of yellow fever as a hidden and
unwelcome passenger caused the medical corps to segregate
the men returning from Cuba. To accomplish this a quarantine station had been established two miles from the debarkation site. After a short rest on the beach, the cavalrymen in
early afternoon began moving for this station. Wagons transported those too ill to march, but several determined Volunteers declined this convenience and tried to stay with the
regiment. Two Arizonans, Corporal George McCarter from
Safford and another man incorrectly identified as William
Whalen of A Troop — the muster rolls show no such man in
the regiment—collapsed alongside the road. While they waited
for the wagons, three New York women saw their plight and
brought them a large basket of fresh fruit. One of the ladies
was reported to have remarked that a good drink of whiskey
would have been more beneficial than a handful of fruit.

At the quarantine station all contact between the veterans and those who had not gone to Cuba was prohibited for
ninety-six hours. To enforce this edict guards were posted just
inside the wire fence of the quarantine station. The officers
unwisely directed that the guards be drawn from the troops
which had been in Cuba. The results were not in accord
with the intent of the quarantine. The Arizona men were in
general agreement that the isolation existed in name only and
that troopers slipped in and out of the station with impunity
during the entire period of theoretical confinement. The only
reason that more did not take advantage of this lack of

discipline was because it was too far to the nearest town of any size.

Four days later, August 19, the Rough Riders in the quarantine station moved to Camp Wikoff. Here they came under the command of Lieutenant Colonel Brodie, the acting regimental commander. Colonel Roosevelt was still in charge of the Second Cavalry Brigade. Nestled between rolling sand hills on the east side of Long Island, the camp lay directly in the path of cool breezes which swept unhindered from the ocean. This, in addition to an absence of mosquitoes, had been factors considered by General Young when he selected the campground. A thick carpet of grass, with interlocking tangles of bayberry bushes, covered the hills in all directions. The men from the barren mountains and deserts of Arizona liked their surroundings. They concluded that the vegetation of Long Island was admirably suited for a thriving cattle industry.

The Arizonans also realized that the Volunteer organizations would soon disband now that the war was over. This camp, they knew, which they considered to be their finest, also would be their last. Tom Grindell of C Troop, in a letter dated August 29 to the editor of the Phoenix *Arizona Republican,* predicted that most of the men would return to "good old Arizona" by October 1.

Lieutenant Colonel Brodie delayed mounted drill a few days to give the men and horses an opportunity to recuperate from their journey. This gave the men time to complete the camp arrangements while the officers and administrative personnel prepared the long-neglected paper work. The Rough Riders never had given much consideration to such routine functions, and the regiment had acquired the reputation of maintaining the most incomplete records of any unit in the Fifth Corps. Colonel Roosevelt himself later admitted: "The paper work of my own regiment was not as high as it should have been."[4] For years afterwards stories made the rounds in the Regular Army that an unbelievable

number of irregularities accompanied the discharge of the
Rough Riders.

When Lieutenant Colonel Brodie finally ordered the
officers to commence mounted drill in the sand hills and along
the beaches, the Arizona troops had so many men scattered
in hospitals throughout the East, on leave or detached on
special duty that scarcely a platoon from each troop could
be formed. On August 31, for example, a typical day in these
twilight hours of the regiment, the three Arizona troops,
which had a combined strength of nine officers and two hundred and seventy-four enlisted men, could muster only seven
officers and one hundred and fifty men fit for duty.

Weakened by tropical dysentery and malaria, which
affected almost every member of the command, the Arizonans
welcomed the opportunity to avoid drill. Many of them were
shadows of what they had been before. Private Webb had
returned from Cuba weighing fifty pounds less than what he
had at enlistment. The other men from Graham County had
fared no better. Out of the ten boys from Graham who went
to Cuba, only three had not spent some time in a hospital
by the time they returned. Two of these three, Private Tuttle
and Corporal McCarter, fell sick shortly after landing at
Long Island. Chaplain Brown was one of the few who did
not return sick. "I am heavier and healthier than I have ever
been before," Brown wrote, "and now at the end I find myself
one of a possible half-dozen who have come through without
sickness."[5]

Illness was not the only reason the men tried to avoid
drill. With the smell of discharge in the air and a successful
campaign behind them, the Rough Riders could not see much
point in practicing military formations and maneuvers.

No single group of fighting men received more publicity
than did "Roosevelt's Cowboys." Many New Yorkers came
to Montauk to get a firsthand look at the popular troopers.
Unlike those who had visited the Rough Riders at San
Antonio, the townspeople brought parcels of food and delicacies to distribute. This was the result of lurid newspaper

accounts describing conditions at the encampment. The New York newspapers in particular devoted considerable space to the situation at Montauk and lost no opportunity to vilify the high command for alleged negligence. The journalists reported that the medical department was failing to adequately provide for sick soldiers and that there was an insufficient supply of rations. They claimed that even the men on sick report were going hungry.

According to the Rough Riders, the stories describing conditions at Montauk typified the worst examples of misleading and erroneous journalistic reporting that characterized the Spanish-American War. It was "yellow journalism" at its worst. In reality, every effort was made by the War Department to provide for the soldiers. Colonel Roosevelt later testified that his command was "admirably treated" at Camp Wikoff. This opinion was shared by the troopers from Arizona. The New York civilians, however, besieged by newspaper accounts of suffering and neglect, came to the camp prepared to help alleviate the reported shortage of rations. So much food arrived in this manner for the Rough Riders that they were forced to give much of it to other cavalry regiments.

Additional assistance came all the way from Arizona. A group of ladies in Florence and another group in Phoenix, upon reading about the reported suffering at Camp Wikoff, solicited donations to be sent to Captain Alexander. On August 30 Alexander received a total of thirty-three dollars and twenty-five cents which he was to use for the "good of the troops."[6] Sixteen dollars and sixty-five cents came from Florence and sixteen dollars and sixty cents came from Phoenix. There is no record of how this money was used, but two weeks later, September 15, Lieutenant Patterson, who had been appointed treasurer, turned the unused balance of three dollars back to Alexander.

Because of the wide publicity given the Rough Riders, the visitors to their bivouac at Camp Wikoff were many and varied. Even President McKinley came to inspect the camp

and visit with the troops. While passing through the area of
the Arizona squadron the President's party came upon a
group of troopers engaged in a crap game, supervised by
"Happy Jack" Hodgdon of A Troop. Unawed by the presence
of his Commander in Chief, Hodgdon invited the President
to make a pass with the dice. The President complied, took the
dice, rattled them in his hand and rolled them out on the blanket. From his vantage point on a box looking over the shoulders of the gamblers, Hodgdon checked the President's roll,
reached down and picked up the fifty-cent piece McKinley
had wagered and announced solemnly: "The President craps
— who is the next lucky guy?"[7] The entire party, including
McKinley, broke into laughter.

The people of New York opened their hearts and homes
to the Rough Riders. The reason for this has not been explained, but it was in accord with the spirit of nationalism
aroused by the epic circulation struggle between the editors
and owners of the *Morning Journal* and the *World* over the
Cuban question. Also there was a need for identification with
a military unit of distinction. The only New York Volunteer
regiment to see action in Cuba, the ill-fated Seventy First
Infantry, had returned under a cloud of cowardice — it reportedly had failed to advance under fire at San Juan. As a
substitute the New Yorkers looked to the First United States
Volunteer Cavalry which, although raised largely in the West,
contained the sons of many prominent New York families.
Some claim to the regiment also could be made because
Roosevelt, already mentioned publicly as a gubernatorial
candidate, as well as Brodie, had been born in the Empire
State. Under such conditions it is not surprising that many
sick troopers were taken into private homes. Roosevelt reported that a Bayard Cutting, a Mrs. Ridisch and a Mrs.
Armitage took forty or fifty sick Rough Riders and placed
them in private residences. Private Charles O. Hopping, a
member of F Troop from Santa Fe, later related that he and
ten others stayed in the home of Fred C. Cocheau, where a
well-stocked wine cellar proved to be a popular attraction.

It is not clear under what authority the soldiers were permitted to take up temporary residence in private homes. Both Lieutenant Colonel Brodie and Colonel Roosevelt made extensive use of what was termed convalescent leave. Apparently, the permission of a regimental or brigade commander was all that was necessary to justify the absence of a sick trooper.

The Arizona Volunteers enjoyed the warm receptions given them. "The best the market affords is none too good for the 'Rough Riders,' so think the people of New York," wrote Tom Grindell, who added: "An ovation is tendered the boys, trooper and officer alike, wherever met out of camp; and thousands come to see those 'awfully rough, but awfully brave Rough Riders.' "[8] Many troopers took advantage of Roosevelt's liberal policy of leave established while still on board the *Miami,* and which Brodie continued. Several Arizonans, accompanied by friends, visited relatives in the East; others secured weekend passes and toured the neighboring cities. Everywhere they went the townspeople did everything possible to make the men welcome.

Arthur Tuttle, however, expressed misgivings about his fun-loving comrades in a letter to his mother. He wrote: "There is R.R. scattered all over the town [New York] and they are being treated fine and if they don't abuse it we will go out of here with a fine reputation."[9] Fortunately, Tuttle's fears failed to materialize. The reputation of the regiment did not suffer from the antics of the Arizonans, who found that even the police made allowances for them. One exuberant group, while crossing the Brooklyn bridge on the way to visit Coney Island, stopped in the middle and fired their revolvers into the air. Police officials hurried to the scene but made no arrests when they recognized the distinctive, yellow-trimmed uniforms of the Volunteers. The justices of the peace were found to be equally lenient, one of whom released without penalty one unknown Rough Rider who was arrested for being drunk and disorderly. In addition to those troopers who went to town for excitement or sight see-

ing, some went for a definite purpose. Frank Van Siclin of
Safford, who had an unusual aptitude for poker, went to the
Bowery and played with the professional gamblers. "He gave
the cardsharks of the Bowery a lesson in poker," recalled his
close friend Arthur Tuttle sixty-four years later.[10]

Early in September, as the chill mornings warned of
impending autumn, the officers prepared to disband their
commands. Before the troop commanders could be relieved of
their responsibility, they had to account for, clean and repair
all organizational equipment. Captain Frantz and Lieutenant
Wilcox had a more difficult task than did Captain Alexander
in this respect, for both officers had lost their property records
in Cuba. Duplicates had to be secured from the quartermaster and ordnance departments before the equipment
could be turned in. In addition, much of the property in A
and B Troops had been left in Tampa and transported to
Long Island under the supervision of officers from other units
who had no liability connections. Consequently, much of the
government property had not been well cared for.

The determination of liability for equipment lost in B
Troop posed a knotty problem for Captain McClintock, who
was still in the hospital at Fort Wadsworth, New York. In
his absence the acting commander, Lieutenant Wilcox, concluded that he could disband the unit without financial loss
to McClintock. In a reassuring letter he wrote to the captain:
"I shall clear you by affidavits if paper holds out. Many
revolvers are missing from saddle bags, but 'lost in action and
transit' covers a great deal of ground."[11] Some items, however,
could not be cleared by affidavit. On September 5 Lieutenant
Colonel Brodie convened a survey board composed of regimental officers to investigate the loss of nineteen carbines,
fourteen revolvers, forty haversacks and most of the mess
kits and shelter tents. The board, headed by Captain Robert
H. Bruce who commanded M Troop, recommended that
McClintock be cleared of all responsibility. Wilcox also found

it easy to account for the 3,000 rounds of carbine and revolver ammunition the troop had drawn. Although all the revolvers except those carried by the officers and noncommissioned officers had been left at Tampa, Wilcox wrote off all ammunition as "expended at Las Guasimas and San Juan."[12]

Another problem Lieutenant Wilcox faced concerned Second Lieutenant Tom Rynning, who later would be an honored Arizona Ranger. It is not clear when or why these two officers first had difficulties, but apparently it had started back at Prescott. What little evidence is available indicates that the selection of Wilcox as the second lieutenant of B Troop was the heart of the matter. Rynning clouded the whole situation when he related that both he and Wilcox were nominated to be the first sergeant of McClintock's troop at Prescott. According to Rynning, Wilcox won only after Rynning asked his own friends to vote for Wilcox. Rynning went on to infer that Wilcox became an officer at a later date.

In reality, the election held at Prescott was for the purpose of selecting the troop second lieutenant and not the first sergeant. The morning report book shows that Rynning was the first sergeant from the day the troop was formed until May 21, when he received a commission. It is entirely plausible that Rynning and Wilcox had words at Prescott where both tried to secure the commission. Wilcox won and Rynning accepted the consolation prize of first sergeant.

Ill-feeling between Rynning and Wilcox came to a head at Montauk Point when Captain McClintock requested that his personal belongings be sent to him. Early in September, when Lieutenant Wilcox returned from a visit with relatives in Michigan, he found that during his absence the captain's request had not been complied with. Wilcox immediately made the necessary arrangements. McClintock's revolver, however, had been lost in Cuba by Sergeant Jerry Lee of Globe, and the captain's saber could not be located. Wilcox then wrote McClintock an angry letter of explanation for the

delay and expressing complete dissatisfaction with Tom
Rynning:

> I received your letter the day I left [on leave] and asked Rynning to
> answer and look after your things. I thought until I received your
> letter today that he had done so, but find he neglected to do so. In
> fact he has been of less use to me through the whole campaign than
> a good corporal would be . . . [today] Rynning is absent sick, I don't
> miss him.[13]

There also is some question as to what happened to
Captain McClintock's revolver. It had been left in Cuba when
the captain was shot at Guasimas, but from there on the story
is not clear. Wilcox stated definitely that Sergeant Lee had
lost the weapon sometime during the campaign and after
McClintock had been evacuated. McClintock later related that
Private Bruce Proffitt returned the revolver with a story
of how it had saved his life at San Juan. Proffitt explained
that he had noticed a fine, pearl handled machete lying
beside the body of a Spaniard in a trench on San Juan
Heights. Leaving his carbine on top of the parapet, Proffitt
jumped into the trench to claim the attractive machete. To
his surprise the Spaniard jumped to his feet with the machete
in his hand. "Then I was mighty glad I had the old .45,"
Proffitt explained. "Just a couple of shots and the dead man
lay down for good."[14]

While their harassed officers struggled to bring order out
of the confused mass of reports, invoices and records, the Volunteers enjoyed themselves until they ran out of money. Each
private drew only $15.60 a month, and it did not last long.
Because the regiment neared discharge, even the "professional
twenty-five percenters," as Corporal French of C Troop called
the money lenders, refused to advance more capital. As a
result the dice and poker games finally ceased to operate, and
the soldiers turned to less expensive amusements.

One afternoon some bored Rough Riders watched a cavalry mount in a nearby field throw its rider, a trooper from
the Third Cavalry. The Volunteers reacted with cat-calls and

stinging comments which prompted the Regulars to challenge the Rough Riders to produce a rider who could stay
with the horse. Slender Tom Darnell, a member of H Troop
from Deming, New Mexico, and little Billy McGinty of K
Troop were regarded as the two best riders in the regiment.
They threw dice to determine which of them would accept
the challenge. Darnell won and arrangements were made to
hold the contest the following morning when the horse would
be fresh. That evening the Volunteers gathered all the "long
green" they could muster to lay bets on Darnell. They had
plenty of takers, for the Regulars had as much confidence in
their horse as the Rough Riders had in Darnell.

The next morning Darnell rode the outlaw in the presence of a large crowd composed of men from both regiments.
The sorrel turned out to be a vicious brute, and the trooper
treated the crowd to a display of horsemanship which was
long remembered. Darnell's seat was unshaken in spite of
everything the horse could do. Even Colonel Roosevelt appeared to witness the show, thoroughly enjoying himself as
he pushed forward to cheer and applaud the exhibition. Almost daily thereafter the Rough Riders held some kind of a
bucking horse contest. If they could not arrange a contest
with a neighboring regiment, the Rough Riders competed
among themselves.

Such activities eased monotony during the day, but the
troopers turned to other pastimes in the evenings when they
stayed in camp. It became their custom to gather in the streets
after roll call to talk and reminisce. One evening, when a
group from C Troop had gathered, Wilbur French noticed
that the conversation had started to lag. In an effort to enliven
the gathering, French urged William Asay, an ex-school
teacher from Graham County and one of the few men who
had become friendly with Sergeant John "Boots" McAndrew,
to call on McAndrew for a speech. McAndrew was a tall,
thirty-three-year-old lawyer who had unsuccessfully run for
attorney general in Colorado on either the Socialist or Popu-

list platform before his enlistment. He was living in Congress
Junction, a small settlement some fifty miles southwest of
Prescott, when the war came. He enlisted in O'Neill's troop
on April 30. A taciturn man, McAndrew had kept his own
counsel and had made few friends, but he had demonstrated
on previous occasions his oratorical ability. Asay approached
the sergeant, seated comfortably on the ground with his long
arms entwined about his knees, and requested that he address
the group on the "Brotherhood of Man." From all those
versatile members of C Troop, French could not have selected
a more suitable orator.

McAndrew arose, smoothed the gray ringlets on the sides
of his elongated head, thrust one arm forward in the classical
oratorical pose of the era, and broke forth a display of oratory
which reverberated through the camp for three-quarters of
an hour. Many off duty soldiers were attracted to C Troop's
area by the sergeant's booming voice. Even Colonel Roosevelt
joined Captain Alexander to listen. McAndrew's eloquence,
nurtured on the campaign platform and in the courtroom,
emerged full blown that evening to make a great impression
on his audience. Not only did he have the ability to arrange
words, but he also had the voice necessary to deliver them.
French later wrote:

He had the most far-reaching, bellowing voice I ever heard. He had
Bryan beat before the start, and that's traveling in pretty fast company
. . . I have been privileged to hear many of the gold and silver tongued
orators, from Wendell Phillips and Bob Ingersoll on down to Bill Bryan
and Hiram Johnson, not omitting Will Rogers, but I never heard the
like of that speech that flowed from his vocal organs without a break
for forty-five minutes.[15]

The personality and flamboyant manner of Colonel
Roosevelt, coupled with his unquestioned courage, had earned
for him the respect and affection of the men of the First
Volunteer Cavalry regiment. The officers and men contributed to a fund to buy a gift to show their appreciation. They
decided on a reproduction of Frederick Remington's bronze
sculpture the "Broncho Buster."

On Tuesday, September 13, the Arizona troopers joined with the rest of the unit as Lieutenant Colonel Brodie formed the regiment in a hollow square near Colonel Roosevelt's tent. He then escorted Roosevelt to the center of the square where Trooper William Murphey, of M Troop, waited at a blanket draped table to make the presentation. As Murphey uncovered the gleaming statue at the conclusion of his speech, the troopers howled their appreciation as Colonel Roosevelt examined the gift closely. No other symbol could have caught the spirit of the Rough Riders more effectively than did the vibrant excitement of horse and rider as immortalized in the glistening bronze.

After the cheering subsided, Colonel Roosevelt, visibly moved, made a nostalgic speech of acceptance. He praised almost everyone — from the eastern recruits to the Negro troopers of the Ninth and Tenth regiments who had fought so well beside the Rough Riders at San Juan. Many of them had drifted over to stand on the sidelines and watch the presentation. Roosevelt extended special praise, however, to the men from the West when he said: "the cow-puncher was the foundation of the regiment, and we have got him here in bronze."[16] When the ceremony ended, Roosevelt requested that the officers march their troopers past in single file so he could shake hands with each man. As each Volunteer uncovered and stepped up to the table, Roosevelt grasped his hand and called him by name. For some he mentioned a personal incident which had a special meaning for the soldier. This made a great impression on every man present. After the Rough Riders had all passed, Roosevelt shook hands with each member of the Ninth and Tenth Cavalry regiments who was present.

In addition to the gift for Colonel Roosevelt, the Arizonans made presentations to their own favorites. The forty-six members of Robert Patterson's platoon of C Troop purchased and presented to their popular young officer a regulation cavalry saber. It had each man's name engraved

on the polished steel blade and made a beautiful keepsake which Patterson cherished the rest of his life. The gift failed, however, to compensate for having missed the Santiago campaign. On many occasions Patterson admitted that he always regretted not having gone to Cuba.

Two days later, September 15, the three Arizona troops formed for the last time. Their equipment had all been turned in, and their final pay had been drawn. Many of the absent troopers heard of the forthcoming discharge and hurried to Montauk Point in time to participate. Arthur Tuttle and six others, convalescing in the Mount Sinai Hospital in New York, learned of the ceremony and demanded their releases. The doctors refused, but with the clandestine sympathy of the head nurse who showed them where their uniforms had been stored, the eager volunteers managed to slip away. They rode a train to the end of the line, and then walked the remaining two miles to the bivouac. They arrived just in time to stand the last formation of the Arizona squadron.

Colonel Roosevelt bids farewell to the Rough Riders at Camp Wikoff, Long Island, Sept. 13, 1898. Note the presentation bronze bronco buster on the table behind the colonel, his gift from the men of the regiment. (*Courtesy Harvard College Library, Roosevelt Collection.*)

The Arizona squadron had a large percentage absent at the final formation. Only six officers and one hundred and sixty-three men, out of nine officers and two hundred and fifty-two men assigned, stood in the wind-swept street to watch Sergeant Wright take down the regimental flag — their Arizona flag — for the last time. The flag was not as pretty as it was at Prescott when it was presented. The colors had run and there were three bullet holes in it. To the Arizona boys these were merely marks of honor. Out of the original two hundred men who had left Prescott four months before, one hundred and fifty-three were physically present. During that short period of time, two had deserted, seven had been discharged because of disease or injury, two had transferred, three had died of disease and nine had been killed in action. There were twenty-four still hospitalized from wounds or illness. On this day, September 15, 1898, the Arizona contingent of the First United States Volunteer Cavalry, known

Color Sgt. Albert P. Wright with the stained and torn national colors which had been made by the Women's Relief Corps of Phoenix and presented to the Arizona squadron at Prescott. Wright carried the standard, with its identifying satin ribbons at the tip of the staff, in action in Cuba. (*Courtesy Harvard College Library, Roosevelt Collection.*)

popularly and indelibly as "Roosevelt's Rough Riders," ceased
to exist.

The Arizona Rough Riders had ended a short but exciting period of military service. Just four months and thirteen
days before, these two hundred eager Volunteers had marched
out of Prescott on a chilly May evening. As the first recruits
for the regiment to rendezvous at San Antonio, they soon had
been joined by eight hundred others. During the next six
weeks they were trained, organized and moved across the
nation to the sandy beaches of Florida. From there one hundred and twenty-two had been sent to the sweltering jungles
of Cuba. Fighting in two bloody engagements, nine of them
had been killed and nineteen more were wounded. After
fighting for another month they remained in Cuba and
watched their ranks further decimated by tropical disease.
At long last they had rejoined their comrades at Long Island.
Those who had not died or been placed in a government
hospital to recuperate from their military adventure now
started home. They had looked forward to going home for
a long time. Lieutenant Wilcox ably expressed this feeling in
a letter to Captain McClintock: "I hope you will be soon well
enough to return to the only country on earth — Arizona."[17]

Epilogue

ON SEPTEMBER 15, WITH THE INK SCARCELY DRY on their discharges, the Arizona Rough Riders started home. It was not a concerted movement, for the departure of many was delayed because of hospitalization for wounds or illness. Others postponed departure a few days to tour the famous landmarks in such places as Philadelphia or Washington, D.C. Some visited with relatives. Often they took their friends and comrades with them.

Everywhere they went the Rough Riders found themselves the center of attraction. Arthur Tuttle recalled that he was admirably treated when he stopped off at Kansas City with Corporal George "Big Bugs" Bugbee and visited a few days there in the home of Bugbee's parents. Lieutenant "Pat" Patterson of C Troop took several friends with him to visit relatives in Pennsylvania. Wilbur French quickly learned that the people wanted to hear details of the fighting in Cuba. Omitting to explain that he had stayed in Florida, French capitalized on this curiosity by enjoying many free drinks while spinning exciting tales of his hypothetical exploits before Santiago. Others did the same thing. In fact, as is often the case, those who had seen the least talked the most.

Some of the men quickly drank or gambled away their muster out pay and found themselves stranded without money to get home. When Colonel Roosevelt, Lieutenant Colonel Brodie and other ranking officers learned of this situation, they provided funds to furnish the troopers with one-way train tickets home. They knew better than to give them cash.

The receptions given to the boys when they returned to Arizona was no less impressive than those given to them in the East. Arriving singly or in small groups, the Arizona Rough Riders found that their friends and relatives were waiting to greet them with open arms. Each day the territorial papers carefully noted the arrival or expected arrival of local boys. When the reporters in Williams learned that Henry Sellers was expected home, they announced the townspeople's preparation: "Henry will be the most petted lad in this neck-o-the-woods for several days to come, as everybody is proud of him and the record he has made."[1] When the fifteen veterans from Bisbee got back, they were the guests of Mr. and Mrs. Crossey, who treated them to a lavish banquet in the Bessemer Grill Room in Bisbee. The festivities were marred somewhat when Alex Keir suffered a relapse of fever during the meal.

One of the most rousing receptions was the one given at Kingman for Fred A. Pomeroy, a twenty-two-year-old accountant who had served in B Troop. Upon his return Pomeroy, according to the Kingman *Mohave County Miner,* was welcomed "with open arms and he was made the recipient of an ovation at the town hall that any hero might well be proud of. There he was presented with a beautiful watch, to the purchase of which nearly every person, including the children, had contributed."[2] And so it was. From Bisbee in the south to Kingman in the north; and from Yuma in the

west to Safford in the east, the townspeople greeted their
native Rough Riders. It was a grand homecoming.

As the novelty of being feted as conquering heroes wore
off, the veterans began seeking employment. Most took up
where they had left off six months earlier when they had
answered Brodie's call to arms. Cornelius Cronin got his old
job back as recorder of Yuma County. Lieutenant Rynning
went back into construction work, but this time in Globe
rather than in Tucson where he was working when the war
came. Alex Keir, John Foster, Tom Wiggins, William Snodderly, George McCabe and Jesse Toland all went back to work
in the copper mines at Bisbee. Most of them went under-
ground, but Wiggins got on as night watchman. Clifton
Middleton, Sebird Henderson and Bill Owens went into the
mines at Globe. Daniel Hogan returned to Flagstaff and went
to work for a lumber company. Marshall Bird had returned
to Nogales a few weeks before, and was working with his
father on the Nogales *Oasis*. James C. Goodwin of C Troop
returned to Tempe and enrolled in the Normal School there.
John McAndrew opened a restaurant in Winslow. Fred and
George Bugbee and Nelson Bartoo got back on with the railroads. The Bugbee boys served with the Southern Pacific out
of Benson and other southern towns, while Bartoo worked
for the Santa Fe line in northern Arizona.

Large numbers of the Arizona troopers went into the
cattle business, mostly working as cowpunchers. Many drifted
aimlessly for a time, doing free-lance prospecting, working
small claims, clerking in stores and doing odd jobs wherever
they could find employment.

A few of the men found it difficult to adjust to civilian
life and went back into the army. According to McClintock
they "hadn't had their bellies full of war."[3] Many of them
enlisted in the Thirty-Fourth Infantry, which was formed in
1900 to serve in the Philippines against the revolt led by
Emilio Aguinaldo. There was a rumor that McClintock was
to go with this regiment, but it is doubtful if he was physically

able — even if he had had the inclination. One of the recruiting officers for the Thirty-Fourth who toured Arizona was Maximilian Luna, the Rough Rider who had commanded F Troop. He had good success in this territory, which bordered his ancestral home of New Mexico. Dick Stanton, McClintock's old nemesis, enlisted as did James Murphy, Stephan Pate, John Campbell, Ira Hartzell, Alva Eakin and Frank Schenck. All had been members of B Troop. Pate and Stanton quickly became sergeants, and Campbell became a first sergeant. Murphy, who had been wounded before Santiago, was killed in the vicious guerrilla fighting somewhere in Luzon. Captain Luna was drowned. Walter Gregory, another old B Troop man, also served in the Philippines, but he was a trooper in the Fourth Cavalry.

Another Arizonan who got back into the army was Fred Bugbee. Shortly before the turn of the century the size of the army was expanded and five hundred and eighty-eight new lieutenants were appointed. Bugbee applied for and received one of these appointments. A few months later a newspaper article credited Roosevelt, then the governor of New York, with securing the commission for Bugbee. Roosevelt was quoted as remembering Bugbee's refusal to leave the firing line after being wounded at San Juan. "I couldn't forget such a fellow," Roosevelt said, "and I got him a commission in the regular army. He's now in the Philippines."[4] After the insurrection in the islands had been put down, Bugbee remained in the army. He rose to the rank of colonel and commanded a regiment in France during World War I.

Still riding the wave of adulation which engulfed them at the time of their homecoming, some of the Rough Riders looked to politics as a means of turning this sentiment into profitable channels. Alexander O. Brodie was one. On September 20, 1898, at the Republican convention in Prescott, Brodie was selected to run for territorial delegate to Congress. He took the nomination seriously and actively launched his campaign on October 14, when he arrived in Holbrook on his way home. Governor Nathan Oakes Murphy, Judge Charles Wright and several other leading Republicans were there to help get the campaign off to a fast start.[5] George Smalley, a veteran journalist, accompanied the group to represent the Phoenix *Republican*.[6]

For the next month Brodie and his friends traveled throughout the territory. This was standard campaign procedure in those days in Arizona for anyone who wanted to win an election. Utilizing trains, stages, buckboards and even saddle horses, Brodie campaigned in every town and village that he could reach. On several occasions local Rough Riders took the speaker's platform to give eloquent testimony in their favorite's behalf. Smalley later recalled that both Wright and Governor Murphy made some effective speeches, but that full use of Murphy was limited somewhat, for the governor traveled with the group only when trains were available. Brodie was well received throughout the territory, drawing good sized crowds in the larger towns.

Although Brodie tried to make the question of statehood the main issue of the campaign, his Democratic opponent stuck with the old question of free silver — an issue that always had strong appeal to the miners of the West. In November, when the election returns were in, Brodie had lost by a few hundred votes. The Phoenix *Republican* offered the explanation that the people of Arizona were more concerned with the mythical "sixteen to one" ratio of silver to gold than they were with statehood. Some of Brodie's ex-troopers, however, blamed his defeat on the eight hundred prospective Rough Riders who had been turned away from the enlistment table at Prescott.

James McClintock, George Wilcox and Tom Grindell of C Troop also threw their hats into the political arena. McClintock and Grindell were Republicans, while Wilcox was a Democrat. The ex-captain of B Troop tried to secure a seat on the Phoenix City Council in 1898, and Wilcox sought a similar position in Bisbee. Grindell tried to be the

Alexander Brodie, candidate for delegate to Congress from Arizona in 1898, while campaigning in Safford, visits with two ex-Rough Riders, Wilbur D. French (left) and Arthur L. Tuttle (right).

school superintendent of Maricopa County. All three were defeated. Grindell ran the best race, losing by only forty-three votes out of 3,309 ballots cast. In the fall of 1898, Arizona gave a cool reception to Rough Riders with political aspirations. Two years later, however, Wilcox was elected justice of the peace in Bisbee.

The political fortunes of the Rough Riders took a sudden turn for the better on September 14, 1901. On that day President William McKinley succumbed to a bullet wound inflicted a few days before by an obscure anarchist. Theodore Roosevelt, late colonel of the First United States Volunteer Cavalry, was now President. In the fall of 1898 Roosevelt had been elected governor of New York. Two years later at the Republican convention in Philadelphia he had been selected to run on the same ticket with President McKinley as the candidate for vice-president. After serving as vice-president for only six months, Roosevelt was suddenly thrust into the presidency.

Many Arizona Rough Riders saw an opportunity to advance themselves politically now that Roosevelt was President. The quickness with which some of them reacted to news of McKinley's death was almost macabre. On September 15, only one day after the President's death, Cronin wrote a letter to McClintock which illustrated his awareness of the situation. Cronin wrote:

Friend Jim:
    While we all equally deplore the death of our beloved President, still the fact has created a change which may mean much to you, and the time for action is now. President Roosevelt should recognize you, as one of his men and one of his party, and I would counsel you to get in and rustle *now*. *If there is anything I can do in your behalf at this end, do not hesitate to use me.* I see no reason why you cannot get the Secretaryship. Let me hear from you and believe me.[7]

McClintock's goal at this time was to be the Secretary of State of Arizona Territory. He was deeply disappointed that the appointment was not forthcoming. The following year, however, 1902, he was named postmaster of Phoenix. McClintock always considered this to be a mere political bone, thrown to him in consolation for greater honors — earned, but never received.

In the months following McKinley's death there were a few minor appointments made in Arizona, but the great patronage began in 1902 when Brodie became governor. It is to Brodie's credit, perhaps, that he did not make extensive use of the personal influence that he had with Roosevelt to further his own ambitions. This influence was demonstrated in May, 1902, when George Smalley, the journalist who had reported Brodie's campaign in 1898, sought a postmaster job in Tucson. Brodie wrote Smalley: "Let me know the day you are going to send your papers [petitions] in and I will get in a personal letter to the President on your behalf — This latter keep to yourself as it is a way I have of landing things and I don't wish it known."[8] Brodie evidently felt that a letter would not suffice in every case, for a month later he traveled to Washington to secure the governorship for William Christy, a Phoenix banker. Roosevelt turned on his intense personal charm and got Brodie to accept the job instead. On July 1, 1902, Brodie was inaugurated as the fifteenth governor of Arizona. The Arizona Volunteers were now well fixed. They had a friend in the White House and another in the governor's chair in Phoenix.

Many of the jobs Brodie and Roosevelt provided for their Arizona troopers were connected with law enforcement. Benjamin F. Daniels, an old-time peace officer from Colorado Springs who served in K Troop, was to be a United States marshal in Arizona. Daniels was so sure of his appointment that he publicly named Sam Greenwald a deputy. The Senate at first denied confirmation, however, and Daniels became superintendent of the territorial prison at Yuma while waiting for the Senate to act. He resigned from the prison when his appointment as marshal finally came through. Charles Utling and John Foster were two of his deputies, having been appointed before Daniels was named. Other Arizona men who

served at the prison at Yuma were Walter T. Gregory of B
Troop, the secretary and treasurer, and guards Sebird Henderson and Cliff Middleton, also of B Troop. Henderson
resigned from the prison before Daniels arrived, claiming that
he and Middleton had not been well received by the guards
already there.

At least nine Rough Riders became members of that
obscure group known as the Arizona Rangers. Initially composed of twelve men, this force was formed in 1901 to combat
rustling and other illegal activities. John E. Campbell, John
Foster, William W. Webb, Richard Stanton and David Warford of B Troop were all rangers at various times, as was
Charles McGarr of A Troop and Oscar J. Mullen of C Troop.
Some of these men served under the first captain of the
rangers, Burton C. Mossman, and some under Harbo or
"Tom" Rynning, who was appointed ranger captain by Governor Brodie in 1903. When Rynning took command, the
strength of the organization had been increased from twelve
to twenty-six men.

The Arizona Rangers operated in semi-private, drifting
into troubled spots with as little publicity as possible. Little
is known of their activities. Brodie's wife, who came to know
a great many rangers quite well, often told her granddaughter
that they were the toughest set of men she had ever seen.
They made a good record. When Rynning resigned from the
force to take charge of the new territorial prison at Florence
in 1907, he was replaced by Harry Wheeler. Wheeler had
been the ranger lieutenant under Rynning, and also had
served in the Rough Riders, although not in the Arizona
squadron.

One of the most lucrative political plums in Arizona fell
to George Wilcox. In 1902 Wilcox was appointed clerk of the
district court in Tombstone. He held this position until 1910,
when he was replaced at the insistence of the chairman of
the territorial Republican party, Hovel A. Smith, and delegate Ralph Cameron. Wilcox then went to Phoenix and

bought a drugstore there. When the First World War began Wilcox got back on active duty, serving as a major training recruits in the United States. He died in Warren, Arizona, in 1949.

Frank Frantz, Henry Bardshar and Fenn S. Hildreth of B Troop also received remunerative positions. After returning briefly to Prescott in 1898, Frantz went to Enid, Oklahoma, where he soon became a postmaster. Two years later he was appointed agent for the Osage Indians of Oklahoma. In 1906 Roosevelt made him governor of Oklahoma. At the age of thirty-three Frantz was acclaimed as the youngest governor of any state or territory in the Union. After leaving that position Frantz went into the oil business in Colorado. Apparently he never again took up residence in Arizona. Henry Bardshar, on the other hand, stayed in Arizona until 1905, when he was appointed United States collector of internal revenue for the district of Arizona and New Mexico. Bardshar assumed his new duties in Santa Fe, the district headquarters. Fenn S. Hildreth, a member of B Troop from Tucson, secured an appointment as receiver of the Phoenix land office. Hildreth, however, had a stormy tenure, not being able to get along with Governor Joseph H. Kibbey, who had replaced Brodie in 1905.[9] There were charges and countercharges of incompetence, senility and underhandedness.

Although Brodie received some criticism for showing too much partiality to his Rough Riders, he made a good record as governor. According to George Smalley, Brodie's secretary, the administration was noted for honesty and integrity. The governor supported a fair tax levied on the mines, personally supervised the Arizona Rangers and saved the territory $50,000 annually by pushing the Cowan Bill through the legislature. This act specified that certain fees kept by the Secretary of State would be retained by the territory. There is no evidence that any scandal marred Brodie's administration. He did receive some adverse comment for issuing a pardon to Pearl Hart, the famous girl bandit who had been convicted of robbing the Globe-Florence stage. Brodie accepted the criticism stoically, consistently refusing to make public his reasons. Fifty-two years later Smalley revealed that the young woman had been pardoned because she was with child. It would have been out of character for Brodie to have revealed such intimate knowledge of the woman's life. He also pardoned Richard Goodwin, a former member of B Troop who had been sentenced to two hundred days in the Pima County jail for assaulting his wife. Goodwin's health was failing, and there was some apprehension that the old soldier would not live out his term.

In 1905 Brodie resigned as governor to achieve his long-cherished dream of getting back on active duty. That year he was appointed assistant chief of the War Department's Records and Pension Division, with rank of major. Undoubtedly Roosevelt secured the position for him. Brodie stayed in Washington just a few months, leaving later that year as a lieutenant colonel for service as Military Secretary in the Department of Visayas in the Philippines. In 1907 he returned, being assigned to the Department of the Dakotas as adjutant general. He brought with him an eloquent letter of commendation testifying to his excellent work for General J. M. Lee, Department of the Visayas. In 1912 Brodie was made colonel and transferred to California as adjutant general. He retired shortly before the United States entered the First World War.

In 1918 Brodie's long career came to an end. During his lifetime, which spanned nearly three score and ten, he had watched his adopted home of twenty-three years grow from a sparsely settled wilderness inhabited largely by hostile Indians to the youngest state in the Union. His contributions had been many; he had been a soldier, a miner, a rancher, a water conservationist and a governor. On May 10, 1918, Alexander Oswald Brodie, the organizer and military backbone of the Arizona Rough Riders, was buried at Haddenfield, New Jersey. In his clasped hands was a spray of Highland heather, sent by relatives in Scotland.

During the First World War two Rough Riders figured prominently in one of the most controversial events that ever took place in southern Arizona. There was a great need for copper during the war, and the mines at Bisbee were producing large amounts of the desired metal. In 1917 certain labor unions called their workers out on strike. According to local tradition, many of the striking miners were members of the Industrial Workers of the World, or "wobblies" as they were called. Many residents of Cochise County, including members of rival unions, considered the strike to be nothing more than a thinly veiled effort to curtail the war-making capabilities of the United States. These people decided to act. What happened next is still not clear.

In July some two thousand deputies, led by Sheriff Harry Wheeler, rounded up more than a thousand strikers and forcibly loaded them on freight cars. They were then escorted across the state line into New Mexico and abandoned. Another Rough Rider who played a part in this "Bisbee Deportation" was John C. Greenway, general manager of the Calumet and Arizona Mining Company and a former lieutenant in A Troop. To what extent Greenway was involved is still a matter of conjecture. Undoubtedly Greenway, like Wheeler, was sure that harsh methods were necessary in order to maintain necessary copper production. To the Rough Riders it was simply a question of patriotism. Although the strike was finally ended by the efforts of a mediation commission appointed by President Woodrow Wilson, the incident left a bitterness which lasted for years.

By the end of the First World War the Rough Riders had scattered to all parts of the world. Many had been successful; many had met with failure. Large numbers had dropped into complete anonymity. Tragedy had dogged the footsteps of a few. Fred A. Pomeroy of A Troop had been

killed when he fell into a mine shaft near Kingman. He
had just recently become engaged. Tom Darnell, the popular
bronco buster of H Troop, had been shot down in a barroom
fight in New Mexico. Some were in jail. William Proffitt,
the crack shot who had performed such effective work hunting snipers in the hills before Santiago, had been murdered.
No one knows exactly what happened, but Proffitt was killed
while prospecting in the deep canyons of the Bradshaw mountains south of Prescott. His body was eventually recovered,
but no clue was ever found as to the identity of his assailant.
One of the most tragic deaths, however, came to Tom Grindell of C Troop.

In 1905 Grindell led a four man expedition to Tiburon
Island off the west coast of Mexico in the Gulf of California.
Inhabited by Seri Indians, who still occasionally practiced
cannibalism at the turn of the century, the island had long
been rumored as being rich with gold. Grindell was one of
several who tried to find it. Accompanied by three men,
identified only as J. E. Hoffman, Rawlins and Ingraham,
Grindell left Douglas in the summer of 1905. They were all
well armed, being prepared to deal with the still uncivilized
inhabitants of the island. What happened is still obscure. It
seems that the party reached the coast somewhere near Her-
mosillo with but very little water left. Rawlins went on ahead
to search for an Indian village, and Grindell soon followed.
Ingraham, probably delirious, soon wandered off into the
desert. J. E. Hoffman, the only survivor of the ill-fated expedition, never saw the other three again. He stayed near the
coast, distilling sea water with an old tea pot, until he was
finally picked up by a Mexican fishing boat near Guaymas.
The bodies of Grindell and his comrades were never found.
Some of the Rough Riders, who kept in touch with each
other through the Rough Rider Association, and other friends
financed an unsuccessful relief expedition.

Like other soldiers of the era, the Rough Riders had

wanted an organization to keep track of them after they returned to civilian life. Captain O'Neill first suggested that steps be taken to form such an organization while enroute to Cuba. He recommended that the association be called the "Military Order of the Morro." Colonel Wood was interested and suggested that the name be changed to "The Military Order of the Foreign Wars of the Republic."[10] Nothing else was done until the regiment prepared to disband at Montauk. On August 31, 1898, the "Roosevelt Rough Rider Association" was officially formed. Lieutenant Colonel Brodie was elected president; General Wood and Colonel Roosevelt became vice presidents, and Lieutenant Goodrich was named secretary. The main order of business was the preparation of a reunion to be held the following year.

Because slightly more than one third of the regiment came from New Mexico, the first reunion was held in Las Vegas, New Mexico, on June 24, 1899. The date was the anniversary of the battle of Las Guasimas. A year later the second gathering took place in Oklahoma, and the third in 1901 at Colorado Springs. In April, 1902, the fourth reunion was held at San Antonio. Colonel Roosevelt attended the first three reunions, but official duties kept him from coming to San Antonio — the site that he personally had selected.

For the most part these four reunions were successful. The men enjoyed visiting with their comrades, reminiscing about the old days in the regiment, comparing notes on personal successes or failures and in general having a good time. Sometimes they helped someone out of difficulty. At the Oklahoma reunion the men chipped in to buy a wooden leg for Charles Buckholdt, a member of B Troop from Kickapoo Springs, Texas, who had enlisted in the troop at San Antonio. Details are not known, but McClintock later stated that Buckholdt had his leg shot off in "some Texas row."[11] When the Arizona men went to Colorado in 1901, they tried to secure a pardon for Edward G. Collier, a former member of B Troop from Globe. Collier had been convicted of robbery. It is not known if the efforts put forth by McClintock and Wilcox secured Collier's release.

Employment or financial difficulties kept many of the men away from the reunions. Others did not go because of personal reasons. Tom Isbell, a member of L Troop from Vinita, Indian Territory, refused to attend the reunions because he felt that the Rough Riders were getting too much publicity. According to Isbell, the First Volunteer Cavalry was no better than any other regiment which fought in the Spanish-American War.

After 1902 there were no regimental reunions held for forty-six years, although local gatherings in different states did take place. In 1948 Robert Patterson, postmaster at Crown King near Prescott, and Harmon Wynkoop, a former member of E Troop living in Prescott, organized a reunion to commemorate the fiftieth anniversary of the battle of Las Guasimas. It was held in Prescott June 24–25, 1948. By this time the number of living Rough Riders had been reduced to a mere handful, but a surprisingly high number of them attended. Approximately sixty-five of the one hundred and seven known survivors came. Some of the Arizona troopers who participated were: From B Troop, Frank Roberts, a retired judge from Texas, George Wilcox from Warren, Charles Heitman of the *Christian Science Monitor,* Martin L. Crimmins of Texas and David Goodrich from New York. Charles McGarr, Howard Marine from Yarnell, and Arthur Tuttle from California represented A Troop. Patterson and Oscar J. Mullen, superintendent of the Jerome public schools, had served in C Troop.

The reunion agenda included several banquets, a trip to the Grand Canyon and selection of a new slate of officers. Many of the veterans had their pictures taken at the famous monument commemorating the Arizona Rough Riders, usually referred to as the "Buckey O'Neill statue." This monument was in a fitting location, having been erected quite close to the spot where the Volunteers had lined up in the plaza to listen to Governor McCord's farewell and receive their flag on May 5, 1898.

The "O'Neill statue" has been a Prescott landmark since its dedication on July 1, 1907. Not originally intended to portray any one man, the monument, created by the noted sculptor, Solon Borglum, had been designed to honor all the Arizona Rough Riders. The reason for the association of O'Neill with the statue stems in part from the basic design. It depicts a hell-for-leather cavalryman, mounted and leaning intently over the straining neck of a spirited war horse. The rider is in uniform with a campaign hat, a pair of cavalry boots, a neckerchief and a holstered Colt swinging on his right hip. The spirit is O'Neill's. On a bronze plaque set in the granite base are inscribed the names of the Arizona Volunteers. The monument is located on the edge of the town plaza north of the court house. Truly, it is a magnificent piece of work. The Rough Riders who had never seen the statue until the reunion in 1948 were impressed.

With the Prescott reunion a success beyond expectation, the veterans decided to hold another the following year in Las Vegas, New Mexico. At this meeting the old soldiers voted to hold an annual reunion in that town until such time as only one man was left. There has been a reunion ever since. The gathering is held in the summer, and the event has come to be associated with the Las Vegas rodeo. Each successive year the number attending has grown less and less. In 1955 the last officer of the regiment died at Crown King, Arizona. This was Robert Patterson of C Troop. Realizing that the end was almost in sight, the Rough Rider Association was opened to honorary membership in 1962. There was some talk of limiting membership to the immediate families of the original Rough Riders, but this idea was abandoned. The only prerequisite is for the honorary member to have his card signed by one of the officers of the Association.

On July 9, 1969, another chapter in the history of the Arizona Rough Riders came to a close. Arthur L. Tuttle, the last survivor of the Arizona squadron, died in Salinas, California. He remained active to the last, participating in the Rough Rider Association and other activities. His mind remained crystal clear and he was an excellent source of Arizona history. Few of his kind remain; he was a living link with the past.

Those were stalwart men who left Arizona for Cuba back in 1898. Like other pioneers before them they carved their own peculiar niche in the measuring stick that plumbs the depths of Arizona history. Their nation did not find them lacking.

Appendices

The Volunteer Bill of April 22, 1898, stated that the Secretary of War would appoint all officers of the special volunteer regiments. The commission shown in Appendix 2 reveals that the initial appointments of the company grade officers of the Rough Riders actually came from the territorial governors. It names Robert S. Patterson the second lieutenant of Capt. Wm. O. O'Neill's Company of the First Regiment of Cavalry, United States Volunteers, to rank as such from May 4, 1898. There is no record of a confirming or duplicating commission issued by the War Department.

Two regimental rosters of the Rough Riders are on file in the National Archives. One is the Muster-In roll completed May 17, 1898, at San Antonio, Texas, and the other is the Muster-Out roll completed September 15, 1898, at Camp Wykoff, Long Island. Both rosters contain minor errors. Copies of the Muster-Out roll were included in *The Rough Riders* by Theodore Roosevelt and *The Story of the Rough Riders* by Edward Marshall. Rosters based on the Muster-In rolls never before have appeared in print.

The rosters shown in Appendix 3 are based on the Muster-In rolls of May 17. Some corrections and deletions have been made for clarity and ease of reference. Names have been arranged alphabetically by rank with last name first and an occasional first name has been added where the individual was enrolled by his initials. The fractional portion of each man's age and certain other information such as next of kin has been omitted. The names of those recruits from areas other than Arizona who enlisted after the squadron left Prescott have been deleted. All known errors in the roster have been identified by inserting the correction in brackets next to the original entry. With the exception of the REMARKS column, which contains entries not on the Muster-In roll, all information added to the roster has been enclosed in brackets.

Office of the Acting Governor
Phoenix.

March 5th. 1898.

Hon. William Mc.Kinley,
President of the United States,
Washington, D. C.

Sir:-

In the event of war and a call for volunteers,I respectfully, recommend that Colonel A. O. Brodie of Prescott, Arizona, be commissioned to organize,and lead on the field of battle , a regiment of cavalry .

Colonel Brodie has tendered his services in the following telegram.

"Prescott, Arizona, March 3rd. 1898.

Hon. M. H. Mc.Cord,
Phoenix.
Governor.
In the event of war and a call for volunteers I have the honor to tender my services to the territory, for the organization of a cavalry regiment for active service in the field. Graduate Military Academy 1870, Seven years service on frontier 3rd.cavalry.
Alex. O. Brodie. "

Having known Colonel Brodie for many years as an Army Officer I can unhesitatingly vouch for him as being an honest and fearless officer, competent in every respect to command a regiment.

Very respectfully,

Charles H Akers
Acting Governor of Arizona.

Brodie's request for authorization to raise a regiment

A Volunteer's commission (*Courtesy of the Patterson family*)

MUSTER-IN ROLL — A TROOP

NAME	RANK	AGE	PLACE OF BIRTH	RESIDENCE
O'Neill, William O.	Captain	38	Ireland	Prescott
Frantz, Frank	1st Lieut.	29	Roanoke, Ill.	Prescott [Richenbar]
Carter, Joshua D.	2nd Lieut.	36	Dubuque, Iowa	Prescott
Greenwood, William W.	1st Sgt.	44	Troy, N.Y.	Prescott [California]
Walsh, George	Q.M. Sgt.	43	Manchester, Eng.	San Francisco
Brown, Robert	Sergeant	38	New Brunswick, N.J.	Prescott
Greenley, James T.	Sergeant	39	Peter Co., Mo.	Prescott
Greenwald, Samuel	Sergeant	37	California	Prescott
Henley, King	Sergeant	43	Henderson Co., Ky.	Winslow
LeRoy, Arthur M.	Sergeant	41	Boston	Prescott
Nash, Henry W.	Sergeant	29	Mt. Sterling, Ind.	Young
Bugbee, George L.	Corporal	28	San Francisco	Lordsburg, N.M. [Safford]
Doherty, George H.	Corporal	30	Detroit	Jerome
Holtzschue, Carl	Corporal	25	St. Joseph, Mo.	Prescott
Howard, John L.	Corporal	25	St. Louis Co., Mo.	St. Louis
Jackson, Cade C.	Corporal	21	Erath Co., Texas	Flagstaff
McGarr, Charles	Corporal	28	Tucson, Ariz.	Tucson
Rhodes, Samuel	Corporal	31	Visalia, Calif.	Porterville, Calif. [Tonto Basin]
White, Harry G.	Corporal	27	Somerville, Mass.	Richenbar
Hamilton, Thomas	Blacksmith	29	Rockford, Ill.	Jerome
Willard, Wallace B.	Farrier	28	Sacramento, Calif.	Cottonwood
Cassi, Emilio	Trumpeter	27	Monte Carlo, Monaco	Jerome
Harner, Frank J.	Trumpeter	24	Tucson	Prescott
Waller, John H.	Wagoner	44	Highland Co., Ohio	Prescott
Whitney, Forest	Saddler	24	Green Bush Co., Wis.	Richenbar
Allen, George L.	Private	41	Cincinnati	Prescott
Azbill, John	Private	27	Tulare Co., Calif.	St. Johns
Azbill, William T.	Private	29	Santa Barbara, Calif.	St. Johns
Bardshar, Henry P.	Private	27	Clyde, Ohio	Prescott
Bartoo, Nelson E.	Private	25	Potter Co., Pa.	Winslow
Boyle, James	Private	31	Carbon Co., Pa.	Prescott
Bugbee, Fred W.	Private	22	Oakland, Calif.	Tucson [Safford]
Champlin, Fred E.	Private	30	Saginaw, Mich.	Flagstaff
Fox, Harry B.	Private	26	Campbelltown, Pa.	Jerome
Garrett, Samuel H.	Private	22	Pottsville, Pa.	Prescott

San Antonio, Texas, May 17, 1898

DATE ENROLLED	OCCUPATION	REMARKS
April 29	Lawyer	Killed in action at San Juan, July 1.
April 30	Clerk	Commanded A Troop from July 1 to Sept. 15. Promoted to Captain after the death of O'Neill.
April 30	Clerk	Promoted to 2nd Lieut. from Quartermaster Sergeant on May 7.
April 30	Miner	Wounded in leg and foot at San Juan, July 1.
May 2	Printer	Died of dysentery on **U.S.S. Miami**, Aug. 11.
April 30	Cowboy	
May 2	Blacksmith	Wounded in leg at San Juan, July 1.
April 30	Clerk	Promoted to 2nd Lieut. and transferred to I Troop, August 31.
May 1	Miner	
April 30	Cowboy	
May 2	Cowboy [Teacher]	
May 2	Train Master	On detached duty in Tampa, June 8 to August 8.
May 2	Carpenter	Killed in action at Las Guasimas, June 24.
April 30	Prospector	
May 3	Teamster	On detached duty in Tampa, June 8 to August 8.
May 3	Horseman	
April 30	Soldier	
May 1	Cowboy	
May 3	Electrician	Wounded in leg at San Juan, July 3.
April 30	Blacksmith	
April 30	Cowboy	
May 1	Band Master	Wounded in the head at San Juan, July 2.
April 30	Cowboy	
April 30	Cowboy	Wounded in the arm at San Juan, July 1.
May 2	Saddler	
April 30	Tinner	On detached duty in Tampa, June 8 to August 8.
May 2	Cowboy	On detached duty in Tampa, June 8 to August 8.
May 2	Cowboy	
May 1	Miner	
May 1	Engineer	
May 3	Cowboy	Wounded in neck and body at San Juan, July 1. Died July 2.
May 2	Rancher	Wounded in the head at San Juan, July 1.
May 1	Rancher	Wounded by shrapnel at San Juan, July 1. Died July 2.
April 30	Printer	
April 30	Stenographer	On detached duty in Tampa, June 8 to Aug. 8. Discharged by AGO Special Order NO. 14 dated 24 August.

MUSTER-IN ROLL

NAME	RANK	AGE	PLACE OF BIRTH	RESIDENCE
Griffin, W. W. [Walter]	Private	36	Prince Geo. Co., Md.	Globe [Safford]
Hodgdon, Charles E.	Private	29	Pelatina, Calif.	Prescott [California]
Hogan, Daniel L.	Private	31	Syracuse, N.Y.	Flagstaff
Jackson, Charles B.	Private	26	Hillsdale, Mich.	Prescott
Jackson, John W.	Private	29	Marshall, Texas	Jerome
Johnson, John W.	Private	34	Boston	Kingman
Lefors, Jefferson D.	Private	37	Arkansas City, Ark.	Prescott
Lewis, William T.	Private	37	Dodgeville, Wis.	Congress Jct.
Liggett, Edward	Private	30	Eagleville, Pa.	Jerome
Marine, Rufus H.	Private	24	Green Castle, Miss.	Flagstaff
May, James A.	Private	32	Amador, Calif.	Safford
McCarter, George A.	Private	38	Erie Co., Pa.	Safford
McCarty, Frank M.	Private	30	Platt Co., Ill.	Flagstaff
O'Brien, Edward	Private	32	Charlestown, Mass.	Jerome
Page, William	Private	28	Iowa	Richenbar
Paxton, Frank	Private	24	Barton Co., Mo.	Safford
Petit, Louis P.	Private	30	Sacramento, Calif.	Flagstaff
Reynolds, Lewis	Private	33	Bedford, Ill.	Kingman
Rudebaugh, James D.	Private	26	Kansas	Flagstaff
Sell, Henry	Private	33	Wittenburg, Germany	Flagstaff
Sellers, Henry J.	Private	32	San Benito, Calif.	Williams
Shaw, James A.	Private	31	Shelbyville, Ill.	Prescott
Stark, Wallace J.	Private	21	Barton Co., Mo.	Safford
Sullivan, Patrick J.	Private	30	Sidney, Ohio	Prescott
Tuttle, Arthur L.	Private	21 [18]	Safford	Safford
Van Siclin, Frank	Private	27	Ingham Co., Mich.	Safford
Wager, Oscar G.	Private	20	Wager, Ark.	Jerome
Wallace, Walter D.	Private	25	Hamblin Co., Tenn.	Flagstaff
Wallace, William F.	Private	21	Ontario, Canada	Flagstaff
Weyland, Thomas J.	Private	41	Sherman, Texas	Williams
Webb, Adelbert D.	Private	30	Jefferson, Ohio	Safford
Weil, Henry J.	Private	22	San Francisco	Chloride
Wilson, Jerome	Private	25	Grayville, Ill.	Chloride

Not Mustered:

Hicks, Robert M.	—	—	—	—

A TROOP (Cont.)

DATE ENROLLED	OCCUPATION	REMARKS
May 2	Cowboy	
April 30	Miner	
May 1	Prospector	
May 1	Rancher	Wounded in the neck at San Juan, July 1.
May 1	Carpenter	On detached duty in Tampa, June 8 to July 7. Deserted July 7.
May 2	Miner	
April 30	Cowboy	
May 3	Cowboy	
May 2	Teamster	Killed in action at Las Guasimas, June 24.
May 1	Cowboy	
May 2	Cowboy	
May 2	Cowboy	
May 1	Rancher	
May 3	Miner	Wounded in the head by shrapnel at San Juan, July 2.
May 2	Miner	
May 2	Cowboy	
May 1	Rancher	
May 1	Cowboy	Killed in action at San Juan, July 1.
May 1	Rancher	
May 1	Cook	
April 30	Cowboy	
May 2	Cowboy	
May 2	Cowboy	
April 30	Barber	
May 2	Cowboy [Student]	
May 2	Cowboy	
May 3	Cowboy	
May 1	Rancher	On detached duty in Tampa, June 8 to August 8.
May 1	Cowboy	Wounded in the neck at San Juan, July 1.
April 30	Cowboy	
May 2	Cowboy [Journalist]	
May 1	Clerk	On detached duty in Tampa, June 8 to August 8.
May 2	Cowboy	
—	—	Name not included in Muster-In Rolls because he deserted after leaving Prescott on May 5 with the Arizona squadron.

MUSTER-IN ROLL — B TROOP

NAME	RANK	AGE	PLACE OF BIRTH	RESIDENCE
McClintock, James H.	Captain	34	Sacramento, Calif.	Phoenix
Wilcox, George B.	1st Lieut.	34	Addison, N. Y.	Phoenix
Rynning, Harbo T.	1st Sgt.	32	Beloit, Wis.	Phoenix [Tucson]
Norton, Edward G.	Q.M. Sgt.	22	Vicksburg, Miss.	Phoenix
Campbell, John E.	Sergeant	31	Pittsburgh, Pa.	[Phoenix]
Cronin, Cornelius P.	Sergeant	27	Boston	Yuma
Davidson, William A.	Sergeant	32	Cleveland	Phoenix [Globe]
Hawley, Elmer	Sergeant	33	Valparaiso, Ind.	Phoenix
Pate, Stephen A.	Sergeant	38	Clamon, Ohio	[Tucson]
Utting, Charles H.	Sergeant	30	Nofa City, Calif.	Phoenix
Gregory, Walter H.	Corporal	25	Cheyenne, Wyo.	Phoenix
Heitman, Charles E.	Corporal	23	Spencer, Ind.	Phoenix
Hughes, David L.	Corporal	25	Tucson	Tucson [Bisbee]
Lee, Jerry F.	Corporal	28	Wilmington, Del.	Globe
McCabe, George J.	Corporal	30	Delphos, Ohio	[Bisbee]
McCarthy, Calvin	Corporal	23	Pittsburgh	Phoenix
Pemberton, Thomas W.	Corporal	22	Chicago	Phoenix
Waterbury, Eugene W.	Corporal	24	Muskegon, Mich.	Tucson
Harmsen, Frank	Farrier	27	St. Joseph, Mo.	Tucson
Pomeroy, Fred A.	Farrier	22	Dakota, Calif.	[Kingman]
Foster, John	Trumpeter	25	Charleston, S. C.	Seattle [Bisbee]
Walters, Jesse	Trumpeter	21	Ballarrat, Colo.	Phoenix
McGinty, Joseph E.	Wagoner	23	Louisiana	Tucson
Goodwin, Richard E.	Saddler	27	Fresno, Calif.	[Phoenix]
Beebe, Walter T.	Private	21	Wisconsin	[Prescott]
Bird, Marshall N.	Private	21	San Jose, Calif.	[Nogales]
Boggs, Looney L.	Private	21	Central, S. C.	Ludlow, Texas
Collier, Edward B.	Private	25	Chambers Co., Ala.	Globe
Colwell, Grant	Private	31	California	Phoenix
Drachman, Sol B.	Private	18	Tucson	Tucson
Draper, Edward D.	Private	30	Tallahatchie, Miss.	Phoenix
Eakin, Alva L.	Private	29	Jackson, Ill.	[Globe]
Fitzgerald, Frank H.	Private	33	Clinton Co., Iowa	[Tucson]
Hall, Joel R.	Private	28	Syracuse, N. Y.	Seattle [Bisbee]
Hall, John M.	Private	27	Wallace, Texas	Phoenix
Hartzell, Ira C.	Private	21	Greenville, Ohio	Phoenix
Haydon, Roy T.	Private	27	London, Eng.	[Prescott]
Henderson, Sebird	Private	30	Doniphan, Kan.	Globe

San Antonio, Texas, May 17, 1898

DATE ENROLLED	OCCUPATION	REMARKS
April 30	Journalist	Wounded in left ankle at Las Guasimas, June 24.
April 30	Farmer	Promoted from 2nd Lieut. to 1st Lieut. on May 7. Commanded B Troop from June 24 to September 15.
May 1	Contractor	Commissioned a 2nd Lieut. on May 21.
April 30	Nurseryman	
April 30	Farmer	
May 3	County Recorder	Discharged June 13 for chronic rheumatism.
May 4	Miner	Promoted to 1st Sgt. on May 21.
April 30	Farmer	
May 2	Rancher	Wounded in the lungs at San Juan, July 1.
April 30	Cowboy	
April 30	Reporter	
April 30	Machinist	On detached duty in Tampa, June 8 to August 8.
May 2	Blacksmith	Wounded in the head at San Juan, July 1.
May 4	Cook	Wounded in the head at San Juan, July 1.
May 2	Miner	
April 30	Cook	
April 30	Electrician	
May 2	Hotel Clerk	
May 1	Bricklayer	
May 2	Accountant	
May 2	Miner	
May 2	Locomotive Engineer	On detached duty in Tampa, June 8 to August 8.
May 1	Carpenter	
May 2	Miner	
May 4	Rancher	
May 4	Newspaperman	Discharged August 8 for head injury incurred in line of duty at San Antonio.
April 30	Rancher	
May 2	Teamster	On detached duty in Tampa, June 8 to August 8.
May 1	Rancher	
May 3	Clerk	On detached duty in Tampa, June 8 to August 8.
May 1	Salesman	
May 4	Printer	
May 2	Miner	
May 2	Rancher [Journalist]	Killed in action at San Juan, July 1.
May 1	Letter Carrier	Wounded in the shoulder by shrapnel at San Juan, July 1.
April 30	Rancher	
May 2	Cowboy	
May 4	Cowboy	

MUSTER-IN ROLL

NAME	RANK	AGE	PLACE OF BIRTH	RESIDENCE
Hildenbrand, Louis H.	Private	23	New Orleans	[Prescott]
Hildreth, Fenn S.	Private	23	Ukiah, Calif.	[Tucson]
James, William H.	Private	20	Mass.	[Jerome]
Johnson, Anton E.	Private	27	Round Valley, Utah	[Prescott]
Keir, Alex	Private	33	San Bernardino, Calif.	Bisbee
King, George B.	Private	24	Sacramento, Calif.	San Francisco
Laird, Thomas J.	Private	34	Wisconsin	Bisbee
Logue, David	Private	26	Springfield, Mo.	Leavenworth, Kan. [Globe]
McCann, Walter J.	Private	30	Canada	Phoenix
Merritt, Fred M.	Private	24	Florence	[Tucson]
Middleton, Cliff	Private	21	Globe	[Globe]
Misner, J. Harvey	Private	24	Dayton, Ohio	Bisbee
Murphy, James E.	Private	27	Texas	[Del Rio]
Orme, Norman L.	Private	22	Rockwell, Texas	[Phoenix]
Owens, William A.	Private	24	Wilson Co., Texas	[Globe]
Proffitt, William B.	Private	24	Madison Co., Texas	[Prescott]
Schenck, Frank W.	Private	29	Cincinnati, Ohio	[Phoenix]
Snodderly, William L.	Private	27	Tennessee	[Bisbee]
Stanton, Richard H.	Private	24	New York	[Phoenix]
Swetman, John W.	Private	24	Wolfe Co., Ky.	[Globe]
Toland, Jesse H.	Private	23	St. Helena, Calif.	[Bisbee]
Tomlinson, Leroy B.	Private	21	Trenton, Mo.	
Townsend, Albert B.	Private	24	New York	[Tucson]
Van Treese, Louis H.	Private	21	Greenville, Ill.	Tucson [Nogales]
Ward, Frank	Private	38	Edinburgh, Scotland	[Globe]
Warford, David E.	Private	21	Troy, N. Y.	[Globe]
Webb, William W.	Private	30	Dallas, Texas	[Prescott]
Wiggins, Thomas W.	Private	30	Florida	Bisbee
Young, Thomas H.	Private	23	Lancaster, Ky.	Phoenix

B TROOP (Cont.)

DATE ENROLLED	OCCUPATION	REMARKS
May 4	Butcher	
May 2	Pharmist [sic]	
May 4	Miner	
May 3	Cowboy	
May 2	Miner	
May 2	Packer	
May 2	Miner	
May 4	Miner	Killed in action at San Juan, July 1.
May 30	Clerk	Injured by a falling iron stanchion on June 21 while on board the **Yucatan.**
May 4	Miner	
May 4	Miner	
May 2	Locomotive Fireman	
May 3	Cowboy	Wounded in the head at San Juan, July 1. Discharged Sept. 10.
May 1	Postal Clerk	Wounded in the lungs at Las Guasimas, June 24.
May 1	Miner	
May 1	Rancher	
May 3	Cook	Absent without leave May 17–22. Mustered into service May 22. On detached duty in Tampa, June 8 to August 8.
May 2	Miner	
April 30	Policeman	
May 4	Cowboy	Killed in action at San Juan, July 1.
May 2	Cook	
May 4	Painter	Died June 23 of typhoid on board the hospital ship **Olivette.**
May 2	Lineman	On detached duty in Tampa, June 8 to August 8.
May 2	Clerk	
May 4	Rancher	
May 4	Cowboy	Wounded in both legs at San Juan, July 1.
May 3	Cowboy	
May 2	Cowboy	Wounded in the right hip at Las Guasimas, June 24.
May 1	Salesman	

MUSTER-IN ROLL — C TROOP

NAME	RANK	AGE	PLACE OF BIRTH	RESIDENCE
Alexander, Joseph L. B.	Captain	40	Los Angeles	Phoenix
Patterson, Robert S.	1st Lieut.	30	Bean Co., Pa.	Safford
Huson, Willis O.	1st Sgt.	34	Iowa	Yuma
Maxey, James H.	Q.M. Sgt.	31	Marion, Ill.	Yuma
Grindell, Thomas F.	Sergeant	26	Platteville, Wis.	Tempe
Klingman, Adam H.	Sergeant	30	Wayne Co., Ind.	Flagstaff
Marti, Frank	Sergeant	31	Berne, Switzerland	Jerome
Noyes, Sam W.	Sergeant	22	Sanders, Wyo.	Tucson
Pearson, Rufus M.	Sergeant	21	Bear Creek, Tenn.	Phoenix
Perry, Arthur R.	Sergeant	34	Devonshire, Eng.	Phoenix
French, Wilbur D.	Corporal	35	Vermont	Safford
Hill, Wesley	Corporal	21	Dundee, Ill.	Tempe
Jordan, Eldridge E.	Corporal	23	Glen Rose, Texas	Phoenix
Kastens, Harry E.	Corporal	22	Berkeley, Calif.	Winslow
McAndrew, John	Corporal	33	Pennsylvania	Congress Jct.
Trowbridge, Lafayette	Corporal	25	Johnson Co., Wis.	Prescott
Warren, Hedrick M.	Corporal	21	Pueblo, Colo.	Phoenix
Gaughan, James	Blacksmith	29	Nashville, Tenn.	Phoenix
Reed, George W.	Farrier	27	Ritchey, W. Vir.	Tucson
Somers, Fred B.	Trumpeter	27	Detroit	Flagstaff
Lankford, Jerome W.	Wagoner	38	Grayson Co., Texas	White Hills
Morgan, Francis L.	Saddler	26	Illinois	Prescott
Asay, William	Private	26	Salt Lake, Utah	Safford
Barthel, Peter K.	Private	28	Ontario, Canada	Kingman
Bradley, Peter	Private	28	Parkensville, W. Vir.	Jerome
Burks, Robert E.	Private	21	Hancock Co., Ill.	Prescott
Byrnes, Olando C.	Private	21	Dubuque Co., Iowa	Prescott
Carleton, William C.	Private	21	Geneseo, Ill.	Bisbee
Carlson, Carl	Private	26	Mrnaa, Sweden	Tempe
Castledge, Crantz	Private	20	Georgia	Tempe
Danforth, Clyde L.	Private	30	Eugene, Ore.	Flagstaff
Danforth, William H.	Private	26	Johnson Co., Ore.	Flagstaff
Engel, Edwin P.	Private	24	Rochester, Minn.	Phoenix
Gibbons, Floyd J.	Private	21	Sterling, Kan.	Prescott
Goodwin, James C.	Private	32	Missouri	Tempe [Globe]
Hanson, Ivan M.	Private	21	Bates Co., Mo.	Phoenix
Hanson, William	Private	34	Denmark	Prescott
Herold, Philip M.	Private	24	Seneca, Kan.	Phoenix
Howland, Harry	Private	36	Fulton Co., Ohio	Flagstaff
Marvin, William E.	Private	29	Milan, Mich.	Yuma
Moffett, Edward B.	Private	24	Visalia, Calif.	Yuma
Mullen, J. Oscar	Private	21	Butte Co., Calif.	Tempe

San Antonio, Texas, May 17, 1898

DATE ENROLLED	OCCUPATION	REMARKS
April 30	Lawyer	Promoted from 1st Lieut. to Captain and transferred from B Troop on May 7.
May 2	Rancher	Promoted from 2nd Lieut. to 1st Lieut. and transferred from A Troop on May 7.
May 2	Lawyer	
May 2	Cowboy	
April 30	Teacher	Discharged September 8 by order of Secretary of War.
May 1	Cowboy	
May 2	Cowboy	
May 2	Insurance Agent	
April 30	Lawyer	Discharged August 26 by order of Secretary of War.
May 1	Contractor	
May 2	Rancher	
May 2	School Teacher	Discharged September 8 by order of Secretary of War.
April 30	Rancher	
May 1	Mechanic	
April 30	Lawyer	
April 30	Cook	
May 1	Rancher	
April 30	Farmer	
May 1	Laborer	
May 1	Lawyer	
May 2	Miner	
April 30	Laborer	
May 2	Rancher	
May 1	Salesman	
May 3	Cowboy	
May 2	Rancher	
May 2	Miner	
May 2	Photographer	
April 30	Farmer	
May 4	Student	
May 2	Miner	
May 2	Miner	
May 1	Ranger	
May 2	Prospector	
May 4	Rancher	
April 30	Farmer	
April 30	Cowboy	
May 2	Bookkeeper	
May 1	Rancher	
May 2	Surveyor	
May 2	Engineer	
May 2	Rancher	

MUSTER-IN ROLL

NAME	RANK	AGE	PLACE OF BIRTH	RESIDENCE
Neville, George A.	Private	40	Albany, Mo.	Yuma
Newnhome, Thomas M.	Private	35	Pike Co., Ill.	Phoenix
O'Leary, Daniel	Private	24	Ontario, Canada	Phoenix
Parker, John W.	Private	21	Arkansas	Safford
Payne, Forest B.	Private	22	Sweet Springs, Mo.	Phoenix
Rowdin, John E.	Private	28	Richmond, Va.	Jerome
Ricketts, William L.	Private	21	Indiana	Phoenix
Roderer, John	Private	18	Weiden, Germany	Prescott
Rupert, Charles W.	Private	32	Scranton, Pa.	Prescott
Scharf, Charles A.	Private	24	Butler Co., Kan.	Flagstaff
Sexsmith, William	Private	28	Fayette Co., Ky.	Yuma
Shackelford, Marcus S.	Private	25	California	Jerome
Shoemaker, John	Private	29	Scott Co., Va.	Phoenix
Skogsberg, Charles G.	Private	21	Sweden	Safford
Stelzriede, John A. W.	Private	21	Belleville, Ill.	Tempe
Vines, Jesse G.	Private	21	San Bernardino, Calif.	Phoenix
Weathers, Bruce C.	Private	33	Brownsville, Ind.	Safford
Woodin, Frank A.	Private	24	Skyland, Neb.	Phoenix
Wormell, John A.	Private	21	Phoenix	Phoenix
Wright, Albert P.	Private	39	Fairfax, Va.	Yuma
Yost, James G.	Private	25	Iowa	Prescott
Younger, Charles	Private	22	Dennison, Texas	Winslow

C TROOP (Cont.)

DATE ENROLLED	OCCUPATION	REMARKS
May 2	Cowboy	
May 1	Rancher	Died of typhoid on August 4 at the post hospital at Fort McPherson, Georgia.
April 30	Farmer	
May 2	Cowboy	
May 1	Salesman	
May 2	Cowboy	Transferred to Regimental Medical Section on June 8.
May 1	Rancher	
May 3	Baker	
April 30	Teamster	
May 1	Farmer	
May 2	Rancher	
May 1	Rancher	
May 2	Cowboy	
May 2	Cowboy	
April 30	Foreman (R.R.)	
May 1	Cowboy	
May 2	Cowboy	
April 30	Clerk	
May 1	Rancher	
May 2	Cowboy	Accompanied the regiment to Cuba as the Color Sergeant.
April 30	Cowboy	
May 1	Fireman	

Notes

Chapter 1
pages 9–14

1. Born in Pennsylvania in 1840, Myron H. McCord started his political career shortly after moving to Wisconsin. He served in the state senate, had been a delegate to the Republican National Convention in 1876 and had been elected to the House of Representatives in 1888. While in Congress he had formed a close friendship with a fellow Republican sitting next to him, Representative William McKinley of Ohio. Shortly after failing in his bid to be returned to Congress, McCord moved to Phoenix and became part owner of the Phoenix *Gazette*. In 1897 he was appointed Governor of Arizona by his old friend, President McKinley.

2. George Crook, a native of Ohio, graduated from West Point in 1854. He had a distinguished record in the Union Army in the Civil War, rising to the rank of major general of volunteers by 1865. A noted Indian fighter, Crook was commander of the Department of Arizona from 1871 to 1875. Seven years later he returned to that command because of a fresh outbreak of trouble with Chiricahua Apaches. He resigned from the department in 1886 when the President and his immediate superior, General Phil Sheridan, lost confidence in his Indian policy.

3. Adna Romanza Chaffee was another famous Indian fighter. A native of Ohio, he enlisted in the Sixth Cavalry in 1861 and

was commissioned a second lieutenant in 1863. Captain Chaffee was one of the principal participants in the Battle of Big Dry Wash along Chevelon Creek in northern Arizona in 1882.

4. Born in 1844 in Philadelphia, Emmett Crawford enlisted in the Union Army in 1861 and was commissioned a first lieutenant in 1864 to command Negro troops. In 1870 he came to Arizona for service with the Third Cavalry. On January 11, 1886, while in Mexico arranging for a surrender of Geronimo, he was shot and killed by Mexican irregulars some sixty miles southeast of Nacori, Sonora.

5. Interview with Arthur L. Tuttle, formerly of A Troop, February 20–23, 1963, in Tucson, Arizona. Tuttle enlisted at the age of eighteen on May 3, 1898. He was the last survivor of the Arizona contingent of the First United States Volunteer Cavalry. Cited hereafter as Tuttle Interview.

6. Born in Tempe, Arizona, in 1877, Hayden was elected to the House of Representatives when Arizona became a state in 1912. He served in that capacity until 1926 when he was elected to the Senate. He voluntarily retired from the Senate in 1967.

7. Alexander Brodie to the President, March 10, 1898, Adjutant General's Office, Record Group 94, National Archives. Cited hereafter as AGO.

8. Charles Akers to the President, March 5, 1898, AGO.

9. Myron McCord to the President, April 2, 1898, AGO.

10. James McClintock to Brodie, April 5, 1898, Brodie Papers, Arizona Historical Foundation, Tempe, Arizona.

11. Tucson *Arizona Weekly Star,* April 14, 1898.

12. William O'Neill to McClintock, April 23, 1898, in folder entitled "Rough Riders — Pre-Organization," McClintock Papers, Phoenix Public Library, Phoenix, Arizona.

13. *United States Statutes at Large, March, 1897 to March, 1899,* 55 Cong., XXX, p. 362.

14. War Department Memorandum, April 28, 1898, Record and Pension Office, Record Group 94, National Archives. Cited hereafter as RPO.

15. For additional information, see Ralph Keithley, *Buckey O'Neill: He Stayed With 'Em While He Lasted* (Caldwell, Idaho, 1949), 217-18.

16. Phoenix *Arizona Republican,* April 30, 1898.

17. Tucson *Arizona Weekly Star,* May 5, 1898.

18. A native of Wales, Sam Hughes came to the United States in 1837, arriving in Tucson twenty-one years later. As adjutant general of Arizona, he was implicated in the massacre of peaceful Apaches at Camp Grant in 1871. He died in Tucson in 1917.

19. Captain William P. Long was well known in Arizona, being active in the Negley Post of the Grand Army of the Republic in Tucson. He was killed in a mine accident in Bisbee in 1899.

20. A graduate of West Point in the class of 1896, Second Lieutenant Tupes arrived at Whipple Barracks in April, 1898, in connection with the abandonment of that post.

21. McClintock to Brodie, April 5, 1898, Brodie Papers, Arizona Historical Foundation.

22. McCord to McClintock, May 3, 1898, McClintock Papers, Arizona Historical Foundation.

23. There is some evidence that the first lieutenant of O'Neill's troop was to be Wiley S. Jones, the county attorney of Graham County. A full court docket kept him from accepting the appointment.

24. G. M. Sargent to McCord, July 23, 1898, in folder entitled "Military Affairs — Territorial Volunteers — Rough Riders," State Department of Library and Archives, Phoenix, Arizona.

25. A native of Maine, Nathan Oakes Murphy came to Arizona in 1883. He was appointed governor in 1892 and resigned the following year. He was reappointed governor on July 16, 1898, and served until 1902. He died in 1908.

26. Prescott *Weekly Journal Miner,* May 11, 1898.

27. *Ibid.*

Chapter 2

1. Prescott *Weekly Journal Miner,* May 11, 1898.

2. Quoted in Clifford P. Westermeier, *Who Rush to Glory, the Cowboy Volunteers of 1898: Grigsby's Cowboys, Roosevelt's Rough Riders, Torrey's Rocky Mountain Riders* (Caldwell, Idaho, 1958), p. 57. Cited with permission of Caxton Printers, Ltd.

3. San Antonio *Daily Express,* May 8, 1898.

4. Allyn Kissam Capron, son of Captain Allyn Capron who graduated from West Point in 1867, began his military career in 1890 when he enlisted in the Fourth Cavalry. He was appointed a second lieutenant in the Fifth Infantry a year later and transferred to the Seventh Cavalry in 1894.

5. David L. Hughes, "A Story of the Rough Riders," David L. Hughes Papers, Arizona Pioneers' Historical Society, Tucson, Arizona. Cited hereafter as Hughes Manuscript, APHS.

6. Adjutant General's Office to Lieutenant Herschel Tupes, May 19, 1898, RPO.

7. A native of Ohio, Lawton saw considerable service with Indiana troops during the Civil War. He stayed in the army after the war and was appointed a second lieutenant in the Forty-First Infantry in 1866. Five years later, as a first lieutenant, he transferred to the Fourth Cavalry. He rose to the rank of brigadier general and was killed in the Philippines in 1899.

8. For a detailed account of the Geronimo Campaign of 1886, see Odie B. Faulk, *The Geronimo Campaign* (New York, N.Y., 1969).

9. Hughes Manuscript, APHS.

10. Wilbur D. French Statement, Hermann Hagedorn, Notes on the Rough Riders, Harvard University Library, II. Cited hereafter as Hagedorn Notes. Compiled by Hagedorn in 1924 for a proposed movie, the statements collected by Hagedorn fill five volumes. This is the best single collection of Rough Rider material. More than forty veterans contributed.

11. Lieutenant Tupes to the Adjutant General, May 26, 1898, RPO.

12. Theodore Roosevelt, *The Rough Riders* (New York, 1899), p. 1.

13. Unidentified newspaper clipping, Tuttle Papers.

14. Quoted in Hermann Hagedorn, *Leonard Wood: A Biography* (2 vols., New York, 1931), I, p. 148. Cited with permission of Harper and Row, Publishers, Inc.

15. French Statement, Hagedorn Notes, II.

16. Charles D. Reppy to "Whom it May Concern," June 11, 1898, George L. Truman Papers, APHS.

17. L.F. Eggers to Brodie, May 5, 1898, Brodie Papers, Arizona Historical Foundation.

18. French Statement, Hagedorn Notes, II.

19. Solomonville *Arizona Bulletin*, May 27, 1898.

20. Tuttle Interview, February 20–23, 1963.

21. James McClintock Statement, Hagedorn Notes, II.

22. Morning Report Book, A Troop, May 18, 1898, AGO.

23. Solomonville *Arizona Bulletin*, June 10, 1898.

24. Quoted in Chris Emmett, *In the Path of Events With Colonel Martin Lalor Crimmins, Soldier, Naturalist, Historian* (Waco, Texas, 1959), p. 113. Cited with permission of Chris Emmett.

25. Tuttle to his Mother, May 25, 1898, Tuttle Papers.

Chapter 3

1. Solomonville *Arizona Bulletin,* June 17, 1898.

2. *Ibid.*

3. Captain Thomas H. Rynning, *Gun Notches: The Life Story of a Cowboy-Soldier by Captain Thomas H. Rynning, as told to Al Cohn and Joe Chisholm* (New York, 1931), p. 158. Cited with permission of J. B. Lippincott Co.

4. Theodore Roosevelt Testimony, *Report of the Commission Appointed by the President to Investigate the Conduct of the War Department in the War With Spain* as reported by General Grenville Dodge, Senate Doc. 221 [8 vols.], 56 Cong., I Sess., Serial 3859, VI, p. 2257. Cited hereafter as *Dodge Report.*

5. Jacob Ford Kent was born in Philadelphia and graduated from the United States Military Academy in 1861. At the outbreak of the Spanish-American War, Colonel Kent was appointed brigadier general of volunteers on May 4, 1898.

6. A native of Missouri, John Coalter Bates served as a captain in the Union Army in the Civil War. He stayed in the army after the war, rising to the rank of colonel in 1892. He was made brigadier general of volunteers on May 4, 1898.

7. Wheeler was born in Augusta, Georgia, in 1836. After graduating from West Point in 1859, he served two years in the cavalry, resigning in 1861 to join the Confederacy. In command of cavalry in western operations, Wheeler was a lieutenant general at the end of the Civil War.

8. A native of Pennsylvania, Sumner was appointed second lieutenant in the Union Army in 1861. By 1865 he was a brevet major. A colonel in the Regular Army at the outbreak of the war with Spain, Sumner was appointed brigadier general of volunteers on May 4, 1898.

9. Samuel B. M. Young, born in Pittsburgh in 1840, enlisted in the Twelfth Pennsylvania Volunteers in 1861. Within a few weeks he was appointed a captain in the Fourth Pennsylvania. At the end of the Civil War he became a second lieutenant in the Regular Army and had risen to colonel by 1897. On May 4, 1898, he was made brigadier general of volunteers.

10. French Statement, Hagedorn Notes, III.

11. Edward Marshall, *The Story of the Rough Riders: First United States Volunteer Cavalry, The Regiment in Camp and on the Battlefield* (New York, 1899), p. 258.

12. Burr McIntosh, *The Little I Saw of Cuba* (New York, 1899), pp. 90-91.

13. Hughes Manuscript, APHS.

14. Solomonville *Arizona Bulletin,* June 10, 1898.

15. Quoted in Emmett, *In the Path of Events,* p. 124. Cited with permission.

16. Interview with Jesse D. Langdon, formerly of K Troop, June 24, 1963, Las Vegas, New Mexico. Now living in New York, Langdon was an eighteen-year-old native of South Dakota when he enlisted in the Rough Riders.

17. Roosevelt Testimony, *Dodge Report,* VI, p. 2257.

18. Marshall, *Story of the Rough Riders,* p. 55.

19. Prescott *Weekly Journal Miner,* June 22, 1898.

20. Solomonville *Arizona Bulletin,* July 15, 1898.

21. Major General O. O. Howard, "Transport Service in the Present War," *The Independent* (August 18, 1898), p. 465.

Chapter 4

1. Tucson *Arizona Weekly Star,* July 14, 1898.

2. Solomonville *Arizona Bulletin,* July 15, 1898.

3. James H. McClintock, *Arizona: Prehistoric, Aboriginal, Pioneer and Modern* (3 vols., Chicago, 1916), II, p. 518.

4. Hughes Manuscript, APHS.

5. McClintock, *Arizona,* II, p. 519.

6. William R. Shafter, "Capture of Santiago," *Century Magazine* (February, 1899), pp. 617-19.

7. *Ibid.*

8. Joseph Wheeler's Battle Report, June 26, 1898, in *Report of the Secretary of War, November 29, 1898,* Serial 3744 (2 vols.), I, p. 162.

9. Quoted in Hagedorn, *Leonard Wood,* I, p. 162. Cited with permission.

10. Roosevelt, *Rough Riders,* p. 18.

11. Marshall, *Story of the Rough Riders,* p. 96.

12. Roosevelt, *Rough Riders,* p. 293.

13. Solomonville *Arizona Bulletin,* July 22, 1898.

14. Thomas Wiggins to McClintock, January 15, 1898, McClintock Papers, Arizona Historical Foundation.

15. Unidentified newspaper clipping, Tuttle Papers.

16. Roosevelt, *Rough Riders,* p. 94.

17. *Ibid.,* p. 130.

18. Unidentified newspaper clipping, Tuttle Papers.

19. Hughes Manuscript, APHS.

20. John Fox, Jr., "Las Guasimas," *Harper's Weekly* (July 30, 1898), p. 751.

21. McClintock, *Arizona,* II, p. 521.

22. Roosevelt, *Rough Riders,* p. 105.

23. Rynning, *Gun Notches,* p. 179. Cited with permission.

24. Tucson *Arizona Weekly Star,* July 21, 1898.

25. *Ibid.,* July 28, 1898.

26. Solomonville *Arizona Bulletin,* July 22, 1898.

27. McIntosh, *The Little I Saw of Cuba,* p. 89.

28. Unidentified newspaper clipping, Tuttle Papers.

29. *Ibid.*

30. Samuel B. M. Young's Battle Report, June 29, 1898, in *Report of the Secretary of War, November 29, 1898,* Serial 3744 (2 vols.), I, p. 333.

Chapter 5

1. Hughes Manuscript, APHS.

2. Roosevelt Testimony, *Dodge Report,* IV, pp. 2263-64.

3. Entry for July 1, 1898, in Leonard Wood Diary (May 29, 1898– July 3, 1898) in Leonard Wood Papers, Box 2, Library of Congress. A typescript copy of the original used.

4. Tuttle Interview, February 20–23, 1963.

5. *Ibid.*

6. *Ibid.*

7. This famous statement, or a minor variation thereof, is repeated in practically all secondary and most primary accounts. There is considerable controversy as to when O'Neill made the statement. See chapter 6.

8. Tuttle Interview, February 20–23, 1963.

9. Solomonville *Arizona Bulletin,* August 19, 1898.

10. Rynning, *Gun Notches,* p. 176. Cited with permission.

11. Roosevelt, *Rough Riders,* p. 126.

12. *Ibid.,* p. 130.

13. In contrast to the clean hole made by a Mauser bullet, the .45 caliber rifle used by the Spanish guerrillas and the American

Volunteer infantry regiments inflicted a ghastly wound. Jesse Langdon of K Troop always maintained that the soldiers killed at San Juan by these heavy bullets were shot by their own Volunteer troops deployed behind them. He never accepted Roosevelt's explanation that the Rough Riders and their comrades were fired upon by Spanish guerrillas in trees behind the American lines. There is very little evidence to support Langdon in his opinion.

14. Roosevelt's Operations Report, July 20, 1898, in *Report of the Secretary of War, November 29, 1898,* I, p. 686. Cited hereafter as Roosevelt's Operations Report.

15. Roosevelt's Battle Report, July 4, 1898, in *Ibid.,* p. 688. Cited hereafter as Roosevelt's Battle Report.

16. Hughes Manuscript, APHS.

17. Unidentified newspaper clipping, Hagedorn Notes, IV.

18. Thomas P. Ledgwidge Statement, Hagedorn Notes, IV. Ledgwidge, a member of F Troop from Santa Fe, wrote an interesting and accurate account of his experiences as a Rough Rider.

19. Muster-Out Rolls, B Troop, September 15, 1898, AGO.

20. Roosevelt's Battle Report, July 4, 1898.

21. Ledgwidge Statement, Hagedorn Notes, IV.

22. Jesse Langdon to the author, December 13, 1962, author's files.

23. Solomonville *Arizona Bulletin,* August 19, 1898.

Chapter 6

1. Rynning, *Gun Notches,* p. 173. Cited with permission.

2. Hughes Manuscript, APHS.

3. Cornelius Cronin to McClintock, August 15, 1898, McClintock Papers, Arizona Historical Foundation.

4. Phoenix *Arizona Republican,* July 18, 1898.

5. Solomonville *Arizona Bulletin,* August 19, 1898.

6. Prescott *Weekly Journal Miner,* July 27, 1898.

7. *Ibid.*

8. Tuttle Interview, February 20–23, 1963.

9. Roosevelt, *Rough Riders,* p. 198.

10. Unidentified newspaper clipping, Tuttle Papers.

11. Solomonville *Arizona Bulletin,* August 19, 1898.

12. Roosevelt's Operations Report, July 20, 1898.

13. Phoenix *Arizona Republican,* April 26, 1929.

14. Henry W. Nash Testimony, *Dodge Report,* VIII, p. 417.

15. Hughes Manuscript, APHS.

16. Solomonville *Arizona Bulletin,* September 2, 1898.

17. Russell A. Alger, *The Spanish-American War* (New York, 1901), pp. 255-73.

18. Sherrard Coleman Statement, Hagedorn Notes, I. Coleman originally was the first lieutenant of E Troop, but he later became the regimental quartermaster.

19. Roosevelt to Maxwell Keyes, January 4, 1899, Maxwell Keyes Papers, in the possession of General Geoffrey Keyes (Ret.), Tucson, Arizona.

20. Tuttle to his brothers, August 4, 1898, Tuttle Papers.

21. Solomonville *Arizona Bulletin,* August 19, 1898.

22. George P. Hamner's autobiography, George Hamner Papers, Hollywood, Florida. A member of F Troop, Hamner recently completed a two hundred page still unpublished autobiography.

23. Unidentified newspaper clipping, Hagedorn Notes, V.

24. Tuttle Interview, February 20–23, 1963.

25. Entry for August 7, 1898, in the Diary of Roger S. Fitch, Roger Fitch Papers, Las Vegas City Museum, Las Vegas, New Mexico.

26. Tucson *Arizona Weekly Star,* July 28, 1898.

Chapter 7

1. General Shafter to Secretary Alger, June 28, 1898, *Dodge Report,* II, p. 924.

2. Phoenix *Arizona Republican,* June 27, 1898.

3. Tampa *Morning Tribune,* July 30, 1898.

4. *Ibid.,* July 1, 1898.

5. Marshall, *Story of the Rough Riders,* p. 209.

6. Tampa *Morning Tribune,* June 23, 1898.

7. French Statement, Hagedorn Notes, III.

8. Tampa *Morning Tribune,* July 29, 1898.

9. *Ibid.,* July 30, 1898.

10. Radio Address by James McClintock, January 14, 1931, in "Forward Arizona" series, sponsored by Union Oil Company of Arizona. Copy in Special Collections, University of Arizona Library.

11. See Eppley's letter, quoted in Westermeier, *Who Rush to Glory,* p. 241. Cited with permission.

12. Unidentified newspaper clipping, Tuttle Papers.

Chapter 8

1. Roosevelt, *Rough Riders,* p. 123.

2. *Ibid.,* p. 217.

3. *New York Times,* August 16, 1898.

4. Roosevelt Testimony, *Dodge Report,* V, p. 2269.

5. Unidentified newspaper clipping, Tuttle Papers.

6. Robert S. Patterson's Notebook, Patterson Papers, author's files.

7. Ledgwidge Statement, Hagedorn Notes, V.

8. Phoenix *Arizona Republican,* September 5, 1898.

9. Tuttle to his Mother, n. d., Tuttle Papers.

10. Tuttle Interview, February 20–23, 1963.

11. Wilcox to McClintock, September 6, 1898, McClintock Papers, Arizona Historical Foundation.

12. Abstract of Expenditures, Quarterly Return of Ordnance, McClintock Papers, Phoenix Public Library.

13. Wilcox to McClintock, September 6, 1898, McClintock Papers, Arizona Historical Foundation.

14. McClintock's Radio Address, January 7, 1931.

15. French Statement, Hagedorn Notes, V.

16. *New York Times,* September 15, 1898.

17. Wilcox to McClintock, September 6, 1898, McClintock Papers, Arizona Historical Foundation.

Epilogue

1. Phoenix *Arizona Republican,* October 2, 1898.

2. Kingman *Mohave County Miner,* March 14, 1903.

3. McClintock to Eugene Waterbury, January 24, 1901, McClintock Papers, Arizona Historical Foundation.

4. Unidentified newspaper clipping, McClintock Papers, Arizona Historical Foundation.

5. Judge Charles Weston Wright came to Arizona from Missouri in 1888. He was a graduate of the University of Michigan law school and died in Tucson in 1900.

6. George Smalley was born in Minnesota in 1872. He came to Arizona in 1896 for his health. He served as private secretary to Governor Brodie from 1902 to 1905. He died in Tucson in 1961.

7. Cronin to McClintock, September 15, 1901, McClintock Papers, Arizona Historical Foundation.

8. Brodie to Smalley, May 2, 1902, Smalley Papers, APHS.

9. A native of Indiana, Joseph Henry Kibbey was an attorney for the Florence Canal Company and later an associate justice of the Territory of Arizona. He became Governor of Arizona in 1905.

10. Hall, *Fun and Fighting of the Rough Riders,* p. 157.

11. McClintock to Waterbury, January 24, 1901, McClintock Papers, Arizona Historical Foundation.

Selected Bibliography

ALGER, RUSSELL A. *The Spanish-American War.* New York: Harper and Brothers, 1901.

AZOY, A. C. M. *Charge: The Story of the Battle of San Juan Hill.* New York: David McKay Co., 1961.

CURRY, GEORGE. *George Curry, 1861–1947: An Autobiography.* Edited by H. B. Henning. Albuquerque: University of New Mexico Press, 1958.

DAVIS, RICHARD HARDING. *The Cuban and Porto Rican Campaigns.* New York: Frederick A. Stokes Co., 1899.

EMMETT, CHRIS. *In the Path of Events with Colonel Martin Lalor Crimmins: Soldier-Naturalist-Historian.* Waco, Texas: Jones and Morrison, 1959.

FREIDEL, FRANK. *The Splendid Little War.* Boston: Little Brown and Co., 1958.

HAGEDORN, HERMANN. *Leonard Wood: A Biography.* 2 vols. New York: Harper and Brothers, 1931.

HALL, TOM. *The Fun and Fighting of the Rough Riders.* New York: Frederick A. Stokes Co., 1899.

MARSHALL, EDWARD. *The Story of the Rough Riders: 1st United States Volunteer Cavalry, The Regiment in Camp and on the Battlefield.* New York: G. W. Dillingham Co., 1899.

McClintock, James H. *Arizona: Prehistoric, Aboriginal, Pioneer and Modern.* 3 vols. Chicago: S. J. Clarke Co., 1916.

McIntosh, Burr. *The Little I Saw of Cuba.* New York: F. Tennyson Neely, 1899.

Millis, Walter. *The Martial Spirit: A Study of Our War With Spain.* Cambridge: Houghton Mifflin Co., 1931.

Parker, John H. *The Gatlings at Santiago: History of the Gatling Gun Detachment, Fifth Army Corps at Santiago.* Kansas City: Hudson Kimberly Co., 1898.

Post, Charles J. *The Little War of Private Post.* Boston: Little Brown and Co., 1960.

Pratt, Julius W. *Expansionists of 1898: The Acquisition of Hawaii and the Spanish Islands.* Baltimore: Johns Hopkins Press, 1936.

Report of the Commission Appointed by the President to Investigate the Conduct of the War Department in the War With Spain. Senate Doc. 221 [8 vols.], 56 Congress, First Session, Serial 3859. Washington: Government Printing Office, 1899.

Report of the Secretary of War, November 29, 1898 [2 vols.], Serial 3744. Washington: Government Printing Office, 1899.

Roosevelt, Theodore. *The Rough Riders.* New York: Scribner's and Sons, 1899.

Rynning, Thomas H. *Gun Notches: The Life Story of a Cowboy-Soldier by Captain Thomas H. Rynning, As Told to Al Cohn and Joe Chisholm.* New York: J. B. Lippincott Co., 1931.

Sergeant, Herbert H. *The Campaign of Santiago de Cuba.* 3 vols. Chicago: A. C. McClurg and Co., 1907.

Steele, Matthew Forney. *American Campaigns.* 2 vols. Washington: United States Infantry Association, 1922.

Westermeier, Clifford P. *Who Rush to Glory, the Cowboy Volunteers of 1898: Grigsby's Cowboys, Roosevelt's Rough Riders, Torrey's Rocky Mountain Riders.* Caldwell, Idaho: Caxton Printers Ltd., 1958.

Index